# VULGARITY
## and
# AUTHENTICITY

# Vulgarity

AND

# Authenticity

DIMENSIONS OF OTHERNESS

IN THE WORLD OF

JEAN-PAUL SARTRE

Stuart Zane Charmé

The University of Massachusetts Press

AMHERST

Copyright © 1991 by
The University of Massachusetts Press
All rights reserved
Printed in the United States of America
LC 90-23296
ISBN 0-87023-740-3
Designed by Jack Harrison
Set in Electra by Keystone Typesetting, Inc.
Printed and bound by Thomson-Shore, Inc.
Library of Congress Cataloging-in-Publication Data
Charmé, Stuart L.
     Vulgarity and authenticity : dimensions of otherness in the world of Jean-Paul Sartre /
Stuart Zane Charmé.
          p.    cm.
     Includes bibliographical references and index.
     ISBN 0-87023-740-3 (alk. paper)
     1. Sartre, Jean Paul, 1905-    .    2. Civilization—Philosophy—History—20th century.
3. Group identity—Philosophy—History—20th century.    4. Authenticity (Philosophy)—
History—20th century.    5. Self—History—20th century.    6. Existentialism—History
I. Title.
B2430.S34C5248    1991
194—dc20                                                                    90-23296
                                                                                 CIP


British Library Cataloguing in Publication data are available.

The author would like to express his appreciation to the American Council of Learned Societies
and the Rutgers Faculty Academic Study Program for their support during the preparation of
this book.

To Nancie and Sara,
who fill my life with joy

# CONTENTS

# ABBREVIATIONS

| | |
|---|---|
| A | *Adieux: A Farewell to Sartre* |
| AR | *The Age of Reason* |
| B | *Baudelaire* |
| BN | *Being and Nothingness* |
| BO | *Black Orpheus* |
| CA | *The Condemned of Altona* |
| CDR | *Critique of Dialectical Reason* |
| CL | "The Childhood of a Leader" |
| CPM | *Cahiers pour une morale* |
| DGL | *The Devil and the Good Lord* |
| EH | "Existentialism Is a Humanism" |
| FI | *The Family Idiot* (3 volumes) |
| FS | *The Freud Scenario* |
| I | *Intimacy* |
| IF | *L'Idiot de la famille* (3 volumes) |
| IM | *Imagination* |
| K | *Kean* (in DGL) |
| LC | *Lettres au Castor, 1926–1939* |
| LPE | *Literary and Philosophical Essays* |
| LS | *Life/Situations* |
| M | *Mallarmé* |
| N | *Nausea* |
| NE | *No Exit* |
| PB1 | "A Conversation about Sex and Women . . . " (*Playboy*) |
| PB2 | "Jean-Paul Sartre: A Candid Conversation . . . " (*Playboy*) |
| PI | *Psychology of the Imagination* |
| PN | "Présence noire" |
| R | *The Reprieve* |
| RP | *The Respectful Prostitute* (in NE) |
| S | *Situations* |

| | |
|---|---|
| SG | *Saint Genet* |
| SH | *Sartre by Himself* |
| SM | *Search for a Method* |
| ST | *Sartre on Theater* |
| TH | "Today's Hope . . . " |
| W | *The Words* |
| WD | *The War Diaries* |
| WE | "Preface" to *The Wretched of the Earth* (Fanon) |
| WL | *What Is Literature?* |
| WS | *Writings of Jean-Paul Sartre* |

**VULGARITY**
and
**AUTHENTICITY**

# Introduction

At the Liberation we were still strangely stuck in the history of philosophy. . . . Fortunately there was Sartre. Sartre was our Outside, he was
really the breath of fresh air from the backyard. . . . And Sartre has never
stopped being that, not a model, a method or an example, but a little
fresh air. . . . It is idiotic to wonder whether Sartre was the beginning or
the end of something. Like all creative things and people, he is in the
middle, he grows from the middle.

—Gilles Deleuze, *Dialogues*

As surely as rebellious sons grow up to find themselves the targets of new
revolts by their own sons, the cultural renegades of the last generation
are inevitably challenged by their own intellectual progeny. Only later,
perhaps, do thematic or structural similarities of their respective revolts
emerge, offering a bridge between the generations. Long before the
death of Jean-Paul Sartre in 1980, a new generation of "post-Sartrean"
philosophers and intellectuals had taken aim at the heirless father of
French existentialism and outspoken champion of oppressed groups,
and obituaries were being written for the era of Sartre. As radical and
iconoclastic as Sartre seemed at the height of his influence, it is now not
difficult to find post-Sartreans who consider his central categories and
interpretations anything from quaintly outdated to perniciously contaminated by questionable assumptions.

While it is important to acknowledge the limitations of Sartre's
analysis of many issues, it is likewise true that his anticipation of many
of the concerns of "postmodernists" has not been sufficiently appreciated. Since his death, there has been a slow but steady resurgence of

interest and scholarship regarding Sartre's life and work, as interpreters have searched for the threads that link together the incredibly diverse elements of a Sartrean corpus that continues to grow with the regular appearance of new posthumous works.

Sartre's own life presents us with an archetypal figure in whom qualities of individual personality and powerful cultural themes intersected in a remarkable way. Taken together, his life and work embody many of the conflicts and dilemmas of twentieth-century social thought. Regarding his autobiography, Sartre himself remarked with just a touch of grandiosity, "I am not only concerned with the particular meaning of one life. I want to recall the rather curious evolution of a generation."[1] Beyond even his own generation, Sartre's life and work help illuminate long-standing issues regarding the boundaries of identity within Western civilization.

This book grows out of my earlier work on Sartre, *Meaning and Myth in the Study of Lives*, in which I examined the underlying hermeneutical and philosophical assumptions in his theory of "existential psychoanalysis." Sartre provides an opportunity to consider not only the philosophical and psychological issues involved in the constitution of the self, but also the religious or "mythic" dimensions of biography and autobiography. The problematic nature of personal identity that preoccupies postmodern consciousness attracted Sartre's attention from the start of his career. In such early works as *Nausea* and *The Transcendence of the Ego*, he confronted the dispersion of our consciousness in the world and the fragmentary data of our lived experience. It is out of these that we construct a self that distorts and hides as much as it reveals, for we perceive some patterns only by not perceiving others. Sartre appreciated that how we ultimately frame the narrative we tell about ourselves is conditioned by the assumptions and ideologies of the period in which we live.

One of the major issues unanswered in my earlier work on Sartre was the question of how the sense of self is constituted not only by our assumptions about who we are, but also by a sense of who or what we are *not*. In *Being and Nothingness*, Sartre emphasized that our consciousness of other people reflects back to us a significant part of who we are to which we have no other access, namely, our "being-for-others."[2]

---

1. "Jean-Paul Sartre on His Autobiography," *Listener*, 6 June 1957, p. 915.
2. Psychoanalytic object relations theory has also emphasized the importance of the Other in the emergence of the sense of self.

A totally private life lacks the reality and differentiation that emerges from interacting with others, being seen and heard by them. As Hannah Arendt puts it, "The privation of privacy is the absence of others."[3]

What Sartre did not explicitly say, however, was that the *image* we construct of the "Other," or of otherness in general, also emerges out of a particular sense of self. In other words, at the root of every "self-image" lies an idea of the Other, an "Other-image" that delineates what one's own self is *not*, or at least what it refuses to accept about itself. The stories we tell and write about our lives describe the adventures of a self that we must create in a world of Others. To the extent that our consciousness forges a model of who we are, a mythic self, it also creates a world of mythic Others with whom we interact. Thus, it is not simply that the Other's consciousness mirrors back to us certain constitutive elements of our selves, or that we learn about ourselves from our contact with others. The crucial point is that our awareness of the Other's "otherness" is filtered through the creations and distortions of our own consciousness.

I call these images "mythic" to indicate that the essential qualities by which we define self and other, as well as the boundaries we trace between them, consist of a delicate web of our most primordial assumptions about what is real and of value. It is mythic in the original religious sense that sees myths as the stories that both construct and determine the meaning of the world we inhabit. The others who travel in that world are also ultimately mythic or paradigmatic of what lies beyond the limits of self. At the extremes, we experience what is other as potentially sacred or demonic. It may represent an enemy that frightens the self to contract, to flee in terror, to fragment, or to strike out in defensive fury; but it may also appear as an alluring invitation to the self to expand itself, to transcend the self's boundaries, and to redefine the self in new ways. As a result, any attempt to demythologize the self will immediately enter the tangle of connections that marks the border with otherness, where one finds that the distinction between self and other has no fixed or natural dimensions, but shifts in an endlessly fluctuating dialectic.

Our models of otherness, however, are not simply generated by the individual self alone. Within any society, there are collective images of otherness that reflect the dominant group's norms for a self which is

3. Hannah Arendt, *The Human Condition* (Chicago: University of Chicago Press, 1958), pp. 58–59.

relatively stable and reliable. A society preserves and protects its collective identity only by clarifying the qualities and values that lie beyond the norms of selfhood and by identifying those persons or things that embody these qualities. The solidification of these categories is often a source of oppressive practices in society, and social change must therefore be accompanied by a destabilization of the foundations of the self.

The present study investigates the complex interrelationship of self and otherness in Sartre's work with particular attention to a critical psychosocial component of personal identity, the theme of *civility* and *vulgarity*. The development of a sense of self in relation to others inevitably requires some accommodation to a group's notion of appropriate human behavior. For most people, a "mature" self will also be a self that has been "civilized." Those who violate accepted notions of civility are threats to more than social cohesion; they challenge the bases of selfhood for all the other members of their group. On this level, it is clear that civility is a design for a self to be created out of, and protected from, the realm of uncivilized vulgarity.

On the other hand, the structure of civility may also be experienced as an imposition of others on the natural tendencies of the self. What appears to be vulgar in the eyes of the civilized may in fact represent a form of rejection of this collective power of the dominant Other to influence the self. Thus, while it is impossible to make any direct correlation between the civility/vulgarity axis and the self/other axis, it would also be wrong to overlook the reciprocal interactions between them. There is a profound ambivalence in our attitudes toward both civility and vulgarity that manifests itself in our inner sense of self and other. Conversely, our images of self and other will doubtless require some careful negotiation of the line between civility and vulgarity.

In Sartre's case, socialization as a privileged bourgeois child made him deeply aware of the conventions of respectability and proper public behavior that govern the world of the Other. As he became convinced that such public, civilized behavior was contaminated by hypocrisy and inauthenticity, he determined that his struggle to become civilized had only undermined his own inner sense of self. Throughout his life, authenticity remained the existential grail of Sartre's quest, the exquisite fruit of embracing and exercising one's own freedom. Yet Sartre did not offer a romantic notion of authenticity as an inner essence to which one must remain true or honest. Such an idea would merely be an example of "the spirit of seriousness" or the ideal of "sincerity" that Sartre specifically repudiated as forms of bad faith or inauthenticity

(*BN*, 62–63, 580). In fact, like the Buddha describing enlightenment, Sartre says more about what authenticity is *not* than he does about what it is. The inauthentic self is one that finds security in the fixed roles and values of the world of civility, one that refuses to call into question the structures and institutions that protect us from confronting the absence of all foundation for those structures.

It is the desire to maintain distance from those structures, to call them into question and to change them that marks the person of authenticity (*WD*, 221). Authenticity is therefore a subversive power that destabilizes the orderly categories and certainties that constantly tempt us. It is not a stable state of being that one might achieve. Rather, it lurks in the shadows of our lives, waging guerilla warfare on the manifold forms of bad faith.[4] Vulgarity, likewise, represented to Sartre a defiant revolt against bourgeois good taste and "bad faith." For this reason, he turned toward vulgarity as a vehicle of authenticity within personal identity.

Sartre struggled with the tension between civility and vulgarity throughout his life. On the one hand, he rejected and sought to escape the hypocritical civility that he associated with the values of the bourgeoisie. On the other hand, he identified a different dimension of civility with the means by which human consciousness transcended the realm of nature and the body. The human condition is balanced on the edge of this existential oxymoron. Our consciousness and imagination rise above nature yet they are inextricably linked to natural processes. In the words of Ernest Becker, only a human being is simultaneously "up in the stars yet housed in a heart-pumping, breath-gasping body that once belonged to fish and still carries the gill-marks to prove it."[5] Sartre further understood that when civility collides with vulgarity, or culture with nature, a dialectical balance is necessary. Thus, he described human reality as simultaneously "natural culture and cultivated nature" (*FI*, 1:28). Accordingly, we might think of his position as one which tied selfhood with both "civilized vulgarity" and "vulgar civility." He was constantly aware of the various ways in which vulgarity oozes through the cracks of civility, as can be seen in his ideas about themes such as obscenity, ugliness, scatology, laughter, and body odors. These

---

4. While Sartre discussed authenticity to some degree in his *War Diaries*, by the time he wrote *Being and Nothingness* he was more concerned with describing the structure of bad faith, the primary obstacle to authenticity. The only mention of authenticity is relegated to a single footnote (*BN*, 70).

5. Ernest Becker, *The Denial of Death* (New York: Free Press, 1973), p. 26.

arose to a great extent from the vulgar qualities of nature. Nevertheless, in other contexts, the revolting qualities of vulgarity also represented the power to revolt against the conservative forces of civility.

In time, Sartre found himself attracted to blacks, women, homosexuals, Jews, and other marginalized groups. Not only did they represent paradigmatic Others in his culture, that is, inverted images of the normative archetypes of white, male, heterosexual, Christian culture; they were models of other forms of selfhood or subjectivity whose voices need to be heard. If bad faith and inauthenticity are required to support the dominant group's image of itself, then those who are both excluded from that group and aware of their exclusion might have a greater opportunity to achieve authenticity. Authenticity requires an acceptance of one's being for others (*CPM*, 26), the fact that, "the other is precisely the I for whom we are Other" (*CPM*, 35). Those who never escape from their own certainty of self, and accordingly never appreciate the reality of their objectness for others, remain in narcissistic bad faith. Ultimately, they can never escape the reality of their being-for-others. To Sartre, the members of marginal groups were oases of potential authenticity in a desert of bad faith. He believed he could rescue himself only if he could fully identify or transform himself into a symbolic outsider like them.

This book will use Sartre's philosophical system as well as his literary and critical works to explore an underlying mythology of the *vulgar Other* in his work and to discuss its implications for the notion of self. While I will discuss some of the central ideas of Sartre's best-known works, I have also tried to excavate the rich veins of lesser known works where he struggles to grasp the meaning of being Jewish, black, or homosexual. It is not my purpose to examine the economic or political causes for the oppression of such minority groups, or to reduce the reality of oppression to issues of vulgarity. Rather, I wish to show how images of otherness that help to create and maintain the marginality of the oppressed may also contain a way of contesting the legitimacy of the system that oppresses. When fully understood, the vulgarity of the Other stands as a manifestation of the inner tension all people experience at the heart of their own humanity. In his appreciation of the liberating potential of vulgarity, Sartre envisioned the possibility of a reappropriation of otherness that would ultimately bring about a reconsideration of the problematic categories of self and other.

Sartre's own ambivalence about the experience of otherness is related in part to the anthropological distinction between nature and culture, and the fact that white males have historically claimed autonomy over the realm of culture, while the Other is associated with the realm of nature. Of course, the polarity between nature and culture is itself an artificial construction linked to various social and political ideologies. At times, the link with nature is romanticized as the original life-force that has become atrophied in civilized people, while at other times it is devalued as that which threatens to destroy the victories of civilization. Examples of both attitudes can be found in Sartre's work. Thus when he considered the imposition of European colonialism on Africa, he described the African peoples in images of nature that represented a purity of human possibility before it was deformed by propriety and civility. Blackness was a metaphor for the power, energy, and creative human capacities that held the cure for the disease of being overcivilized. On the other hand, when Sartre contemplated the nature of "femaleness," he recoiled at the repellent, threatening, engulfing manifestation of nature he saw in women. In both cases, it is an association with nature that provides these groups with an escape from the artificiality of the dominant cultural powers.

It is in our attitude toward nature and its processes that we find the areas of otherness within ourselves. Sartre maintained an ambivalent attitude toward nature, sometimes seeing it as what must be transcended by the freedom of human consciousness and sometimes as a realm of freedom from a deadly civility. Either way, nature represented what has been called "a category of challenge,"[6] defined in opposition to what Sartre either approved of or disapproved of.

While women and blacks were particularly appealing to Sartre as different symbolic representations of the Other, the image of the Jew as Other stood out both in his work and personal life. This image of the Jew is especially interesting, since it cannot be categorized by any simple opposition or polarity. Rather, it seems that the otherness or marginality of the Jew stems from the non-Jew's perception of the Jew as a foil to the dominant cultural presuppositions about the self. In this sense, the symbolic function of the Jew is similar for an antisemite on the one hand, and for a philo-semite like Sartre on the other. In either case, the Jew marks an outer limit. The major difference between the antisemite and the philo-semite lies in their different attitudes toward the normative model of the self. Their evaluations of the core image or

6. See Maurice Bloch and Jean H. Bloch, "Women and the Dialectics of Nature in Eighteenth Century Thought," in Carol P. MacCormack and Marilyn Strathern, eds., *Nature, Culture, Gender* (Cambridge: Cambridge University Press, 1980).

values that the Jew demarcates determine the value of those who occupy the margin. Insofar as Sartre found the central cultural image of the bourgeoisie suspect, if not bankrupt, those who represented the margins of either civility or vulgarity—as the Jew did—acquired a positive valorization.

Sartre's romanticizing of the marginal and his portrayal of the Jew as the marker of *both* civility and vulgarity are common cultural phenomena. Conversely, for the antisemite, the figure of the Jew defines the *devalued* margin of both civility and vulgarity. This explains in part the paradoxical symbolic valence of the antisemitic image of the Jew. At one end of the spectrum, the Jew represents what is horribly natural, crude, carnal, vulgar, and perverse—in short, the threat to civility. Yet, on the other end of the spectrum, the Jew represents the "excesses" of civilization—the threats of cosmopolitanism, decadence, overrefinement, rootlessness, internationalism—in short, the fear of modernity, the city, and the threat of civility itself.

For the Jew, as for other inhabitants of the margin, to be Other is to be seen as sacred in a certain sense. People experience otherness with all the ambivalence evoked by the sacred: it represents a power simultaneously fearful and enticing, repulsive and desirable. The sacred defines the *central* ordering principles of reality (as well as that which is ontologically "wholly other"), but it also indicates the *margins* of reality (which are charged with a kind of negative sacrality or otherness). These two elements of the sacred contribute to the normative images of self and other contained within a particular religious system.

John Murray Cuddihy's *Ordeal of Civility* offered a provocative analysis of the social dilemma that political emancipation presented to Jews of nineteenth-century Europe. Political emancipation in itself could not compensate the Jews for lack of expertise in the area of proper social etiquette and public behavior in the Gentile society at large. To a great extent, the continuing "Jewish problem," the question of whether the Jews could ever fully assimilate into respectable European society, stemmed from the Jews' lack of bourgeois ritual competence. Despite their newly attained political rights, Jews were still regarded as vulgar and uncultivated by the mainstream society. Beneath this problem lay the larger question of what happens when there is a clash of different models of the self.

The central distinction in civilized society between the public and the private was alien to the European Jewish subculture where emotion was directly expressed and a clearly delineated realm of the private was mostly absent. As the Jews moved from social and cultural marginality toward the center of bourgeois society, they had to learn to conceal or restrain private emotions or channel them into appropriate, respectable, public behavior. "Jews were being asked, in effect, to become bourgeois."[7] The sense of cultural awkwardness, of a residual coarseness or rudeness which could never be completely removed, led Jewish intellectual giants to develop theories which simultaneously accounted for the Jewish lack of refinement, aimed at "civilizing" the Jews, and unmasked the "Protestant etiquette" which had both excluded them and stigmatized them as social pariahs. In different ways, they showed both the triviality and hypocrisy of the courtesies and rituals which constituted respectability and civility. The net effect of this critique was to relocate the boundaries of the self.

Freud, for example, shifted the focus from proper social behavior to the nonsocial, uncivilized instincts within *everyone*. Marx showed bourgeois etiquette and religion to be merely a spiritualized refinement of the genuine crudity of economic struggle. Lévi-Strauss showed the cultural equality of the raw, vulgar, naked, and primitive to the cooked, refined, clothed, and civilized.

The dilemma over civility in Sartre's life and thought reflects the reverse image of the pariah's ordeal with civility. Sartre's well-known hostility to bourgeois culture was fundamentally a hostility to civility and the form of selfhood that it supported. Yet Sartre's problem was neither the marginality and social ineptitude of the freshly emancipated Jew nor the stigmatization of the black or homosexual. He had been born into a proper middle-class family and had been socialized from birth into correct public behavior and the institutionalized rituals of social interaction. Sartre's ordeal lay in fighting off the total engulfment of his private self by his public civilized role in society. Those who appropriate civility too completely or identify too strongly with their public roles may find that they have endangered any sense of a true or authentic self. As Cuddihy puts it, "Civility tries to make Marranos of us all."[8] Yet Marranos, those Spanish Jews who passed themselves off as Christians during the Inquisition, always knew inwardly who they really were beneath their social acting. Sartre's identity was that of a Marrano who could not figure out who he was when he stopped acting.

7. John Murray Cuddihy, *The Ordeal of Civility: Freud, Marx, Lévi-Strauss, and the Jewish Struggle with Modernity* (New York: Basic Books, 1974), p. 13.
8. John Murray Cuddihy, *No Offense: Civil Religion and Protestant Taste* (New York: Seabury Press, 1978), p. 120.

While Jewish Freud was concerned with "passing" in bourgeois civilized society, young bourgeois Sartre would try to become more like a Jew. His problem was not forcing his way into an exclusive social realm, but rather escaping from a social realm that he saw as artificial and inauthentic. Consequently, many of Sartre's ideas, like Freud's, reflected his experience of the tension and discrepancy between civilized public demeanor and private consciousness of the self; it raised the general question of whether the public or private self is more real or authentic. His ambivalence toward his cultural background, moreover, was crystallized in the problem of civility. He recognized that he was a product of that culture, yet he ceaselessly tried to strip away its effects on him. Like the Jewish intellectual giants described by Cuddihy, Sartre saw civility as artificial and contrived. Believing that rejection of bourgeois etiquette was necessary to avoid bad faith, Sartre looked to the "uncivilized" Jew, bastard, homosexual, or black as his models of authenticity and struggled to find similarities to them in himself.

Modern civility has had a particular impact in two areas which are significant for the evolution of Sartre's thought. These are the nature of community and the nature of religion. Bourgeois civility has been accompanied by the loss of the intimate communal ties characteristic of traditional religious or tribal society. Civility requires merely a show of respect for others, that is, a sense of solidarity only as deep as manners and courtesy demand. But it can be untrustworthy and unreliable, as when we act politely interested in people we find boring, or smile politely rather than complain about something annoying.

Sartre noted that as modern religion was infused by values of civility, genuine community was sacrificed in the process. As religious belief became privatized and individualized, it no longer offered a sense of belonging in a community. Bourgeois religion tended to be bifurcated into deeply held beliefs or disbeliefs which were a matter of individual, private decision, and appropriate public religious behavior. Too much or too little public religious expression ran the risk of seeming fanatical, disreputable, or vulgar. It is important to recognize that much of Sartre's hostility to religion was based less on philosophical disputes than on his perception that religion had become an important element of civility. To be Christian was to be "civilized." People participated in religion for the sake of appearance, not out of commitment.

Sartre's own response to the issue of civility was expressed in two major ideological directions. His early philosophy of existentialism rejected civility in favor of the isolated individual who withdraws into a somewhat narcissistic dream of hermeneutical omnipotence and self-apotheosis. His Marxist turn, on the other hand, represented the quest for a revolutionary community in which authenticity would arise with the death of etiquette, manners, and the values which marginalize certain groups as Other. Having seen the hypocrisy behind the "priestly" religion of civility, Sartre assumed a "prophetic," even utopian, role, and suggested the possibility of genuine communal existence. These two responses to the consequences of civility epitomize two major streams of disaffection with modernity: withdrawal into a heightened sense of godlike self or romantic visions of a future community which blur the divisions and soothe the alienation that exists between self and other. By the end of his life, Sartre had stepped back from Marxism and had just begun to reconsider religious imagery as a way to describe a future for humanity that might include both existential authenticity and a new form of communal existence.

# PART 1

## THE STRUGGLE BETWEEN THE CIVIL AND THE VULGAR

# ONE

# Vulgarity and the Rise of Otherness

It's worse than wicked, my dear, it's vulgar.
—Old *Punch* Cartoon

Shit is a more onerous theological problem than is evil.
—Milan Kundera, *The Unbearable Lightness of Being*

I am not as fond of shit as people say I am. (SG, 246)
—Jean-Paul Sartre

## Vulgarity and the Other

Sartre once amused an audience by recounting the story of a woman who occasionally let slip a vulgar expression when she was nervous. She would then excuse herself by exclaiming, "I believe I am becoming an existentialist" (*EH*, 288). As his notoriety grew, Sartre found himself the target of absurd stories in "respectable papers," including tales of his luring virgins to his room to look at etchings (*S*, 171). Despite his objection to popular associations of vulgarity and ugliness with existentialism, it would also be wrong to dismiss casually such associations as a prudish response of the uninformed. Ironically, Sartre did imply that vulgarity might be a necessary component of existential authenticity.

What then does the vulgar represent and why should Sartre have encouraged it? On one level, vulgarity is a phenomenon of social class and custom. It is the quality that the dominant social class attributes to other classes as a way of maintaining its position. In its original sense, the word "vulgar" referred to the common people of a society and their

kind of language. These common people were considered only marginally civilized. They were basically uneducated and ignorant; their language was foul and crude.[1] Since they lacked culture, breeding, taste,
and refinement, they were excluded from "good" society.

Sartre's companion, Simone de Beauvoir, admitted having had just
such ideas in her childhood. She learned from her father that the
common people lacked the refinement necessary to appreciate the
world in the enlightened way that she did. Vulgarity permeated their
being and emanated from them like a vile odor. She remembered
thinking:

> Certain individuals from the lower classes might perform feats of intellec-
> tual prowess, but they would always retain something of their original lowly
> condition. . . . On the other hand, every man who came from a good family
> had "that certain something" which distinguished him from the common
> herd. . . . It seemed obvious to me that morally, and therefore absolutely, the
> class to which I belonged was far superior to the rest of society. Whenever I
> went with mama to call on grandfather's tenant-farmers, the stink of ma-
> nure, the dirty rooms where the hens were always scratching and the
> rusticity of their furniture seemed to me to reflect the coarseness of their
> souls; I would watch them laboring in the fields, covered in mud, smelling
> of sweat and earth, and they never once paused to contemplate the beauty of
> the landscape; they were ignorant of the splendors of the sunset; they didn't
> read, they had no ideas; Papa used to say, though quite without animosity,
> that they were "brutes."[2]

A member of the bourgeois elite, she saw nothing wrong with the fact
that she was not allowed to play with other little girls in the park—"This
was obviously because we were made of finer stuff. Unlike the vulgar
race of boys and girls"[3]—or that she went to elite private schools so as
not to have to mix with the herd of common children. As a member of
the dominant class in her society, Beauvoir equated "civilized" with her
own class and disdained the vulgarity of the lower classes.

The *prise de conscience* that finally enabled Beauvoir to renounce the
bourgeois ideals of her father corresponded to a vulgarization of her

1. Compare, "By *genteelism* is here to be understood the substituting, for the ordinary natural word
that first suggests itself to the mind, of a synonym that is thought to be less soiled by the lips of the
common herd, less familiar, less plebian, less vulgar, less improper, less apt to come un-
handsomely betwixt the wind and our nobility." H. W. Fowler, A *Dictionary of Modern English
Usage*, quoted in Marston Bates, *Gluttons and Libertines: Human Problems of Being Natural*
(New York: Random House, 1967), p. 129.
2. Simone de Beauvoir, *Memoirs of a Dutiful Daughter* (New York: Harper and Row, 1959),
p. 130.
3. Ibid., p. 47.

own behavior. Politeness and truth seemed to exclude one another. "I was seeking for the absolute truth: this preoccupation did not exactly encourage polite conversation." Her family and friends began to remark at her lack of manners and neatness. She soon became known as "a kind of monster of incivility."[4]

In *On the Genealogy of Morals*, Nietzsche traced the origin of the ideas of good and bad back to their social roots. He noted the fact that "Everywhere 'noble,' 'aristocratic' in the social sense, is the basic concept from which 'good' in the sense of 'with aristocratic soul,' 'noble,' 'with a soul of a high order,' 'with a privileged soul' necessarily developed: a development which always runs parallel with that other in which 'common,' 'plebian,' 'low,' are finally transformed into the concept 'bad.' "[5] Nietzsche further observed that the German "schlicht" (plain, simple, as in the common man) was transformed into "schlecht" (bad). Thus vulgarity comes to signify lack of social standing at best and outright evil at worst.

Somewhat earlier, Montaigne had observed a similar situation in relation to a close cousin of vulgarity—barbarism. He pointed out that what we call barbarism is simply that which is *other* than our own practice, opinion, or custom. Our ethnocentrism makes us see our own manners as the most perfect and sophisticated. Although we label the manners of "cannibals" as "wild," like the fruits that they eat, observed Montaigne,

> really it is those that we have changed artificially and led astray from the common order, that we should rather call wild. The former retain alive and vigorous their genuine, their most useful and natural, virtues and properties, which we have debased in the latter in adapting them to gratify our corrupted taste.[6]

It is obvious that respectability and civility define themselves in contrast to both the vulgarity within society and the vulgarity of those outside it. Thus, the issue of vulgarity ultimately relates to who or what has been defined as *other*. The basis of all vulgarity or barbarism is the perception of *otherness*, the determination that a person or thing is different from how we are or would like to be, or what we consider

---

4. Ibid., pp. 179, 182. Ironically, by the time Beauvoir met Sartre, she had—in some respects— left behind more of her upbringing than he. "My lack of common courtesy often embarrassed Sartre, who in those days was a surprisingly polite person." *The Prime of Life* (New York: Harper and Row, 1976), p. 105.
5. Fredrich Nietzsche, *On the Genealogy of Morals* (New York: Vintage Books, 1969), p. 27.
6. "On Cannibals," in *The Complete Essays of Montaigne* (Stanford: Stanford University Press, 1958), pp. 152–53.

healthy and good. In short, the Other usually is regarded as *vulgar*, and the vulgar is almost always seen as *other*. Disdain at vulgarity is rooted in fear of the Other's difference, for difference by its very nature is subversive and carries the seeds of loss of control. By relativizing one's assumptions about the way the world is and ought to be, the Other's difference threatens the easy stability and security of seeing in the world only a reflection of ourselves. To neutralize this threat, it is necessary to devalue (and thus disempower) the Other as uncivilized, vulgar, dangerous, or even mad.

## Revenge of the Vulgar

Since respectability and civility have regularly served merely to cloak the exploitation and repression of individuals and groups who are not in power, those who question the societal status quo have sometimes transformed their stigma of vulgarity into a badge of authenticity. This "stigma" symbolizes their rejection of respectability, gentility, and elegance. A conservative Ortega y Gasset was astonished at what he saw as the audacity of the vulgar crowd in the modern age. The revolting masses, he despaired, not only were shameless about their vulgarity, but also "proclaim and impose the rights of vulgarity, of vulgarity as a right."[7] Indeed, Sartre himself regarded vulgarity as a heroic stance expressing a bold and refreshing passion for life in place of insipid respectability. He admired the heroic vulgarity of the young "countercultural" rebels of the 1960s who rejected not only the ideas and values of the older generation, but also their rituals, ceremonies, and sense of propriety. The protests of the 1960s involved a willingness to "make a scene," and to violate rules of public behavior.[8] The celebration of the vulgar in language, fashion, or behavior was not intended as loud exhibitionism; the counterculture was not simply narcissistic self-indulgence. Rather, the counterculture often turned to "countercivility" to express its rejection of the technological, functional rationality characteristic of modern society. The ultimate goal was genuine connection with the group, and the main virtue was openness—emotional, physical, verbal. It brought the public/private distinction into question. Public copulation and defecation, or violation of linguistic taboos in public, expressed a rejection of the private realm.

Another product of the 1960s, the human potential movement, also offered an implicit critique of civility in its focus on honest and sponta-

7. Ortega y Gasset, *The Revolt of the Masses* (New York: W. W. Norton, 1932), p. 70.
8. See Philip Slater, *The Pursuit of Loneliness* (Boston: Beacon Press, 1970), p. 55.

neous expression of feelings. Manners and civility were seen as obstacles to "self-actualization" to the extent that they elevated dispassionate control and restraint over feelings. The American etiquettician Judith Martin (a.k.a. Miss Manners), a popular spokesperson for civility, reacted predictably to the "anticivilizing" results of total openness and honesty. She responded with a Jewish family maxim she had inherited: "People shouldn't act naturally, but civilly."

But civility often requires an absence or suppression of real affect. Much of the force behind the vulgarity of the counterculture was a search for intense experience and uncensored relationships. Vulgarity recognizes the power and reality of our own desires. It acknowledges the natural or instinctual side of our being. It is "the vulgar" who question the need always to delay gratification or disguise the sexual side of their existence. The vulgar unapologetically glory in a level of stimulation that frightens those with "good taste."

One of the major forms of vulgarity for which Sartre was criticized was linguistic. In part, he may have used vulgar language in his literary works to shock the complacency of respectable folk and because he believed that crude and vulgar language was often essential for speaking the truth. Those who have been excluded from the power and culture of the dominant class within a society must find a way to talk about their experience without deforming it into the language of their oppressors. Sartre appreciated the linguistic challenge posed to black writers, homosexual writers, and others in search of an authentic voice. He was particularly aware of the problems of language that arise when one attacks the conventional forms of thought. He noted that the "acceptable" leftist writers were those who maintained a moderate tone in their protest, and thus were coopted. In the late 1960s he became involved with the banned Maoist newspaper, *La Cause du peuple*, which refused to use bourgeois language and reasoning. Sartre seemed to equate the paper's vulgarity of expression with the authenticity of its feeling.

> Their rough, primitive, and violent language deeply shocks the bourgeois. . . . None of the accepted forms are there. . . . Here the people speak to the people. . . . It is the popular language that accompanies a certain stage in the struggle—exactly the kind of language the bourgeois does not want to recognize, because it ignores bourgeois subtleties and consistently affirms the popular morality and the popular meaning of justice.[9]

Throughout his life Sartre gravitated toward those who preserved this kind of "vulgar" relation to life. Simone de Beauvoir remembered the

9. *Sartre in the Seventies: Interviews and Essays* (London: Andre Deutsch, 1978), pp. 180–81.

time early in their lives when she and Sartre especially enjoyed being jostled in a crowd and felt special affection for grimy shops, warehouses, and factories. "Such objects were not works of art: they lacked all baroque and poetic charm. These unlovely houses and streets neither rose above the condition of mankind nor sought to escape it: they were its concrete embodiment."[10] Even as an old man, Sartre found himself attracted to the vitality and vulgarity of young people.

Sartre's strong feelings about the disreputable and vulgar elements of society stemmed in part from his own childhood experience. He had been raised to be a pretentious, snobby child. Only in retrospect did he see that this special treatment had inhibited him from developing a "real" identity. The playmates from whom his grandfather shielded him, however, were those whose language was repulsive. In *The Words* he recalled his own panicked reaction to seeing his teacher's name written on the wall—"Old man Barrault is a prick [*con*]" (W, 50):

> My heart began thumping violently. I stood there utterly stupefied. I was afraid. "Prick" could only be one of the "dirty words" that swarm in the disreputable areas of vocabulary and that a well-bred child never encounters. It was short and brutal and had the horrible simplicity of rudimentary insects. Merely to have read it was too much. I forbade myself to pronounce it, even in a whisper. I didn't want that cockroach on the wall to jump into my mouth and change into a loud, evil blast. . . . It seemed to me both that some cruel lunatic was jeering at my politeness, my respect, my zeal, the pleasure I took in doffing my cap and saying, "Good morning, Monsieur l'Instituteur," and that I myself was that lunatic, that the dirty words and evil thoughts swarmed in my heart. (W, 50–51)

Here is an excellent example of Sartre's own split consciousness, and his discovery of the power of the vulgar within himself. As an adult, he came to relish the opportunity to shock the proper and respectable bourgeoisie. Indeed, breeding and good taste were elements of a bourgeois civility for which Sartre had lost all patience and respect.

In his personal life as well as his intellectual thought, Sartre carried a deep ambivalence toward his own bourgeois background and the bourgeoisie in general. He oscillated between the part of himself that had assimilated bourgeois culture and the part that vehemently condemned it for having cheated him. In fact, he did continue to shine as a creator of culture, but he always searched for that group—outside his cultural family—whose crude slang and gestures he could imitate and with

10. Beauvoir, *The Prime of Life*, p. 122.

whom he could laugh in chorus. On the one hand, Sartre recognized that he was a product of the age in general and his family in particular, while on the other hand he struggled endlessly to uproot himself from that background. Fighting to belong everywhere, he ended by not truly belonging anywhere, not even—by the end of his life—in the Sartrean "family" that had coalesced around him. Of course, he could say that it was not his fault. Was it not the fate of human consciousness to define itself in terms of what it is not, and where it does not belong? Looking back, he reflected with some satisfaction, "What infuriates people is that I'm doubly a 'traitor.' I'm a bourgeois and I speak harshly of the bourgeoisie" (*PB2*, 70).

Could it be that in this position of double treason, Sartre found some basis for his identity? The "I" that is bourgeois exists over against the common people who represent its negation. To the extent that they are oppressed and I stand apart from them, I have betrayed them. To be totally accepted and socially legitimate is also to be a faker, to be existentially illegitimate. The "I" that flees its bourgeois roots by seeking a kind of solidarity and existential legitimacy with the nonbourgeois Other suffers a different sort of alienation, that is, a betrayal of its own foundation. Out of this double negation, Sartre hoped to find something positive, an identity based on a perpetual revolution at its core. Two negatives make a positive. Loser wins!

## From Vulgarity to Scatology

It is not without some reason that Sartre's existentialism was called "excrementalism" by certain people, or that one of his critics remarked, "*Nous avions le mouvement dada, voici maintenant, le mouvement caca.*"[11] Indeed, Sartre's attraction to the vulgar inevitably involved him in questions of scatology. Although he defended himself against his critics' charges, he also rejected their attempts to sanitize the discussion of human existence. Most people are socialized to ignore or deny physical life. For Lucien Fleurier in Sartre's story, "Childhood of a Leader," toilet training made a major contribution to his transformation into a "respectable" adult. "You could never imagine they [adults] forgot themselves in bed or did all the other little things that boys do, because they have so many dark clothes on their bodies and you can't imagine what's underneath. When they're all together they eat every-

11. Alfred Stern, *Sartre: His Philosophy and Existential Psychoanalysis* (New York: Delta Books, 1969), p. 199.

thing and talk and even their laughs are serious, it's beautiful, like at mass" (*INT*, 85–86). Confronting the reality of bodily functions, therefore, is one way of piercing bourgeois civility and is necessary for the sake of truth. Like Freud, Sartre felt he had an obligation to recognize and publicize the less civilized and less tasteful side of human existence.

> The reason why we must speak of even the most humble functions of the body is that we must not pretend to have forgotten that the spirit descends into the body, or in other words, the psychological into the physiological. . . . I don't speak of these things for my amusement but because in my view a writer ought to grasp man whole. . . . There is an interaction between sex and thought as we have been taught by psychoanalysis, which is not sufficiently known. (*EH*, 258)

During the period that Sartre was held by the Nazis in a prisoner of war camp, he noticed that though the common toilet facilities offered no privacy, they had contributed to the sense of community he experienced there. He did not feel degraded or dehumanized by the impossibility of maintaining traditional customs of civility in regard to personal hygiene, as others may have been. Nor did he focus on the fact of regularly being seen by others as he was involved in the normally private act of defecation. Rather, he felt linked to the other inmates because of it. As Barrington Moore has noted, "The acceptance of another person as observer or participant in the major secretions and excretions is likely to imply a high degree of intimacy."[12] To force strangers to do so may likewise help create that intimacy in an immediate way.

Under most circumstances, defecation provides children with one of their earliest experiences of privacy (see, *INT*, 89). It requires temporarily suspending the solidarity of the group. As David Bakan has pointed out, the early socialization of children strives (through toilet training) to bring defecation under the control of their will, and to isolate it in a proper space and time.[13] This suppression of anality, he argued, is characteristic of the repressiveness of bourgeois society and contributes to the emergence of modern individualism. Mastering the anus requires the segregation of a realm which is private and vulgarly natural. Propriety reinforces this idea by teaching shame and disgust at the actions and products of the anus.

Accordingly, it is the anal area that speaks the body language of

12. Barrington Moore, Jr., *Privacy: Studies in Social and Cultural History* (Armonk, N. Y.: M. E. Sharpe, Inc., 1984), pp. 59–60.
13. David Bakan, *The Duality of Human Existence* (Boston: Beacon Press, 1966), p. 86.

defiance. If anal control is one of the earliest experiences of civilizing the inescapably organic aspect of life, then public farting or exposing one's buttocks registers one's disdain for conventional civility. In his study of Jean Genet, Sartre uncovers two anal dimensions to Genet's alienation from proper society. First, as a foundling given up by his mother, Genet must have felt, Sartre supposed, like little more than excrement in his mother's eyes, a waste product to be gotten rid of. Second, when Genet is caught *from behind* in the act of stealing, the shock to his sense of self is symbolically tantamount to an anal rape.

Shit is a very ambivalent symbol for Sartre. On the one hand, it is yet another expression of the vulgar and repugnant dimensions of existence that must be confronted to perceive the truth. On the other hand, social attitudes toward it display the rotten core of all attempts at civility. While most "decent folk" are offended by scatology as a violation of propriety, the bourgeoisie simultaneously manages, Sartre observed, a "friendly feeling . . . for his excrement" (SG, 246n). The French bourgeois, he added, "doesn't dislike shit, provided it is served up to him at the right time." Indeed, Sartre thought that coprophilia was the ultimate symbol of "our civilization of solitude and individualism." Isolated in an indifferent or hostile society that fails to provide meaningful social transcendence, individuals and families turn inward for security. Sartre said he was *not* fond of shit when it merely represented this pursuit of an identification with the organic world.

In his discussion of Flaubert, Sartre took note of other scatological themes. Strangely enough, he considered coprophagy, eating excrement, to be a perfect symbol of the quest for self-sufficiency within bourgeois marriage. Just as the family represents a self-sustaining unit in contrast to the cruel outside world, coprophagy represents nutritional self-sufficiency. One eats what one eliminates and eliminates what one eats. Furthermore, coprophagy was a symbol of bourgeois utilitarianism, of the greed and egoism that makes us want to make use of even the wastes of our own activities. To this extent, Sartre insisted, we are all figurative shit-eaters (FI, 3:208–9).

Concern with excrement and scatology may thus represent a rejection of transcendence in favor of immanence. Feces are a powerful symbol of the boundary between the inorganic and the organic, between mere matter and life. It is matter out of which life has been leached. At the same time, it is produced by the body in an involuntary way during which time the body is temporarily immobilized and helpless.[14] On the other hand, facing the underworld of scatology may

14. Moore, *Privacy*, p. 61.

indirectly be a form of transcendence, as one breaks through the disguises that alienate consciousness from its own embodiment.

## The Curse of Ugliness

The pervasive disgust at scatology is a protective reaction to this kind of violent confrontation with the utterly natural side of human life, one that is normally disguised by civility. A major trauma in Sartre's childhood stemmed from his sudden intuition of another aspect of this natural side of his existence from which his family's civility had shielded him. It happened in confronting his own appearance. "The mirror taught me what I had always known: I was horribly natural. I have never got over that" (W, 69). Why should it be so horrible to be "natural"? For Sartre, it was a shattering experience of internal otherness, an awareness of that which is beyond human consciousness and intention, namely the formlessness of his flesh that made him cousin to the jellyfish (W, 69). In *Nausea*, Roquentin also notices this strange "natural" quality of his face in the mirror.

> What I see is well below the monkey, on the fringe of the vegetable world, at the level of jellyfish. . . . I see a slight tremor, I see the insipid flesh blossoming and palpitating with abandon. The eyes especially are horrible seen so close. They are glassy, soft, blind, red-rimmed, they look like fish scales. . . . I draw my face closer until it touches the mirror. The eyes, nose and mouth disappear: nothing human is left. . . . People who live in society have learned how to see themselves in mirrors as they appear to their friends. I have no friends. Is that why my flesh is so naked? You might say—yes you might say, nature without humanity. (N, 27–29)

It is obvious that nature appeared to Sartre as that which undermined and destroyed one's human quality in a nauseating display of naked flesh. He himself suffered from a profound sense of alienation from his own body, in which he never quite felt very much at home (A, 311).

In the previous passage, Roquentin not only saw his own face as disgustingly natural, he experienced the chaotic existence of the whole physical world as overwhelmingly ugly. Beauty could only exist, he thought, as a creative product of human imagination and freedom. Roquentin reflected:

> All the things around me were made of the same material as I, a sort of messy suffering. The world was so ugly, outside of me, these dirty glasses on the table were so ugly, and the brown stains on the mirror and Madeleine's

apron and the friendly look of the gross lover of the patronne, the very existence of the world so ugly that I felt comfortable, at home. (*N*, 232–33)

This association of the contingent quality of nature with ugliness took on very personal dimensions for Sartre. His early life was shaped by a traumatic discovery of his own physical ugliness. This revelation was precipitated by his first haircut at the age of seven. Without his long hair, it was no longer possible for everyone to "deny my obvious ugliness." His falling locks had transformed him from a "little wonder" into a "toad" (*W*, 66).[15] At the end of *Words*, Sartre promised later to "tell when and how I served my apprenticeship to violence [his adolescence] and discovered my ugliness—which for a long time was my negative principle, the quicklime in which the wonderful child was dissolved" (*W*, 158).

Although Sartre spoke of his ugliness with some remorse, it also symbolized a path of escape. To be sure, Sartre was neither deformed nor physically grotesque in any way. Photos reveal a reasonably attractive (though walleyed) young man. Simone de Beauvoir denied that she found Sartre any uglier than other men (*A*, 288), though she also remembered that he had stood out from his friends when she first met him, because he was "the dirtiest, the most poorly dressed, the ugliest" (*SH*, 22). Whatever the reality, however, Sartre clung to an exaggerated sense of ugliness as though it were a life preserver. At last there was something he could use to crack his world of privilege, to spoil his perfect identity, and perhaps to identify with those who are outsiders. Since his life as a "wonderful child" was also that of an impostor and fake, the crumbling of that life under the corrosive acid of ugliness was a way to become more authentic. Indeed, Sartre's discovery of his own ugliness corresponded with his discovery of his imposture. Ugliness became associated with cutting through illusions and lies, and looking reality in the face. Existential authenticity isn't pretty!

Sartre never wrote the promised sequel to *The Words* that would explore violence and ugliness. Nevertheless, in his later interviews with Simone de Beauvoir, he explained how it was women who revealed his ugliness to him. In particular, he recalled an event that occurred when he was an adolescent. He had told his friends that he wanted to meet a certain pretty young girl. His friends told him to approach her as she

---

15. Sartre has offered several different versions of this episode. In *Words*, he contended that his mother reacted to his haircut by kindly saying nothing about his looks. But in a later interview, he recalled the incident differently: "Naturally my mother and grandmother let out shrieks of horror and declared that I looked vile" (*PB1*, 104).

went along the street. The girl, who had been warned, tried to elicit something amusing from Sartre, and then left. The next day she turned to Sartre, in front of his friends, and called him (depending on which of Sartre's accounts one accepts): "Ugly fool" (A, 289); "Old fool, with his spectacles and his big hat" (A, 292); "swollen-headed guttersnipe" (PB1, 104); or "old bum with one eye that says shit to the other."[16] Sartre reacted to this episode with both anger and despair. Following it, he claimed that his friends continued to mock him on account of his ugliness. Henceforth, Sartre reported that ugliness was a part of him, and he had the persistent feeling that other people found him physically repulsive. He felt that even in asking directions of a stranger in the street, he was inflicting "a disagreeable presence" on the person (A, 288). Obviously, the stigma of ugliness had a secondary benefit. Here at least was Sartre's opportunity to experience a hostility to his being that he could compare to the antisemitic, homophobic, or racist experiences of stigmatized groups.

In his study of Flaubert, Sartre briefly analyzed the paradox that people regard physical ugliness as something over which one has no control, and yet they are offended by it, as though an ugly person deliberately chose to look this way. In other words, we accept ugliness as "a received determination subject to an external law and which, as the passive result of heredity, intrauterine accident, etc. is maintained through passivity"; but on a deeper and more primitive level, we hold the ugly responsible for their ugliness in some way (FI, 1:297).

A person's face, observed Sartre, represents the intersection of contingency and freedom. On the one hand, it is an example of "chained freedom," since human consciousness is here limited by a certain material form. On the other hand, it is also a "surpassed materiality," since all people assume and surpass their physical beauty or ugliness in the mode of existence they determine for themselves. In looking at a face, Sartre said, we often confuse the aesthetic (which is contingent and involuntary) and the moral (which is a matter of freedom). Thus a beautiful face is reassuring, and an ugly one "seems to reveal the hideousness of a soul" (FI, 1:298). "A truly ugly woman is arresting, discordant in the midst of dull, run-of-the-mill human faces, and there is not doubt at all that she is unhappy" (FI, 1:298), at least in the popular mind. The ugly woman (and one could add, *mutatis mutan-*

---

16. Quoted in John Gerassi, *Jean-Paul Sartre: Hated Conscience of His Century* (Chicago: University of Chicago Press, 1989), p. 61.

*dis*, women in general, Jews, blacks, etc.) learns to internalize her ugliness (or Jewishness or blackness) "as the permanent principle governing her perceptions, her feelings, and her conduct" (*FI*, 1:299). She assumes her ugliness and takes responsibility for it with each of her decisions. "The way others look at her and behave toward her constantly reveal to her the afflictions she would like to forget, and consequently this unmasked ugliness is the basis of the antagonistic relationship she maintains with them" (*FI*, 1:299).

Sartre's attitudes toward ugliness reflect a parallel ambivalence to his feelings about civility. Ugliness can be a shocking revelation of the contingency and absurdity of existence. But in so doing it can also be a symbol of those who are authentically in touch with the reality of life. On the other hand, ugliness is something to be mastered and transcended by the manner in which one incorporates it into a mode of being in the world.

Curiously, Sartre did not mention how the impact of ugliness on a person's existence depends to a great extent on his or her gender. For himself, as a man, ugliness awakened him from bourgeois bad faith. The discovery of his ugliness corresponded with the emergence of his own masculinity. Part of what had been destroyed by the haircut was his childhood femininity. Ugliness represented the unspoken truth that lay beneath the veneer of appearances. It also meant moving from a life of mere self-display, which Sartre characterized as feminine, to finding something more real. His own life showed the power of raw consciousness to rise above the accidents of birth, be they ugly or beautiful. But it was his privilege as a man to define himself and to be responded to by others on the basis of what he did and thought, and not how he looked.

When it came to his taste in female companions, however, Sartre's intolerance of ugly women revealed a different attitude. One of the reasons Sartre gave for always trying to go out with women possessing charm or beauty was to balance his own ugliness. The effect of an ugly man with an ugly woman, he said, would be too much (*A*, 311). In this case, he seemed to require the veneer of a pleasing appearance in a woman to complement his being. He ignored the ways in which attitudes of civility toward women exacted higher costs for ugliness and invested greater energy in their beauty as a way to distract them from more power and authentic existence.

In *Being and Nothingness*, Sartre discussed certain characteristics that he called "unrealizables" (*BN*, 527). These are characteristics that people may possess, but that they cannot fully realize by themselves. As illustrations of such qualities, Sartre described the nature of being Jewish or Aryan, ugly or handsome, vulgar or distinguished. He explained: "If I am told that I am *vulgar*, for example, I have often grasped by intuition as regards others the nature of vulgarity; thus I can apply the word 'vulgar' to my person. But I can not join the meaning of this word to my person" (*BN*, 527). For myself, I am never any of these qualities. It is part of my being-for-others, a product of my interaction with others. To be labelled with one of the negatively valued of these "unrealizables" (Jewish, ugly, vulgar) is immediately to be exiled to social marginality. Yet the society of the marginalized also offers a kind of freedom not available to those preserving conventional values. For Sartre, to internalize ugliness as an important part of his identity is just one of his many attempts to ally himself with the negative Other of bourgeois society. Ugliness would be a visa stamped on his face that might gain him admission to the ranks of the authentically marginal and a way out of the world of the marginally authentic.

## The Obscene and the Collapse of Human Significance

Vulgarity, scatology, and ugliness all raise issues of either deliberate violation of civility or uncontrollable breaches in it. All of them demonstrate aspects of a collapse of order and meaning. Civilized behavior requires that our actions or words be suited to the context or situation at hand. When we break a given society's "rules of seemliness," whether through our words or actions, the infractions are the simplest form of obscenity.[17] The obscene represents a slightly different kind of threat to civility than vulgarity, though certainly the extreme cases of vulgarity might be considered obscene. That which is obscene violates the prevailing sense of civility and propriety. In the case of the vulgar or ugly, the violation is primarily aesthetic; when the violation is obscene, however, we sense a moral transgression as well.

In this general sense of the word, Sartre did not hesitate to include elements in his work that have been regarded as obscene by some people. Sartre felt that honesty compelled him to face the ugly underside of reality, regardless of how distasteful it was. An early interpreter of Sartre was revolted by the sex and scatology of Sartre's novels, and especially his book on Genet. Liselotte Richter spoke of Sartre's "repul-

---

17. Geoffrey Gorer, quoted in Carl D. Schneider, *Shame, Exposure, and Privacy* (Boston: Beacon Press, 1977), p. 155.

sive excessives," "pornographic descriptions," and passages in many of
his books that are "totally lacking in all breeding and good taste."[18]
Thomas Molnar concurred that the book on Genet was "one of the
most obscure, verbose, and above all, *obscene* texts of the century,
comparable in content and style to the divagations of the Marquis de
Sade."[19] To the extent that "obscene" refers to a violation of the rules of
propriety, Sartre would surely not have been disturbed that such a label
was applied to his work.

There is a more specific sense of the obscene that Sartre discussed,
however, toward which he was considerably less inclined. Interpreters
of Sartre have long noted his discomfort when faced with brute bodily
existence. Sartre himself admitted that he had never felt quite at ease
even with his own body. In *Being and Nothingness*, he argued that the
realm of the obscene appeared when the human body and its activities
were stripped of all human meaning and were reduced to a purely
animal or physical level. The obscene isolates and publicizes one part
of the body or one action and cuts it off from its larger human significance. Harry Clor echoes Sartre when he mentions two crucial elements in identifying obscenity. First, it *exposes* intimate, private, physical processes, and second, it *degrades* them to a purely animal or
physical level.[20] Obscenity exposes the intimacies of life to public view
in order to depreciate them and depreciate humanity.

The obscene does not have to be manifested through the human
body, however. To Sartre, it appeared anywhere that nature overflows
the controlling structures of consciousness. In *Nausea*, he described
Roquentin's encounter with the unmediated existence of a tree as
something obscene.

> The root, the park gates, the bench, the sparse grass, all that had vanished:
> the diversity of things, their individuality, were only an appearance, a
> veneer. This veneer had melted, leaving soft, monstrous masses, all in
> disorder-naked, in a frightful, *obscene* nakedness. (*N*, 171–72; emphasis
> added)

In short, the bile-laden guts of existence spewed forth, raw, undisguised, and undigested.

18. Liselotte Richter, *Jean-Paul Sartre* (New York: Frederick Ungar Publishing Co., 1970), p. 78.
19. Thomas Molnar, *Sartre: Ideologue of Our Time* (New York: Funk and Wagnalls, 1968), p. 22
[emphasis added].
20. Harry Clor, *Obscenity and Public Morality* (Chicago: University of Chicago Press, 1969),
p. 225.

In nearly all societies, those activities or processes which most remind us of our physical needs are protected by a system of civility. In particular, eating, sexual relations, sleeping, and defecation are either shielded from public view or disguised with cultural meanings and ritualized behavior. These social customs surrounding one's eating and sexual life are intended to prevent persons from being reduced to the merely physical level. When this system of civility fails to operate, is suspended, or is willfully violated, we may be in the presence of the obscene. Most cultures have developed some idea of privacy to protect certain areas of biological functioning from public exposure. To grossly violate such individual boundaries of privacy expresses a more serious form of dehumanization than mere vulgarity or crudeness.

In general, human beings feel humiliated when they lack control over their natural functions and appearance, either because *they* have *lost control* or because *others* have *taken control* (e.g., inmates in concentration camps). One of the major difficulties of disease and old age, for example, is the loss of control over various physical functions, resulting in a gradual deterioration of the veneer of civilized rituals.[21] When one is healthy, the body exists transparently as a means of expressing human will. In illness, the body reasserts itself over the claims of civility. Illness and oldness remind us of the inevitability of civility's defeat. Such loss of control over one's own body also means a frightening chasm of otherness has opened between it and oneself.

A sick or old person may often lose what Sartre considered the major weapon against the obscene—gracefulness. Ordinarily, Sartre observed, we disguise our bodily nature from ourselves, either through clothing, cosmetics, or graceful movement (*BN*, 389). The graceful movement of the dancer, even an ugly dancer, transcends the contingency of her body, without the use of clothing or makeup. "Nothing is less 'in the flesh' than a dancer even though she is nude" (*BN*, 389), said Sartre. He considered grace to be a victory of consciousness over the body. "In grace the body is the instrument which manifests freedom" (*BN*, 400). Thus, when a graceful act uses the body as a tool to achieve some goal of consciousness, the body is spiritualized and manifests the transcendent quality of consciousness.

Facticity then is clothed and disguised by grace; the nudity of the flesh is wholly present, but it cannot be seen. Therefore the supreme coquetry and

---

21. Beauvoir offers a painful example of this in her account of Sartre's physical decline in the last years of his life. See *Adieux: A Farewell to Sartre* (New York: Pantheon Books, 1984).

the supreme challenge of grace is to exhibit the body unveiled with no clothing, with no veil except grace itself. The most graceful body is the naked body whose acts enclose it with an invisible garment while entirely disrobing its flesh. (*BN*, 400–401)

In contrast to the gracefulness of a dancer, there are also moments that call attention to the contingency of the body. A clown, for example, despite his use of costume and makeup, presents the naked facticity of the body by accentuating his clumsiness, his tendency to fall, to trip, and so on. The clown has already started in the direction of the obscene. What saves it from being obscene is the fact that his clumsiness is, in fact, intentional, and that is the reason for the comic effect. On the other hand, those who are genuinely ungraceful or awkward display their bodies in a mechanical way, lacking in transcendent meaning. This brings the body's underlying "facticity" into view. The obscene appears when the body or part of it appears as inert flesh, lacking in intentionality.

Sartre noticed something obscene about "certain involuntary waddlings of the rump" (*BN*, 401) which are "passive," "contingent," and "unjustifiable." In other words, its movements are not part of any meaningful or "graceful" action. Fat seemed to be particularly revelatory of the obscene for Sartre. He made special mention of "flabbiness" in movement and "deformity in its structure (for example the proliferation of the fat cells)" (*BN*, 401–2) as potential manifestations of the fleshiness of the body.[22] Fat is a concrete manifestation of loss of control, both in its origin (most people do not choose to be fat) and in its essential quality as inert flesh that is less responsive to human will.

If consciousness represents the human ability to transcend the fleshiness of human existence, another threat to civility emerges when consciousness is damaged or distorted. An illness of consciousness, that is, psychopathology, is profoundly disturbing to both the victim and those who witness it, since it illustrates the tenuousness of consciousness's dominion over the world of flesh and nature. Sartre was fascinated by the idea of madness. The loss of control over the self, and over language and thought terrified him. Around the age of thirty, Sartre tried mescaline and watched shoes and umbrellas become transformed into skeletons and vultures. He felt as though he was being pursued by insects, crabs, and an orangutan. Later he felt depressed, his vision was distorted, and houses looked like leering faces. For a while he told

22. Sartre had a horror of fat people and feared becoming a "bald little fatty" (*WD*, 123).

Simone de Beauvoir that he feared the onset of "hallucinatory psychosis." Beauvoir said it was just his difficulty accepting adulthood. [23]

It was as though forces of nature beyond the self were able to overwhelm consciousness. And yet madness intrigued Sartre as the kind of experience from the margins of human reality that could also be a way for consciousness to escape the straitjacket of conventional thinking.

## Civilized Scents and Vulgar Vapors

In *Being and Nothingness,* Sartre offered a lengthy analysis of "the look of the other" as the core of relationships between people. With the realization that one has become an object in the consciousness of another person, he argued, a wave of ontological shame sweeps over one's existence, to the extent that one feels part of the meaning of one's existence hemorrhaging through the hole created by the Other's look. The Other has determined part of who I am. Certainly, shame at my own vulgarity will occur when I let the Other *see* the uncivilized parts of myself. The nature of this relationship with the Other, however, is very much conditioned by Sartre's focus on the sense of sight to epitomize encounters between people. Of all the senses, sight is in some ways the purest. I can look at a person from a distance without becoming entangled in their actual physical reality. I see the person *there* where he or she is, and I can look away when I am done. We remain distinct and separate.

There are other forms that consciousness of another person can take, and they raise important issues about our assumptions about others. The sense of smell, for example, is a largely overlooked form of consciousness. As civilization progressed, human posture stretched upward and away from the smells of the earth. As Freud observed, civilization has meant a separation of the organ *of* smell from the organs *that* smell. Yet both the odors that I emit myself as well as the scent of the Other that I detect comprise elements in a highly charged medium undulating between the civil and the vulgar. For Sartre, some smells are deeply disturbing reminders of the biological facts of life that consciousness and civility constantly try to transcend. Other odors, however, capture the bad faith of civilized life and seep through its cracks.

The odors that we give off are a unique manifestation of both our being and nonbeing. An odor is simultaneously detached from and yet

23. Beauvoir, *The Prime of Life,* pp. 169–70.

attached to its source. Even when I cannot see the Other, I may be able to smell his or her presence. A scent may linger after the person who produced it has gone. And while it is passive and inert, yet I cannot master it or avoid it. Odors can reveal the presence of a person or a kind of absence, their bodily existence or their spiritual essence. In contrast to the fullness and being of the visible world, a fragrance may be more elusive, more delicate, more absence than pleasure (*FI*, 1:430).

> The smell of a body is the body itself which we breathe in with our nose and mouth, which we suddenly possess as though it were its most secret substance and, to put the matter in a nutshell, its nature. The smell which is in me is the fusion of the body of the other person with my body; but it is the other person's body with the flesh removed, a vaporized body which has remained completely itself but which has become a volatile spirit. Baudelaire was particularly fond of this spiritualized possession. We often have the impression that he "smelt" women rather than made love to them; but in addition to this, perfumes had a special power for him. While giving themselves unreservedly they evoked an inaccessible beyond. They were at once bodies and, as it were, the negation of the body. (*B*, 174)

But smells are closely tied to the most disgusting aspects of the body, too. We ingest savory food, only then to return it (either as vomit or excrement) altered by the addition of our own odor, the odor of decay and decomposition. Our odors also reveal to us the fluidity of the body's boundaries. We cannot control the smells that leak from our bodies and betray us to others. Nor can we defend ourselves against the odors of others that can penetrate our bodies effortlessly. They reach out and grab us. We can neither hold nor contain them.

As Alain Corbin has brilliantly documented, during the nineteenth century there was a concerted movement of the bourgeoisie to control the sense of smell.[24] Their goal was one of "decorporalization," to deny or disguise the unavoidable organic aspects of life. Control of bodily odors meant confining personal hygiene to private regions of the home. A refined man was one who was clean and relatively odorless. The more that he deodorized his own body, however, the more he became attuned to the offensive smells of other groups of people, particularly those who were very different from himself. Thus, the bourgeoisie extended its concern with "distinction" to the area of odors, which were seen as a barometer of social status. Sartre was pleased to find in Flaubert a writer

24. Alain Corbin, *The Foul and Fragrant: Odor and the French Social Imagination* (Cambridge: Harvard University Press, 1986), p. 141.

who joyfully unmasked the "carrion stench" beneath the dignified and respectable appearances of the bourgeoisie, "not that he likes those gamey odors for themselves, he is simply pleased that our species smells bad" (FI, 1:429).

As for bourgeois women, the importance of their scent increased as decency required them to hide more and more of their bodies.[25] Pleasant scents were now enlisted to disguise the natural smells of things. A perfumed woman does not give off the natural odors that link her with fertility and sexuality. Instead, her sex appeal was focused on the delicate floral fragrances that surrounded her. This was less obvious and crude than the coarse sexuality and musky smell of the prostitute or peasant woman.

Strong odors of any sort were both physically and morally offensive. "The absence of intrusive odor enabled the individual to distinguish himself from the putrid masses, stinking like death, like sin, and at the same time implicitly to justify the treatment meted out to them."[26] Similarly, the habitat of the masses, the countryside, was described not as the fragrant natural area that Rousseau had exalted, but as stinking of peasants, filth, excrement, and decomposition.

Smell has traditionally been used as a way of differentiating the civilized from the vulgar. "Civilized" people have generally sought to give off a fresh, clean scent, or to be as completely odorless as possible. Conversely, those who embody otherness for the dominant class in society usually are thought to have repulsive smells. For example, Jews, homosexuals, prostitutes, the mad were often disparaged for their filth and smell.[27] Shunning social and economic analysis, Freud once proposed that cleanliness was one of the most important indicators of civilization: "Dirtiness of any kind seems to us incompatible with civilization. We extend our demand for cleanliness to the human body, too. . . . Indeed, we are not surprised by the idea of setting up the use of soap as an actual yardstick of civilization."[28] To be dirty and smelly was clear evidence of lesser development, of being closer to barbarism and animal instinct. It is no accident that the stereotype of pretentious civility is "snootiness," the image of the nose straining even higher.

To a great extent, many of Sartre's own references to odors were

25. Ibid., p. 176.
26. Ibid., p. 143.
27. See Sander L. Gilman, Difference and Pathology: Stereotypes of Sexuality, Race, and Madness (Ithaca, N.Y.: Cornell University Press, 1985).
28. Sigmund Freud, Civilization and Its Discontents (New York: Norton, 1962), p. 40.

tinged with his own sense of disgust and nausea over "uncivilized" reality.[29] He often reacted to odors as far-reaching tentacles of an overflowing nature that threatened to engulf and suffocate the human realm. They were the most obvious residue of the cycle of organic birth, death, and decay that so terrified Sartre. In *Nausea*, Roquentin describes how nature has slowly infiltrated the lives of city-dwellers like a great cloud of gas. "It doesn't move, it stays quietly, and they are full of it inside, they breathe it, and they don't see it, they imagine it to be outside, twenty miles from the city. I *see* it, I *see* this nature" (*N*, 212). Roquentin is horrified to find this oozing of nature all around him, even in the midst of apparently civilized life.

For Sartre, the comfort of the civilized world of intellectual abstraction is no real defense against this layer of reality. We may try to establish an order by infusing reality with our thought and senses, but that appearance of order is only a superficial layer. Roquentin's climactic epiphany of the brute reality of the world calls into question the validity of all our civilized perceptions, for he sees everything melting into the flow of nature.

> Colors, tastes, smells were never real, never themselves, and nothing by themselves. . . . It looked like a color, but also . . . like a bruise or a secretion, like an oozing—and something else, an odor, for example, it melted into the odor of wet earth, warm, moist, wood, into a black odor that spread like varnish over this sensitive wood, in a flavor of chewed sweet fiber. (*N*, 175–76)

For many of Sartre's literary characters, odors also convey their disgust surrounding sexuality. In "Intimacy," Lulu recoils at the idea of sleeping in her man's arms, since she would then have to "smell his odor" (*INT*, 11). Later, they stay in a hotel that "stinks of love" (*I*, 32). In "Childhood of a Leader," the seduction of Lucien by a homosexual friend is intertwined with civilized smells—"silk pajamas that smelled of lavender," "the smell of whisky in his throat," "the stifling smell of eau-de-cologne" (*CL*, 121)—that try to mask the reality of the moment. Later in the story, when Lucien has forgotten almost all the details of the trip and his seduction, the episode remains linked with "a dismal odor of flesh and eau-de-cologne" in his memory. After seducing a woman himself, Lucien sits empty and tired in the metro "saturated with a smell of absinthe and fresh fish" (*CL*, 150); that is, the aromatic smell of seduction and the foul odor of the naked flesh. In *No Exit*,

29. Cf. Gerald Prince, "L'Odeur de la nausée," *Esprit créateur* 17 (Spring 1977): 29–35.

Garcin remembers the many times he came home "stinking of wine and women" (*NE*, 25).

Smell is thus something sticky that cannot be washed off easily. It lingers even after its cause is gone. Fred, the "respectable" senator's son in Sartre's *Respectful Prostitute*, complains to the prostitute Lizzie about "the smell of sin" coming from the bed where they spent the night. By the end of the play, he is drawn back to her coarse sexuality, unable to shake her scent. He tells her, "You stick to me like the teeth in my gums. I see your belly, your dirty whorish belly, I feel your heat in my hands, your smell in my nostrils" (*NE*, 279). Sartre considered this kind of concern with the smell of sex to be a symbol of the immanence of existence, of that which reduces a person to the level of animal instinct. "The couple really tries to become a single animal that smells itself, broods over itself, sniffs at itself, touches itself with its eight groping paws" (*SG*, 246n). The intermingling of odors strips away the transcendent pretensions of civility.

In *Nausea*, Sartre offered some of his strongest olfactory images as Roquentin contemplates the various women of Bouville. There is the cashier at the cafe who is "rotting quietly under her skirts . . . , like the odor of violets given off by a decomposing body" (*N*, 78). The patronne at the restaurant fills Roquentin with disgust, "and besides, she smells like a newborn child" (*N*, 82). During sex with her, he dreams of a park filled with insects, and he shouts, "This park smells of vomit" (*N*, 83). In fact, when Roquentin's most powerful attack of nausea at the superfluity of existence occurs, he is in an actual park where nature oozes forth in a disgustingly obscene way. At this moment his "nostrils overflowed with a green, putrid odor" (*N*, 172).

Women's bodies have a horribly cloying smell to Roquentin as they seem to dissolve him between their lips. He asks himself,

> Am I going to . . . caress in the opening of the white sheets the white ecstatic flesh which falls back gently, touch the blossoming moisture of armpits, the elixirs and cordials and florescence of flesh, enter into the existence of another, into the red mucus with the heavy, sweet, sweet odor of existence, feel myself exist between these soft, wet lips, the lips red with pale blood, throbbing lips yawning, all wet with existence, all wet with clear pus, between the wet sugary lips weeping like eyes? (*N*, 138)

Thus, Roquentin's sexual experiences are linked to female odors of either vomit or something thick, heavy, and sweet. In either case, strong odors indicate the vulgar, obscene oozing of nature in general and female sexuality in particular.[30] Sartre's male characters feel engulfed by women's sexual scent.

On the other hand, Sartre associated foul odors with those representing the inauthenticity and bad faith of the bourgeois world. In *Words*, he contrasted the "sweet-smelling skin" of his mother with the disgust he felt at his teacher's terrible breath. During the time that he accepted the values that the teacher stood for, he also "zealously inhaled the repellent odor of his virtues" (*W*, 50). Only after his respectful attitude toward the teacher starts to crumble in the face of the vulgar thoughts his classmates stimulate in him, does he refuse to breathe in the teacher's foul breath. By holding his breath he staves off the temptation to yell, "That old monkey stinks like a pig" (*W*, 51).

In this case, Sartre experienced the split in himself between the part that is well behaved and polite and the part which mocks and rejects that civility. The teacher's stinking breath demonstrates the impossibility of containing the foul underside of civility. Odors awaken us to the presence of something rotten and bad beneath the appearance of things. In a stronger use of the same metaphor, Sartre condemned the evil of French colonialism. Seeing the condition of blacks in Africa, he said, would be enough "to hit us in the face with the hot breath of Africa, the bitter smell of oppression and misery" (*WS*, 188). The truth, Sartre implied elsewhere, is like "a fart in a soap bubble" (*M*, 25). It does not bother your nose at first, but eventually you know when the delicate bubble containing it has burst.

In the play *The Flies*, odors take on a moral quality. The people of Argos stink with such guilt and remorse that the Flies are attracted to them like pieces of dung. One man falls on his knees before Zeus crying: "I stink! Oh, how I stink! I am a mass of rottenness. See how the flies are teeming round me, like carrion crows. . . . I am a sink of ordure, and I reek to heaven" (*NE*, 77). What he smells, suggests Sartre, is the odor of bad faith. The people's religion has reinforced their sense of remorse for an act they have not even committed, and it maintains their abject submission to the Gods. The high priest in the play invokes the smell of the dead to perpetuate their dread and guilt.

> You, the dead, arise; this is your day of days. Come up, pour forth like a thick cloud of fumes of brimstone driven by the wind; rise from the bowels of the earth, ye who have died a hundred deaths. . . . Come forth and scatter

30. On the odor of women, see also Andrew N. Leak, *The Perverted Consciousness: Sexuality and Sartre* (New York: St. Martin's Press, 1989), pp. 27–29.

like a dark miasma in our streets, weave between the mother and her child, the lover and his beloved. . . . Arise and have at them like a great rushing wind, and gnaw them to the bone. (*NE*, 78–79)

When Electra defies this collective submission to Zeus, she taunts him with her own fragrance. "Now smell me for a change, smell the perfume of a fresh, clean body. But, of course, I'm young, I'm alive— and you loathe youth and life" (*NE*, 64). Orestes, too, presents Zeus with his own odorous offering: "I'll rip open the bellies of those stolid houses and there will steam up from the gashes a stench of rotting food and incense" (*NE*, 93). Here we have the stench of bad faith versus the refreshing fragrance of freedom.

For Jean Genet, Sartre pointed out, there was a deliberate effort to be unnatural, to reject the assumptions of society as to what is acceptable and natural. He communicated this sentiment through outrageous smells. "Violent perfumes justify the homosexual's artificialism: they are as far removed from vague natural scents as the homosexual wants to remove himself from the species" (*SG*, 363). On the other hand, Genet used the most vulgar natural elements of the body to make his art. The irony behind *Our Lady of the Flowers* is evident. It is a work that

smells of bowels and sperm and milk. If it emits at times an odor of violets, it does so in the manner of decaying meat that turns into a preserve; when we poke it, the blood runs and we find ourselves in a belly, amidst gas bubbles and lumps of entrails. . . . Through the prisoner's nostrils we inhale his own odor. (*SG*, 449)

Genet brings together two vulgar extremes of odor to disturb and undermine the consciousness of the respectable: the grossly artificial and the grossly natural.

Sartre's path to existential authenticity requires him to navigate between the dual threat and promise that lie within both civility and nature. Civility can be either a prison of bad faith or a refuge from the onslaught of nature. Conversely, what is natural can be a source of nausea that engulfs consciousness, or it can be an oasis in a desert of pretentious civility. The rude otherness of the vulgar can be a breath of fresh air in the stifling atmosphere of polite role-playing. It can represent a crack in the surface of civility through which one can glimpse at the subversive core of human freedom that rejects bad faith. But there is something else that seeps through the cracks of civility; through them one glimpses the undisguised entrails of existence. If the look of the Other reveals our vulgarity to us, the natural side of our own being— which we experience as both uncontrollably Other and yet indisputably the basis of our own being—repeatedly undoes the gains of civilization. The stinking, ugly, obscene dimension of our bodily presence in the world is a horror that our consciousness struggles valiantly to transcend and our nervous laughter tries to minimize. Perhaps those who see themselves as civilized try to distance themselves from this disturbingly natural part of human life by suppressing its obvious manifestations in themselves and projecting them onto some uncivilized and vulgar Other.

If bourgeois civility was ultimately impotent to protect one from the vulgar realities of existence, then perhaps those who remained in contact with that reality because of their exclusion from civility might offer an alternative perspective. The vulgar, ugly otherness of marginal groups may represent the external viewpoint that will make *respectable* society experience the shame of being judged by the Other. Sartre himself was a bourgeois who needed this Other to teach him who he was. He had originally discussed this subversive function of the Other as a universal human phenomenon. "The appearance of the Other in the world corresponds therefore to a fixed sliding of the whole universe, to a decentralization of the world which undermines the centralization which I am simultaneously effecting" (*BN*, 255). For those whose ideas and values comprise the central power of society, this decentering from the outside may be even more threatening at first, for it undermines the stability of their bad faith. Yet, ultimately, it also may become profoundly liberating. Sartre had a clear sense of this shifting center when he described how the Other situated him ". . . as a European in relation to Asiatics, or to Negroes, as an old man in relation to the young, as a judge in relation to delinquents, as a bourgeois in relation to workers, etc." (*BN*, 279).

Obviously, part of Sartre's own identity had been molded by the traditions and privileges available to middle-class white men, the ultimate judges of his society. His early internalization of the look of the civilized Other, the regard of the public, ultimately contaminated his private sense of self. If the Other is an untrustworthy faker, the image reflected back from the Other is distorted and unreliable. But Sartre had revolted against his background and glimpsed another place to look for self-confirmation. In attempting to decenter himself, he felt drawn to racial and ethnic minorities, the young, the delinquent, and the worker as a way for him not to be what he was and to be what he was not, and to find in them—at the very least—symbols of a more courageous approach to life.

# TWO

## Civility and Its Defenses: Shame, Bad Faith, and Religion

We know ourselves through others; we know others through ourselves. (*FS*, 505)

Laughter is proper to man because man is the only animal who takes himself seriously. (*FI*, 2:164)

—Jean-Paul Sartre

While civility functions well as a mechanism for regulating relations between different individuals and groups within society, Sartre noticed certain ways in which participation within this civilizing process produced a dramatic modification of one's identity. In particular, there are two ways in which traditions of civility may have an impact on the constitution of the self. First, civilized society encourages loyalty to and identification with appropriate social roles. This may produce a collapse in one's sense of freedom to transcend the limitations imposed by all social roles. The most successful internalization of civility requires total belief in the social role one is impersonating. One's identity congeals around a fixed set of socially approved behaviors and thereby falls into the condition of "bad faith." Second, the creation of a class of civilized roles and acts simultaneously erects around it a territory of vulgarity. For those who venture into this territory, the penalty is the realization of the Other's power to inflict shame. Both bad faith and shame help to maintain a stable hierarchy of social roles.

## The Role of Shame in the Protection of Civilization

One of the major instruments by which respectable folk enforce conformity to their society's principles of civility is through the phenomenon of shame. The sense of shame has often been regarded as one of the major steps marking the development from uncivilized to civilized. Indeed, its presence is a primary trait of a civilized person; its absence demonstrates a failure of civility and a potential irritant in the social body. A civilized person maintains a sense of honor and well-being by internalizing society's prescriptions and proscriptions, and by reacting to any personal lapses from this code with a feeling of shame at her or his own vulgarity. To persist deliberately or unknowingly in such violations marks one as shameless and vulgar. The truly vulgar person either rejects or remains ignorant of these rules of civility, or follows an alternate standard of civility. Shame regulates the behavior, thoughts, and feelings that need to be kept private. It is a more powerful safeguard or punishment in the event that honor and modesty have failed to curtail inappropriate behavior.

Only human beings distinguish between what ought to be covered and what may be safely exposed. [1] As primitive societies became known to Western culture in the nineteenth century, the openness of tribal peoples about exposure of their bodies and about basic bodily functions was seen as both shameless and uncivilized. The fear of exposure and the shame that accompanies it only arise in a society that has established a clear dichotomy between the realm of the public and the realm of the private. Modern civilization, which recognizes the importance of the individual, has developed certain rules of propriety to protect each person's privacy. Among the things that are ordinarily considered private are those that link us to the world of nature. Indeed, one of the principles of the public realm has been the effort to disguise or conceal the natural functions of the body and those things that reveal our vulnerability to natural processes. Human dignity requires controlling the open display of bodily functions such as defecation, great pain, sex, even the process of dying. [2] The undisguised demands of nature are both shameful and vulgar and indicate nature's inevitable victory over the civilizing process.

Throughout his life, Sartre was aware of the shameful results of both

---

1. See Schneider, *Shame, Exposure, and Privacy*, pp. 29–39.
2. Ibid., p. 49.

physical and social exposure. A relatively modest man, he noted his embarrassment when he appeared for his military physical and had to strip in front of six soldiers checking documents.

> Our sexes gave that respectable gathering a tinge of melancholy. Wrinkled, wilting, ashamed, they strove vainly to conceal themselves in their hair. The M.O. inspected them with an elegant finger, saying, "Cough." And I understood and approved whole-heartedly the phrase of André Breton's: "I should be ashamed to appear naked before a woman without having an erection." No two ways about that, it's a question of good taste. (WD, 20)

For a man, shame also marks the dimensions of a particular culturally constructed model of masculinity. Here, Sartre's nonerect exposure in front of other men, including a doctor who actually handled his genitals, stimulates a mixture of homosexual shame as well as the potential shame of sexual impotence. Sartre later described his "mild disgust, from seeing all those pricks." Perhaps, he said, his response was "a way of asserting my heterosexuality," or maybe it was merely the natural odor of urine (WD, 20).

The sense of exposure involved in the experience of shame is not always focused on one's body *per se*. Rather, it may be rooted in others' perceptions of the vulgarity that one has demonstrated by a major failure in the rules of civility. The experience of shame frequently arises from a relatively trivial incident. "The cause may be an awkward gesture, a gaucherie in dress or table-manners, a gift or joke that falls flat, an expressed naiveté in taste, a mispronounced word, ignorance of some unimportant detail that everyone else surprisingly knows."[3] In these cases, shame involves a discrepancy between our images of ourselves and the images others have of us. This is the element that Sartre emphasized most, the realization that the self we expose to others is not necessarily the self we think we are. Indeed, the primordial core of shame is this realization of who I am for others. This dimension of myself that I am for the Other permanently escapes my own consciousness, and yet *I am it.*

Although Sartre saw the experience of shame as being grounded in the ontological structure of human experience, he neglected to mention the important sociological dimension of the specific situations of shame he cited. All of his scenarios were related to the kind of bourgeois civility about which he was so troubled. One of the most common

---

3. Helen Merrell Lynd, *On Shame and the Search for Identity* (New York: Harcourt, Brace and World, Inc., 1958), p. 40.

sources of shame that Sartre identified was the case in which a person has been observed making "an awkward or vulgar gesture." He repeatedly suggested a connection between shame and vulgarity, but he did not explore the reasons for that connection. Shame is the traditional civilized response to having one's vulgarity exposed or discovered. Both shame and vulgarity are related to what Sartre called a person's being-for-others. Vulgarity is one of the primary meanings one receives from other people. "The very notion of *vulgarity* implies an inter-monad relation. Nobody can be vulgar all alone!" (*BN*, 222).[4]

In *Being and Nothingness*, Sartre's major example of shame can only be fully understood in relation to modern notions of civility. Sartre posed the following situation for our consideration: "Let us imagine that moved by jealousy, curiosity, or vice I have just glued my ear to the door and looked through a keyhole" (*BN*, 259). In this state, I am aware only of what I hear through the door and see through the keyhole. I am not self-consciously focused on myself doing these things. But suddenly something happens. "I hear footsteps in the hall. Someone is looking at me! What does this mean?" (*BN*, 260). For Sartre, it means the shameful realization that I am an object for the consciousness of another person. The foundation of who I am now lies in the consciousness of this Other. "Shame is only the original feeling of having my being *outside*, engaged in another being and as such without any defense, illuminated by the absolute light which emanates from a pure subject" (*BN*, 288). Sartre believed that this experience of being seen from behind is nothing less than an ontological rape, assault, and even murder, a simultaneous violation and revelation of one's being. He described the Other's look as something that "strips" one's transcendence (*BN*, 266), punctures one's being in a way that makes one's self and relation to the world "hemorrhage" and "decompose" (*BN*, 263), finally resulting in "the death of [one's] possibility" (*BN*, 264).

Although Sartre offered the imaginary situation at the keyhole as though it were an ordinary one that might occur in everyday life, he

---

4. Erving Goffman makes a similar point about the social origins of stigmas. "The normal and the stigmatized are not persons but rather perspectives." *Stigma* (Englewood Cliffs, N.J.: Prentice-Hall, Inc., 1963), pp. 137–38. As Sartre explains,

It will be said that the ego in everyone is a determination of the psyche and that it is entirely conditioned by others, full of alien determinations which we can grasp in their abstract significance but cannot *see* because they appear only *to others*. Others alone can *find* me spiritual or vulgar, intelligent or dull, open or closed, etc. I can *know* that they find me so, understand the sense of the words which designate me, but these qualities—which express the relation to others—essentially escape me. (*FI*, 1:167n) failed to explore certain peculiar features of the example. If we examine the situation he has described more closely, we find that what we are really confronted with is a dual invasion of privacy, the major element that shame is intended to protect. First, there is the invasion of the privacy of the people on whom the keyhole peeper was hypothetically spying. What sort of scene might they have been engaged in? Sartre mentioned "jealousy, curiosity, or vice" as the possible reasons for spying on them. The "spy," therefore, might have been listening to and watching a couple engaged in private conversation or perhaps some act of physical intimacy. The voyeuristic element of Sartre's description suggests a case of observing that which is usually shielded or protected from observation. It is being caught in the act of this violation which is shameful, not just the mere fact that someone is looking at me.[5] Conversely, the people being observed might feel shame as well if they were aware of an observer on the other side of the keyhole, not merely because they were seen and heard, but because the private things that they were doing and saying behind closed doors had been exposed.

In addition, there is clearly a sexual undertone to Sartre's example. After all, what could looking through the keyhole due to *vice* suggest? But, Sartre deliberately dismissed *sexual* modesty or *sexual* shame as only symbolic of the more abstract dimension of shame. "Modesty [*la pudeur*] and in particular the fear of being surprised in a state of nakedness are only a symbolic specification of original shame; the body symbolizes here our defenseless state as objects. To put on clothes is to hide one's object-state; it is to claim the right of seeing without being seen, that is, to be pure subject" (*BN*, 289). Sartre wanted to reduce any sociological factors in shame to mere epiphenomena of intersubjective ontology. "Pure shame is not a feeling of being this or that guilty object but in general of being an object; that is, of *recognizing myself* in this degraded, fixed, dependent being which I am for the Other" (*BN*, 288). Though Sartre displayed a flamboyant shamelessness about bourgeois expectations and civility, at the same time he felt highly sensitive to the more abstract shame that came from his awareness of being in a universe where one is continuously a helpless target of the look of the Other.

5. As Arthur Danto points out, the internalization of social conventions of privacy is the critical ingredient of shame, without which it might not necessarily occur. *Jean-Paul Sartre* (New York: Viking, 1975), p. 122. When William Ralph Schroeder offers a different example from the keyhole-peeper, he chooses a fundamentally equivalent scene: an adolescent sneaking into his sister's room and reading her diary. *Sartre and His Predecessors: The Self and the Other* (London: Routledge and Kegan Paul, 1984), pp. 182–83.

Perhaps we should not be so quick to leap from the concrete social situation to the level of pure philosophical abstraction. Indeed, on the literal level, Sartre's point about clothing is patently false. Being clothed does not make us invisible or less objects to be seen. We may even be ashamed at the way we are dressed when in the company of certain others. But it is true that clothes do disguise the aspect of the body which is a mere mass of flesh and part of the world of nature. Nakedness itself may be symbolic, but not just of "original shame." It reminds one of the naked self beneath the veneer of civility. When Lucien Fleurier plays an adolescent game of imagining someone watching him through the keyhole, he lets them see all sides of his naked body, and he turns his rear to the door and goes down on all fours to insure that he looks "all plump and ridiculous" (*CL*, 96). When he takes to looking through keyholes himself, it is now his mother on the bidet who appears to him as "a gross pink mass" (*CL*, 96).

A more specific source of shame for Sartre's keyhole peepers would be the fact that they have been caught in an act of uncivil behavior, vulgarly displaying their jealousy, curiosity, or vice. Surely, this shame is qualitatively different from any discomfort I might feel at noticing someone looking at me as I stand on a line, for example. Is it not the initial acceptance of certain canons of civility which makes naked jealousy, curiosity, and vice a type of vulgarity, and places rules of propriety around private, intimate life?

Sartre cited Adam and Eve's sense of *nakedness* after the original sin and fall as a symbolic expression of the primordial ontological experience of being an object for another (*BN*, 289). What he did not mention about the Biblical story was that Adam and Eve discovered their nakedness only after they had been caught violating a rule by touching what they should not have touched, eating what they had been forbidden to eat, and learning what they should not have known. It was not simply a question of being objects seen by God. God had seen them as objects from the moment of their creation. In the paradise before there are rules of right and wrong, proper and improper, Adam and Eve live in shameless nakedness.

Shame is not always the result of having exposed oneself as awkward or vulgar, or having violated the rules of civility. Shame also is a difficulty for all those who are excluded from civilized society because of some physical or social stigma. Sartre recognized that the existence of a stigmatized identity, whether the stigma is physical (e.g., being crippled) or social (e.g., being a Jew), presents the stigmatized person with a choice of attempting *either* to hide *or* to reveal the stigmatizing feature, to be ashamed of it or to accept it with pride (*BN*, 328). For most stigmatized persons (Jews, blacks, homosexuals, etc.) Sartre seemed to side with those who chose proud revelation of their stigma rather than shameful concealment. The world's lack of acceptance of stigmatized people may be a source of shame for them, and they may tend to be self-conscious about the impression others have of them to an extent others are not. But other stigmatized persons (e.g., Jean Genet) may abandon any hope or desire for acceptance by society as a whole. Such a person, says Erving Goffman, "bears a stigma but does not seem impressed or repentant about doing so. This possibility is celebrated in exemplary tales about Mennonites, gypsies, shameless scoundrels, and very ortho-dox Jews."[6] In short, it is always possible to reject the authority of those who enforce the stigmatizing label.

Stigmatized people may find support in others who share their stigma, and in those Goffman called "wise." The "wise" are those who understand the secrets of the stigmatized group and are sympathetic to it. "Wise persons are the marginal men before whom the individual with a fault need feel no shame nor exert self-control, knowing that in spite of his failing he will be seen as an ordinary other." In other words, the shame response is influenced by the nature of the other person who sees us. The stigmaphobic response of ordinary people will be balanced by the stigmaphilic response of the wise.[7] In the cases of most stig-matized groups, Sartre offered his support as one of the "wise," and his "look" was one that accepted them, not one that shamed, humiliated, or objectified them.

### Laughing Off Incivility

When a person's deviant behavior challenges the prevailing sense of proper civilized behavior, the collective response in more serious cases may be to control the threat by segregating or expelling the offender, or in less serious ones by shaming and stigmatizing them. Sometimes, however, none of these responses is really appropriate. A drunk, for example, may be totally harmless, and yet he presents a disturbing image of the vulnerability of our human dignity and comportment to a little alcohol. Anyone who has ever been drunk has experienced the

6. Goffman, *Stigma*, pp. 14, 6.
7. Ibid., pp. 28, 31.

rapid decomposition of human dignity, grace, and nobility. Despite our best efforts to maintain the respectable appearance of a *human* being, it is hard to escape Sartre's conclusion that this lofty notion of the human person is merely "an unplayable role unless *all* circumstances are favorable" (*FI*, 2:156). Although everyone recognizes this on some level, Sartre observed, no one wants to be reminded of it. Instead of allowing the drunk's loss of control to ridicule our idea of human civility, we may exercise another method to neutralize this disturbance to our sense of security. We can laugh.[8]

Sartre believed that one of the major weapons of civility against threats to the human structure of meaningfulness was laughter. He followed Bergson's idea that what we laugh at in the comic is the reduction of human action to the level of the inorganic. As Freud observed, "one of the techniques of jokes is to degrade the dignity of individuals by directing attention to the frailties which they share with all humanity, but in particular the dependence of their mental functions on bodily needs."[9] When we laugh at a person, we see him or her as less than fully human. Laughter is a way of dissociating ourselves from a person who has called into question, or ridiculed by means of exaggeration, our assumptions about the dignity of human beings (*FI*, 2:155). It is a measured reaction to the threat of exposing these assumptions as hollow or false, when attacking the threat directly would be excessive. Whatever shows us that our sense of being in control of our lives is merely an illusion can cause us to laugh. In the case of laughing at "famous last words," noted Sartre, we laugh at someone who claims to be in control but really is not (*FI*, 2:158–59). The cartoon of a driver cruising confidently down a road that we see ends in a cliff amuses us, since it shows our feeling of mastery of the surrounding world is, as often as not, an illusion.

More simply, we laugh at the *person* who violates our ideas of civility rather than allow ourselves to question *civility* itself. We laugh at that which threatens "the spirit of seriousness" (*FI*, 2:163), the civilized, refined image we have of ourselves.

> We laugh at bumblers, unfortunate cuckolds, excrement: the scatological makes us collapse with laughter, the pornographic much more rarely, unless its purpose is to ridicule the feminine body, showing beneath a woman's

8. On Sartre's view of laughter, see Peter Caws, "Flaubert's Laughter," *Philosophy and Literature* 8 (October 1984): 167–79.

9. Sigmund Freud, *Jokes and Their Relation to the Unconscious* (New York: Norton, 1963), p. 202.

modesty the female who "wants to be fucked" [sous la réserve de la femme, la femelle qui "veut être foutue"]. (*FI*, 2:158)

Scatology is funny because any focus on bodily functions serves to disparage our efforts to be civilized. Serious threats to civilized life may need to be destroyed, but less serious ones can be sanitized by laughter. Our laughter disqualifies these threats to the human order, as long as they remain confined to the behavior of the Other. Laughter separates the laughter from the object of laughter (*FI*, 2:157). We suspend compassion when we laugh, for we do not want to identify with the object of laughter and thereby realize our own ridiculousness. When we laugh at an official falling on his ass, we laugh to avoid thinking that our respect for his office and power was merely an empty illusion (*FI*, 2:161).

Children's behavior often evokes laughter, since we see in them the halting attempts to become civilized persons. Their behavior breaks down our own actions into their simplest elements, which children then perform clumsily like bad actors (*FI*, 2:170). Children imitating what they do not understand amuse us just as adult behavior stripped of meaning would.

> If in describing a rugby match, I write, "I saw adults in shorts fighting and throwing themselves on the ground in order to send a leather ball between a pair of wooden posts," I have summed up what I have *seen*, but I have intentionally missed its meaning. I am merely trying to be humorous. (*LPE*, 40)

> A cartoon will show some bloated fat men, sweaty and poofed out, dressed in shorts and hacking around on a soccer field. The humor comes from the fact that there's really no question of sport or competition any more—that the meaning of the whole thing has been taken away. (*WS*, 242)

In the first case, the description of the soccer game has removed the reference to the game itself. Without this reference the spectators see only the comic absurdity of the players' actions. In the second case, the notion of sport disappears under the weight of the men's fat, sweaty bodies. Thus, humor is a first line of defense against the idea that our own behavior is merely a game with little more meaning than kicking a ball between two posts, a game, moreover, that is totally dependent on our fragile control over our bodies.

Freud observed that refined people do not permit themselves to laugh at gross, coarse, or obviously obscene jokes. Vulgarity or obscenity can leave a residue of itself on the one who laughs, thereby allowing a fissure to appear in laughter's protective power. Laughter maintains a delicate balance between civility and vulgarity. It gives a taste of unacceptable vulgarity in the same moment that it establishes a safe distance from it. As people become more refined, the jokes they share must also become more refined. Freud noted, "the greater the discrepancy between what is given directly in the form of smut and what it necessarily calls up in the hearer, the more refined becomes the joke, and the higher, too, it may venture to climb into good society." A rise in civilization, in educational and social level, makes it more difficult (especially for women) "to tolerate undisguised sexuality." But the joke allows satisfaction of sexual instincts by circumventing the repression it has undergone due to civilization. The refined person rejects as unacceptable what was formerly experienced as agreeable.

> When we laugh at a refined obscene joke, we are laughing at the same thing that makes a peasant laugh at a coarse piece of smut. In both cases the pleasure springs from the same source. We, however, could never bring ourselves to laugh at coarse smut; we should feel ashamed or it would seem to us disgusting. We can only laugh when a joke has come to our help. [10]

In this case, the refined joke allows us to experience the vulgar satisfaction that we could not openly permit ourselves without shame or disgust.

Nonetheless, there is a subversive quality to laughter that potentially undercuts its protection of civility. Sartre offers the example of the vulgar, gross character of the Garçon that Flaubert created and played at. Although the initial reaction of onlookers to the gross belching and farting of the Garçon is to distance themselves through laughter, they quickly discover that their laughter rebounds on themselves. *"In the name of what should I, a mere sack of stench, withdraw solidarity from this other sack of filth? He displays it and I hide it. So I am the comical one. In short, his obscene and scatological stupidity manifests itself only to reveal our stupid hypocrisy. . . . Thus the onlooker who laughs at the Garçon suddenly finds that he is laughing at himself"* (FI, 3:161). The physiology of laughter itself transforms us, moreover, into something laughable. In the "spasmodic contractions" (FI, 2:156) of laughter, Sartre saw a mimetic reproduction of the main quality of the *object* of laughter, namely, the loss of dignified control of the body. To "burst out" laughing is an explosive way of internalizing the loss of control of human dignity and of revealing the otherness of our own bodies.

While respectable people may use laughter to preserve their self-

10. Ibid., pp. 100–101, 101.

image, the comic person can also evoke their laughter to subtly attack pretentiousness and to question conventions and taboos. The comic represents a more childlike (precivilized) view of the world, a liberation from respectability. The fact that Jews and blacks have been heavily represented in the area of comedy cannot be unrelated to their ambivalent relation to the prevailing conventions of respectability. What makes humor so difficult is the need to keep its cross-purposes in balance. It simultaneously permits the civilized to project their anxieties on the Other and allows the Other to express a suppressed rage that seeks to undermine accepted values. In other words, we must distinguish between the laughter of bad faith and the laughter of authenticity.

## The Social Context of Bad Faith

Bad faith is Sartre's well-known concept for analyzing various forms of human behavior that he deemed "inauthentic." He regarded bad faith as a form of self-deception, a way of protecting ourselves from our real selves, feelings, or intentions as well as from the feelings and intentions of others. In bad faith we pretend *to be* what we *are not*, or *not to be* what we *are*. As in the case of shame, Sartre tried to approach this issue in a rather abstract philosophical way, but his treatment of bad faith was closely related to his discomfort with the bourgeois emphasis on civility and proper public behavior. His unspoken program was to demonstrate the need to break out of the superficial and false world of bourgeois civility.

For Sartre, the issue of civility arose at an early age as he struggled to negotiate the delicate line between what felt natural and what was artificial, that is, between private feeling and public display. Sartre's autobiography *The Words* details his own battle to escape from the hypocrisy and "bad faith" demanded by the bourgeois world into which he had been socialized. As an adult writing retrospectively about his childhood, he depicted his family setting as a stage on which cere-monial rites and fake gestures took place, while natural existence was ignored or suppressed. For many people in modern society, the family is presumed to be a haven of the private, a place for self-fulfillment. For Sartre, it was merely the place where he served his apprenticeship to the traditions of public civility. It was a stage where he played a role in reaction to the roles that others played.

Like Freud, Sartre regarded the social roles we perform in society as false masks which disguise our inner private selves. Both men devel-

oped ideas emphasizing the tension and discrepancy between our pub- √
lic demeanor and our private consciousness or sense of self. However,
while Freud struggled with the problem of gaining entrée into the
excluded social realm of Gentile respectability, Sartre was most concerned with finding an escape from an artificial social realm based on
inauthenticity. He had discovered the dangers of an inadequate sense of
the private from his own childhood, where his family had smothered
privacy by treating domestic life as a public performance.

The death of his father during Sartre's infancy forced Sartre and his
mother to return to her parents' household, where the two of them were
immersed in the dualisms of the bourgeois family. One such dualism
was that between proper social etiquette and role-playing on the one
hand, and a certain underlying coarseness on the other.

The Schweitzer family embodied the basic dichotomy in the French
value system between the sublime and the coarse, the spiritual and the
natural, the theatrical and the private. While grandfather Charles
Schweitzer was a highly esteemed educator dedicated to the teaching of
language, he nevertheless told scatological jokes in provincial dialect
with his brothers. The oxymoronic combination of these two qualities
is evident in Sartre's description of his grandfather's family as "virtuous
playactors" and "coarse spiritualists" (W, 6). Sartre spoke of their
"rough, theatrical life" (W, 6) and their fondness for "crude words
which, though belittling the body in very Christian fashion, manifested
their broad acceptance of natural functions" (W, 7). The Schweitzers
recognized the crude and coarse aspects of life even if they mocked
them with appropriate "Christian" disdain.

Sartre's Lutheran grandfather, however, had married the daughter of
a Catholic lawyer, a woman who preserved the principles of complete
social propriety in the midst of the Schweitzers' vulgarity. The Schweitzers spoke in plain coarse language, *les mots crus*, true to their Lutheran
heritage, while Sartre's grandmother Louise preferred the language of
euphemism, *les mots couverts* (W, 7). Unable to confront reality in
broad daylight for what it was, she lived in semidarkness and would cry
out when her husband Charles would push open the blinds and light all
the lamps. "Gently, mortals, be discreet," was her motto (W, 7).[11]

Sartre's mother, Anne-Marie Schweitzer, was the youngest of the
Schweitzer children. She was brought up a proper bourgeois woman,

11. "Glissez, mortels, n'appuyez pas." Compare Sartre's discussion of sliding in *Being and
Nothingness*, discussed in Chapter 5.

one who was "taught to be bored, to sit up straight, to sew" (W, 8). Her family treated her as a dainty ornament not to be touched. Though she was gifted, they preferred to leave her talents and beauty undeveloped and hidden from her. Sartre mused, "Those proud, modest bourgeois were of the opinion that beauty was beyond their means or below their station; it was all right for a marquise or a whore" (W, 8). In other words, the bourgeoisie was pulled in these two directions, between the aristo- cratic and the common. The "beauty" of the bourgeois woman was neither the simple beauty of the peasant country girl, the coarse sensual beauty of the whore, nor the highly refined, stylized beauty of the upper class. Rather, it was some mixture of them all. Sartre's mother carried this background with her into marriage. She had learned from her own mother that marriage "was an infinite succession of sacrifices broken by nocturnal crudities. Following her mother's example, my mother pre- ferred duty to pleasure" (W, 9). When her husband fell ill, she "nursed him devotedly, but without carrying indecency to the point of loving him" (W, 9). She had learned to accept a clearly defined female role in her society and family, but one which ignored her private feelings completely. Proper public behavior demanded only duty, devotion, and respect. The private inner feelings of love, pleasure, and the like were unnecessary, if not "indecent."

Of course, there is something about Sartre's description that raises suspicions. Anne-Marie's restrained, dutiful relation to her husband will be replaced and improved upon after his death by her intimate, loving involvement with her son, Jean-Paul. The contrast is easy to make out: a loveless, passionless sense of duty toward her husband versus a loving, passionate relation with her son. Whether this picture offers a fair representation of Anne-Marie's own perception or really represents Sartre's own need to neutralize emotionally a father with whom he *claimed* no Oedipal competition, it presents the two relation- ships as models of two radically different modes of interaction.

The social context of his childhood continued to inform Sartre's analysis of bad faith years later. In most of his examples, bad faith seemed to arise most conspicuously in conjunction with bourgeois propriety and in navigating the split between public feelings or actions and private ones. Bad faith occurred when people ignored their sense of  these private feelings and intentions and became concerned only with proper public demeanor, or when they wallowed in private individual- ism at the expense of social solidarity.

The social dimension of bad faith is most obvious in a well-known

example Sartre presented in *Being and Nothingness*. It is the case of a
waiter in a cafe who moves a little too quickly, too precisely, and too
solicitously. Sartre concluded, "All his behavior seems to us a game. . . .
He is playing, he is amusing himself. . . . he is playing at being a waiter
in a cafe" (*BN*, 59). In *The Age of Reason*, Sartre's character Mathieu
came to a similar conclusion about a bartender.

> Around him it was just the same: there were people who did not exist at all,
> mere puffs of smoke, and others who existed rather too much. The bar-
> tender, for instance. A little while ago he had been smoking a cigarette, as
> vague and poetic as a flowering creeper; now he had awakened, he was
> rather too much the bartender, manipulating the shaker, opening it, and
> tipping yellow froth into glasses with slightly superfluous precision: he was
> impersonating a bartender. Mathieu thought of Brunet. "Perhaps it's inevi-
> table; perhaps one has to choose between being nothing at all and imper-
> sonating what one is. That would be terrible" he thought to himself; "it
> would mean that we were naturally bogus." (*AR*, 227)

What disturbed Sartre about the waiter or bartender was that his
behavior was an effort to limit the transcendent quality of his existence
and to submerge it into a false essence. Yet the complex philosophical
terminology does not disguise the sociological dimensions of this situation. The situation of the waiter, like all such social roles,

> is wholly one of ceremony. The public demands of them that they realize it
> as a ceremony; there is the dance of the grocer, of the tailor, of the
> auctioneer, by which they endeavor to persuade their clientele that they are
> nothing but a grocer, an auctioneer, a tailor. A grocer who dreams is
> offensive to the buyer, because such a grocer is not wholly a grocer. Society
> demands that he limit himself to his function as a grocer. . . . There are
> indeed precautions to imprison a man in what he is, as if we lived in
> perpetual fear that he might escape from it, that he might break away and
> suddenly elude his condition. (*BN*, 59)

This passage is significant because it presents a particular view of
society, namely, the bourgeois view that society is a stable order in
which everyone has his or her own assigned place. Social interactions
depend on all players maintaining their correct social roles. Any violation of this order is not only scandalous but also threatening to the
established hierarchy. The notion of "a grocer who dreams" is "offensive" because it not only reminds the bourgeois of the artificiality of the
public social order, but it also reveals a more profound reality beneath
it. A grocer who dreams forces the bourgeois to acknowledge the sphere

of the private where consciousness has complete freedom from public constraints. If human beings' existences precede their essences, then they have no fixed places in society but must define them for themselves. The person who is truly in bad faith is the one who sees the grocer as nothing more than a grocer and does not take notice of the grocer as a free person. Such a person is indifferent or blind to other people as genuinely conscious and free beings. From the perspective of bad faith, people simply are their functions or social roles, and one can learn to manipulate them in the kind of I-It relation that Martin Buber condemned. As Sartre explained,

> I practice then a sort of factual solipsism; others are those forms which pass by in the street, those magic objects which are capable of acting at a distance and upon which I can act by means of determined conduct. I scarcely notice them; I act as if I were alone in the world. I brush against "people" as I brush against a wall. . . . They express what they are, not what I am, and they are the effect of my action upon them. Those "people" are functions: the ticket-collector is only the function of collecting tickets; the cafe waiter is nothing but his function of serving the patrons. In this capacity they will be most useful if I know their *keys* and those "master-words" which can release their mechanisms. Hence is derived that "realist" psychology which the seventeenth century, *How to Succeed [Moyen de parvenir]* by Béroalde de Verville, *Dangerous Connections [Liasions dangereuses]* by Laclos, *Treatise on Ambition [Traité de l'ambition]* by Hérault de Séchelles, all of which give us a *practical* knowledge of the Other and the art of acting upon him. . . . In a sense I am reassured, I am self-confident; . . . I am in a state the very opposite of what we call *shyness* or *timidity*. I am at ease; I am not embarrassed by myself, for I am not outside; I do not feel myself alienated. This state of *blindness* can be maintained for a long time, as long as my fundamental bad faith desires; it can be extended—with relapses—over several years, over a whole life; there are men who die without—save for brief and terrifying flashes of illumination—ever having suspected what the *Other* is. (BN, 380–81)

In contrast to the principle of bad faith, Sartre developed the idea of the absolute freedom of human consciousness, the power to transcend any given situation through our imagination and projects. This emphasis on freedom, imagination, and projects was one way by which he thought one could begin to escape the expectations and demands in the role of a bourgeois gentleman.

When Sartre reflected back on his childhood, he quickly identified his grandfather as his earliest tutor in the practice of "bad faith." It is easy to see a parallel between the example of a waiter who plays too much at being a waiter and a grandfather who plays a bit too hard at being a grandfather. In Sartre's mind, his grandfather was a typical bourgeois gentleman, concerned above all with his public role and performance. Charles's whole life was a performance; he was always on stage, continually "waiting for the next opportunity to show off" (W, 15).[12] Simply being a grandfather was not enough. It was a role he had mastered. Like an actor, he filled his house with photos of himself; these photos were not simply candid snapshots but rather *tableaux vivants*, that is, carefully prepared and posed scenes. The "art of photography" was necessary to capture the "art of being a grandfather." Everything was a pretext for him to strike a pose or act a role.

Because of his grandfather's tendency to assume the proper social role, young Jean-Paul began to wonder whether the adoration he received really reflected his grandfather's private feelings or was just another role he chose to play. "Did he love me? In so public a passion it's hard for me to distinguish sincerity from artifice" (W, 14). Sartre saw that the authenticity of public role-playing was hard to determine. Nonetheless, he proved to be an able apprentice to his grandfather, quickly mastering his part in the endless drama being performed in his grandfather's house. That part was to be the "good child"; he remembered, "I found my role so becoming that I did not step out of it. . . . I know nothing more amusing than to play at being good" (W, 16).[13] Like an actor, Sartre came to define himself by his audience and its attitude toward him. He boasted, "I have the lordly freedom of the actor who holds his audience spellbound and keeps refining his role" (W, 17). Everywhere the young Sartre went he was the star, the center of the stage. "I have only to push open a door to have . . . the feeling of appearing on the scene" (W, 15). Everyday life was simply a series of scenes to perform well, merely opportunities to please one's audience. His sense of self was consumed with the obligation to make people happy: ". . . only one mandate: to please; everything for show. . . . Our life is only a succession of ceremonies, and we spend our time showering each other with tribute. I respect adults on the condition that they idolize me" (W, 20).

Although he may have exaggerated his own theatrical side in retro-

---

12. "Toujours entre deux coups de théâtre."

13. In Sartre's play *Dirty Hands*, one of the characters warns, "It's the well-behaved children that make the most formidable revolutionaries. They don't say a word, they don't hide under the table, they eat only one piece of chocolate at a time. But later on they make society pay dearly. Watch out for good boys" (*NE*, 158).

spect, Sartre did not consider himself unique. Indeed, he thought all bourgeois children were socialized to be little actors (see *FI*, 2:23). Since all their needs were taken care of, all that remained for them was to please others. As actors they experienced themselves solely as objects for others and thus either sacrificed their own senses of self or developed a self determined by others. Sartre lamented that his own first nine years had been dominated by the desire to please. This desire prevented him from ever experiencing genuine love or hatred for anything or anyone. "One cannot be asked both to hate and to please. Or to please and to love" (*W*, 24). Love and hate reflect authentic emotional responses distinct from one's performance for others. But Sartre was too busy trying to get approval from his audience to be aware of, much less communicate, any inner feelings. As a result, he failed to develop any sense of self independent of the appreciative reactions of others.

> Too eager to charm, I forgot myself. After all, it doesn't amuse me very much to make mudpies, to scribble, to perform my natural functions: in order for these to have value in my eyes, at least one grown-up must go into raptures over my products. (*W*, 25)

The mature Sartre, looking back at his childhood notions and experiences realized that something was wrong. In his public role, he felt like an "impostor." He wondered, "How can one put on an act without knowing that one is acting? . . . I was a fake child. . . . I could feel my acts changing into gestures. Play-acting robbed me of the world and of human beings. I saw only roles and props" (*W*, 52–53). This realization of the emptiness of his ceremonial life was a great source of anxiety for Sartre.

> A stranger to the needs, hopes, and pleasures of the species, I squandered myself coldly in order to charm it. It was my audience; I was separated from it by footlights that forced me into a proud exile which quickly turned to anguish. Worst of all, I suspected the adults of faking. . . . I was prepared to grant—if I had been old enough to understand them—all the reactionary maxims that an old liberal taught me by his behavior: that truth and fable are one and the same, that one feigns passion in order to feel it, that human life is a ceremony. I had been convinced that we were created for the purpose of laughing at the act we put on for each other. I accepted the act, but I required that I be the main character. But when lightning struck and left me blasted, I realized that I had a "false major role," that though I had lines to speak and was often on stage, I had no scene "of my own," in short, that I was giving the grown-ups their cues. (*W*, 53–54)

As a result of being "overcivilized" Sartre lost his own private sense of reality or self. He confused his role with his total identity. When he was alone, out of the public spotlight, he no longer could tell what he really felt or thought.[14] There had to be more to identity than merely entertaining each other with our respective roles.

Sartre's discovery of the world of literature seemed to relieve him of the need to perform, but indirectly it allowed him to continue his role-playing for adults. To a certain extent, his literary precociousness was also an act. "I saw myself reading as one listens to oneself talking. . . . the game went on. . . . I faked" (W, 44). If he heard someone coming, he would put down what he was reading and pick up a heavy tome of Corneille. Culture itself was a game that people of a certain class liked to play. Gradually, the intoxication with this game reached its full toxic effect. He had contracted his grandfather's "disease." "Culture permeates me, and I give it off to the family by radiation" (W, 24). "The playing at culture cultivated me in the long run" (W, 45).

Sartre was eventually able to diagnose his dis-ease with culture when he experienced the discrepancy between the role he performed and his "real" self. This realization, likewise, came out of his reading. In addition to high culture, Sartre remembered that he had also read "real things." He especially enjoyed popular literature, the cheap little magazines his mother picked up for him at the newsstand. He could speak only to his mother about this reading material, since it would have been unacceptable in his grandfather's refined circles. "This literature remained clandestine for a long time. . . . Aware of its unworthiness, I said not a word about it to my grandfather. I was slumming. I was taking liberties, I was spending a vacation in a brothel but did not forget that my truth had remained in the temple" (W, 47–48). Yet it was in this "brothel" that he could be healed, that he could detoxify his self from its addiction to the approving looks of adults.

Thus, Sartre led a "double life" (W, 48) between his proper cultured bourgeois role and what was "real" to him. He associated escape from the civility of his grandfather with private times spent with his mother, for example, in the movies, reading popular literature, playing piano. Throughout his life, he remained torn between the world of cultured men and his preference for the simple sensitivity of women. Like his mother, women were able to circumvent civility and help him to

14. Compare D. W. Winnicott, "Ego Distortion in Terms of True and False Self," in *The Maturational Processes and the Facilitating Environment* (New York: International Universities Press, 1965), p. 150.

express his private self. Despite a life lived mostly in the realm of culture, Sartre would seek out other "brothels" where he could peel off the rules of civility and shed the roles he had mastered.

Literature could be a hypocritical game that threatened to swallow up the self, but it also opened the door for Sartre to a realm of imagination that nourished a private or introspective sense of self free of social conventions. In literature, he escaped from the public world of appearance and role-playing that characterized his family and the people who came to visit. He began to feel that his real life had nothing to do with such social games, but lay in the time he spent alone with his books, where he could be reborn in a strange and wondrous wilderness. "Our visitors would leave, I would be left alone, I would escape that graveyard of banalities and go back to life, to the wildness in books" (W, 33). Of course, Sartre was being ironic about his confusion between the reality of life and that of books. But there is also a sense in which the freedom of consciousness in literary imagination provides a greater sense of real identity than a cultivated life that is mired in "bad faith."

By writing for himself without any concern for others, Sartre later began to discover his lost self.

> I was beginning to find myself. . . . I was escaping from play-acting. By writing I was existing, I was escaping from the grown-ups. . . . In any case, I knew joy. The public child was making private appointments with himself. It was too good to last. (W, 95)

Writing ceased to be a way back to authenticity for Sartre, however, as he slowly was seduced by the myth that culture (literature) could provide a kind of salvation for mankind. He absorbed his grandfather's suggestion that he had been called to be one of those guardians of culture who would help lead humanity to the civilized world of truth and beauty.

> The wild beasts of the temporal, large and small, had full leisure to kill each other or to live a dazed and truthless existence, since writers and artists meditated for them on goodness and beauty. In order to rescue the entire species from animality, only two conditions were required: that the relics of dead clerks—paintings, books, statues—be preserved in guarded places; that there remain at least one living clerk to carry on with the job and manufacture future relics. Filthy twaddle: I gulped it down without quite understanding it; I still believed in it at the age of twenty. (W, 111)

This was the cultural mission Sartre accepted: to rescue humanity from animality. He overlooked the unfortunate fact that the process of being civilized, or overcivilized, can leave one stranded in a rarefied world floating above reality. In a tragic twist of fate, his mission became little more than "a refusal to live" (W, 119).

Young Sartre looked in vain for another source of identity, such as following in one's father's footsteps. In his case, his father left him no purpose in the world, no real property of his own, nothing substantial enough to anchor his identity. Even the joy he had once found in other people's approval lost its value to him as soon as he came to suspect them of merely acting, too. Perhaps he could still find an identity by somehow identifying with others, but it would have to be a different kind of Other, one who was real and could be trusted, not someone playing a part.

If it was the adult world that had betrayed him with its duplicitous acting, perhaps other children might have pulled Sartre back into the semicivilized world of childhood where he would have been accepted simply as one of the gang. Unfortunately, Sartre's early socialization had distorted his relations with his peers, his natural allies. At first, he was educated privately at home, coming into contact primarily with adults. Even when his grandfather finally decided to send Sartre to public school, he made it clear that his grandson was to be kept away from the common children who attended public school. At the time, Sartre said he found it "distinguished" to sit bored at his special desk beside the teacher's, while the other children played. Soon young Sartre became envious of the normal carefree life which ordinary children lived. "There was another truth. Children played in the Luxembourg gardens. . . . I had met my true judges, my contemporaries, my peers, and their indifference condemned me. I could not get over discovering myself through them: Neither a wonder nor a jelly-fish.[15] Just a little shrimp in whom no one was interested" (W, 84–85). He wished he could have played with other children as an equal. Indeed, Sartre's haunting feeling of being superfluous and contingent, and his attraction to those who have been excluded, have their earliest roots in a childhood without significant playmates or peers. Later when he finally found some playmates, he felt redeemed from the family charade. He exulted:

> I had playmates at last! . . . I dropped the family play-acting. Far from wanting to shine, I laughed in chorus with the others, I repeated their

---

15. "Ni merveille ni méduse." In addition to the connotation of jellyfish as something dangerous to touch, the allusion to Medusa invokes someone dangerous to look at.

catchwords and phrases, I kept quiet, I imitated my neighbors' gestures, I had only one desire: to be integrated. Keen, tough, and gay, I felt I was made of steel, that I had been delivered at last from the sin of existing. (W, 139)

Being a well-mannered little boy had only alienated Sartre from his peers. He had been *playing a role* while other children had simply been *playing*. He knew the art of being a child as completely as his grandfather knew the art of being a grandfather. Only after he had been accepted by his playmates as their equal, sharing in their fooling around and fighting, did he feel he had become a "true democrat,"[16] finally capable of authentic relations.

## Behaving Oneself in Hell

Sartre's best-known play, *No Exit*, contains the notorious line "Hell is other people." Sartre explained that the reason he set the play in hell with three dead characters was to symbolize the fact that when people become encrusted in their habits, customs, and judgments, they become mere victims, "dead" to authentic living (*ST*, 200). The characters in the play have reduced their existence to a level of bad faith that condemns them to the nonstop light of the public realm without relief or escape, that is, to a total collapse of the private element of their lives. The structure and values of civilized society themselves constitute a kind of hell from which there is no exit.

The fact that Sartre's hell is furnished with "a drawing room [*salon*] in second empire style" (*NE*, 3) is no accident. Indeed, this atmosphere represented the epitome of bourgeois hypocrisy and superficiality to Sartre, not unlike the bourgeois home of his grandfather, "a man of the nineteenth century," "an old republican of the empire" (W, 14–15). This is a life that lacks almost all privacy and reduces people to their public roles. As Garcin confesses at the play's opening, "I had quite a habit of living among furniture that I didn't relish, and in false positions. I'd even come to like it. A false position in a Louis-Philippe dining-room—you know the style?—well, that had its points, you know. Bogus in bogus, so to speak" (*NE*, 3). Garcin's first reaction to his new situation is to preserve the protective facade of respectability. Initially, he tries to hide his private feelings behind a veneer of politeness and playacting, but Inez quickly points out that Garcin's twitching face betrays the underlying fear beneath his politeness. She knows politeness is a shallow game.

16. Gerassi, *Jean-Paul Sartre*, p. 54.

Sartre regarded civility or politeness as one of the major defenses against facing reality. In *No Exit*, Estelle is a character whose entire life has been dedicated to pleasing others, and consequently her sense of identity is dependent on their responses to her. This is the typical form of behavior into which a bourgeois woman is socialized. For Estelle, maintaining a proper appearance is everything. Her biggest worry is that her makeup is on right, as though she were an actress about to go on stage. Her identity rests only on being admired by others as beautiful. She prefers the safety of politeness and propriety wherein conversation remains on an inoffensive, euphemistic level. Thus she is offended when Garcin bluntly observes that the three of them are "dead." She implores: "Please, please don't use that word. It's so—so crude. In terribly bad taste, really" (*NE*, 140). She suggests that they call each other "absent" instead. ("Have you been—been absent for long?") Likewise, when Inez points out that they are all damned souls in hell, Estelle refuses to listen and exclaims, "Keep quite! I forbid you to use such disgusting words" (*NE*, 146).

Politeness and euphemism are ways to avoid confronting reality. In some ways, Estelle resembles Sartre's own grandmother who disliked crude language and the light of day. He portrayed her in *Words* as a model of social propriety. In *No Exit*, the fact that the lights cannot be turned off indicates the impossibility of hiding in the dark behind conventional civility. It is the ubiquitous light of consciousness. During her life, Estelle had spent most of her time trying to maintain a respectable appearance. She could not let it be known, for example, that she had had an illegitimate child by a man of no social class. Nor could she understand why her lover committed suicide after he saw her kill their child. After all, she preserved their reputations and her husband had never suspected a thing (*NE*, 28–29; 159–60).

Clothing is another way in which one protects privacy and presents a pleasing image to others. Estelle's alarm when Garcin starts to remove his jacket is, therefore, no surprise. To remove one's clothes symbolizes shedding one's social habits and roles, and showing one's real self. She cries, "How dare you! No, please don't. I loathe men in their shirt-sleeves" (*NE*, 13). Only later, when she has been forced to confess her real crimes in life does she no longer care that Garcin starts to take off his jacket (*NE*, 29). His disrobing underlines their interaction. Inez says to Garcin, "Now you have us in the nude all right" (*NE*, 29). And Garcin reiterates moments later, "Look at me, we're naked, naked right through, and I can see into your heart" (*NE*, 31).

In *Being and Nothingness*, Sartre discussed the inauthentic behavior of a woman who deals with the obvious sexual desires of her companion by consciously acknowledging only what is respectful and discreet in his attitude. Estelle, likewise, wants Garcin to desire her, but she is only willing to recognize his desire when it is respectable. Garcin bluntly points out her seductive behavior and refuses to play this game of respectability. Surprised at her resistance after he has fondled her neck, he demands: "Why not? We might, anyhow, be natural. . . . So we may as well stop posing, we've nothing to lose. Why trouble about politeness, and decorum, and the rest of it? We're between ourselves. And presently we shall be naked as—as new-born babes" (NE, 23–24).

The situation Sartre has created in this play involves a collapse of the ordinary distinction between public and private, and the breakdown of civility. In a world without darkness, without sleep, without respite from the gaze of other people, the public and the private become one. In Erving Goffman's terms, one is always "on stage"; there is no "backstage." All of the characters in the play experience the constant shame of exposure. They are seen without the ability to conceal any part of themselves, gradually stripped of the protective conventions of civility.

## Religion, Civility, and the Roots of Existential Atheism

The need to please with one's behavior is something that children learn very early in life. It is their earliest apprenticeship in "bad faith" and a way to control the shame of self-exposure. As we have already seen, a major theme of Sartre's autobiography, The Words, is his childhood socialization to these rules of civility and his subsequent disillusionment at discovering their hollowness and superficiality.

Religion, for Sartre, was simply another area where his good behavior would be approvingly monitored by others. He remembered being delighted with the "high spirituality" of the church, which provided him with the opportunity to show off his good behavior.[17] But this good behavior was subtly undermined by Sartre's sacrilegious imagination and determination to violate the rules of decorum. In church he mused about the possibilities: "What if I stood up and yelled 'Boom!'? What if I climbed up the column to make peepee in the holy-water basin?" (W, 17).

On a more serious note, Sartre saw religion as a primary source of the

17. In "The Childhood of a Leader," young Lucien "forced himself to behave so that his mamma would congratulate him after mass" (CL, 90). "When he made his first communion the curé said he was the best behaved little boy and the most pious of all the catechism class" (CL, 91).

hypocrisy and "bad faith" that infected the bourgeoisie. In the nine-teenth century, bourgeois religion became for many something they publicly avowed while privately ridiculing it. The main force behind their religious observance seemed to be simple habit. In *Being and Nothingness*, Sartre described the self-deceptive nature of conscious-ness in "bad faith" as "not-believing-what-one-believes" (*BN*, 70). Yet bad faith is also involved when we pretend to believe what we do not really believe. It lies between the authentic commitment of true belief and the cynicism of open disbelief. Sartre found this attitude of bad faith epitomized by the shallowness of bourgeois religion. He further worried that religion produced bad faith by strengthening certain fixed social roles and inhibiting people's ability to transcend social values and models. Religion tended to discourage people from questioning the routines and pretensions of everyday life.

The conservative social tendencies of religion were of much greater concern to Sartre than philosophical arguments about the concept of God, but they were not responsible for his childhood disillusionment with religion. To truly appreciate the nature of Sartre's childhood experience with religion, one must also consider the traditional bour-geois attitudes toward religion in France.

As early as the eighteenth century, religion was more a matter of appearance than substance for the average bourgeois. Although the bourgeois normally identified himself as a Catholic, his religion had little application to either his daily life or worldly affairs. By the time of the Enlightenment, disbelief was quite respectable, even fashionable, and the educated bourgeois felt it set him apart from the crude super-stitious beliefs of the peasants. Lack of faith was simply part of bourgeois class consciousness.[18]

Even though religion regained some of its influence in the nine-teenth century, the traditional bourgeois was still less concerned with being a religious person or believer than with being an upright, respect-able gentleman. His religion was essentially "extrinsic" in its orienta-tion.[19] It was a vehicle of affiliation with socially respectable society. Thus, its focus was on conformity to clearly defined public rituals and practices, rather than any "intrinsic" moral commitment. A bourgeois

18. Bernard Groethuysen, *The Bourgeois: Catholicism vs. Capitalism in Eighteenth-Century France* (New York: Holt, Rinehart and Winston, 1968), pp. 18, 24.
19. I am using the term "extrinsic" in the sense developed by Gordon Allport and others. See G. W. Allport and J. M. Ross, "Personal Religious Orientation and Prejudice," *Journal of Personality and Social Psychology* 5 (1967): 432–43.

gentleman could tolerate some belief, but mainly he wanted to avoid believing too much. He did not want his religion to go too far, to risk becoming fanatical. Although he might privately consider himself agnostic, he would still call himself a Catholic. It was, after all, France's traditional heritage. For the agnostic, religious practices were "only signs of one's bourgeois status, like clothing, living quarters, furniture, food, and the adoption of a certain way of speech" (FI, 1:492). Religion was a question of bourgeois respectability, "an attenuated faith" by which "the bourgeoisie affirmed its spirituality and acknowledged its distinction" (FI, 1:492). One did not want to disbelieve too much, however, since rabid atheism was only another kind of fanaticism. Belief had become increasingly privatized and individualized for the bourgeois, unlike the peasants of an earlier age for whom religion was a more integral part of collective life.

In his study of Gustave Flaubert, *The Family Idiot*, Sartre discussed the role of religion in the bourgeois family at length. Bourgeois religion retained its social respectability (and therefore its place in public practice), even after it had lost its intellectual respectability (i.e., its place within private belief). It was simultaneously "present and rejected" (FI, 1:492). Sartre noted that Flaubert's father, like many liberal-thinking fathers of his period, was caught in an awkward dilemma. *Privately*, he ridiculed and condemned the rituals and dogmas of the church, whereas *in public* he observed all the rituals and practices. Sartre observed, "By forcing fathers to participate in religious ceremonies, the cops and the defenders of the faith put them in a precarious position in the eyes of their sons; it was difficult to call these rituals rigmarole in private while subscribing to them in public" (FI, 1:491). Thus it was quite natural for Dr. Flaubert to have his sons baptized, to send them to first communion, and to have his daughter married in the church. All this was a matter of social prudence. To ignore the sacraments for himself and his children would have offended his patients. Yet while he tolerated baptism and communion for his children, he no doubt inwardly scorned Catholic rites, dogma, and priests. He demolished his sons' "feeble religiosity," not by direct attack but with smiles and ironic responses to Biblical stories. The result of this situation for Flaubert and others of his generation was that they were "tormented by the need to believe and dechristianized by their parents' agnosticism" (FI, 1:501). "Without being consulted, they had been baptized into unbelief" (M, 22).

The bourgeois attitude toward religion, therefore, was only a microcosm of other general bourgeois attitudes, in particular the dichotomy in bourgeois life between public behavior and private belief. Bourgeois religion was based on maintaining a civilized public appearance, on getting along harmoniously with others in society, regardless of whether there was a deeper sense of solidarity with them or not.[20] The bourgeois ideology of civility required that one behave in a way that was inoffensive to others. Human relations were an art whose rules one had to master.

This sort of residual religion preserved out of habit shows up frequently in Sartre's literary work. The "self-taught man" in *Nausea* says he used to go to mass every Sunday even though he has never been a believer (N, 155). In *The Condemned of Altona*, Leni brings out a large sixteenth-century Bible whenever there is a family conference in case they need to swear an oath. When her sister-in-law points out that Leni believes neither in God nor the Devil, she replies, "That's true. But we go to church, and we swear on the Bible. I've already told you—this family has no longer any justification for living, but it has kept its good habits" (CA, 8). In *The Devil and the Good Lord*, a woman asks the priest Heinrich why her three-year-old son has died of hunger. The priest explains that everything is the will of God and for the good. Even though he admits he does not understand this, he exhorts her simply to believe. The woman accuses Heinrich of insincerity: "You say we must believe and you don't look as though you yourself believe what you are saying." And Heinrich responds: "My sister, I have said the same words so often these last three months that I no longer know if I say them out of conviction or from habit" (DGL, 10–11).

Sociologist Peter Berger noted that one of the functions of religion in many societies is to bolster and guard the socially accepted sense of respectability, which is embodied in class mores.[21] Religious affiliation indicates membership in the community of the respectable.

> Religion is something for those who have a stake in and a commitment to society as it now exists. Those who are excluded from respectability, be it by their own choice or that of others, are *ipso facto* outside the religious institution which is a pillar of that respectability. . . . Social religion has little toleration for the intellectual or moral radical, or anyone who flaunts the canons of respectability.[22]

20. See Cuddihy, *No Offense.*
21. Peter Berger, *The Precarious Vision* (Garden City, N.Y.: Doubleday, 1961), pp. 174–75.
22. Peter Berger, *The Noise of Solemn Assemblies* (Garden City, N.Y.: Doubleday and Co., 1961), p. 89.

An atheist is not only outside the religious community; he is also beyond the pale of respectability. Enemies of bourgeois respectability are also enemies of religion, and vice versa. Despite the merely luke-warm faith in his own family when he was a child, Sartre found that outright atheism was considered crude and uncivil. He noted with sarcasm why the deeply held convictions of the atheist were out of place in polite circles.

> Declared disbelief had the violence and raucousness of passion. An atheist was a "character," a wild man whom one did not invite to dinner lest he "lash out," a fanatic encumbered with taboos who refused the right to kneel in church, to weep sweetly there, to give his daughters a religious wedding, who took it upon himself to prove the truth of his doctrine by the purity of his morals, who hounded himself and his happiness to the point of depriv-ing himself of the means of dying comforted, a God-obsessed crank who saw His absence everywhere and who could not open his mouth without utter-ing His name; in short, a gentleman who had religious convictions. The believer had none. (W, 61–62)

Thus, the religious disbelief of the bourgeoisie was quite "timid" in the late nineteenth and early twentieth centuries. Conspicuous atheism was still shocking. "One could be an atheist but within the Christian religion" (FI, 1:492). It was simply more comfortable to make polite nods in the direction of the church. Sartre observed, "Good society believed in God in order not to speak of him" (W, 62). Ironically, God was more of an issue to the impassioned atheist than to the indifferent Christian. The religious problem of the bourgeois, in Sartre's view, is not that he believes too much, but rather that he believes too little.

Sartre recognized the important role of Christianity as the currency of social affiliation for the bourgeoisie. The primary symbol of induc-tion into this social group is baptism. In his *Critique of Dialectical Reason*, Sartre referred to "lukewarm or skeptical Catholics (or even free-thinkers)" (CDR, 485), who were Catholic in origin rather than in faith. He found it peculiar that when such Catholics had children, they were certain to have the children baptized. The reason they gave for doing this was that the children would be free to choose for themselves when they grew up. Ironically, they felt that if they had done nothing they would have deprived the child of freedom to share in a sense of identity with the Christian community.

> From the point of view of the group (to which the lukewarm or unbelieving but respectful Catholics still belong, the cousin possibly being a seminarist, the maternal aunts being pious, etc.) . . . baptism is a way of creating

freedom in the common individual at the same time as qualifying him by his function and his reciprocal relation to everyone; he interiorises common freedom as the true power of his individual freedom. ( *CDR*, 486n)

Sartre implied that the mere fact of being baptized and receiving first communion installed in the child a system of religious symbolism, a form that later could receive its contents. It made the child a "virtual member of the Church" (*FI*, 1:500). He explained that in his own case, "I had been baptized, like so many others, to preserve my independence; in denying me baptism, the family would have feared that it was doing violence to my soul. As a registered Catholic, I was free, I was normal, 'Later,' they said, 'he'll do as he likes.' It was deemed at the time that is was much harder to gain faith than to lose it" (*W*, 62). Mostly, however, performing these rituals meant little in terms of genuine religious affirmation. Not to do them, on the other hand, would have meant a radical step of rejecting the outward signs of respectable society.

Growing up in a bourgeois family at the start of the twentieth century, Sartre experienced his family's religious ambivalence at a young age. While his mother and grandmother brought him up as a Catholic, his grandfather, a Protestant, tended to poke fun at religion. His family had been affected by the general de-Christianization or weakening of faith among the bourgeoisie. The fact that his grandmother, a Catholic young lady from the provinces, could marry a Lutheran was evidence of this weakening (*W*, 61). Sartre said of his grandfather: "In private life, out of loyalty to our lost provinces, to the coarse gaiety of his anti-papist brothers, he never missed an opportunity to ridicule Catholicism. His table-talk resembled that of Luther" (*W*, 62–63). His grandfather's suspicion about the church and priests transformed young Sartre's religious school into "enemy territory." That training lasted only six months. Each time he returned home from school, his grandfather poked fun at the religious ideas he had learned (*W*, 63).

Sartre admitted that the mystical and saintly paths of a religious calling might have seduced him, if they had not been discredited by the scornful attitude of the adults around him. It was not that he was denied religion, but that he was taught to believe in a "fashionable God" and became disenchanted with the official doctrine (*W*, 61). "My grandfather disgusted me with it forever. I saw it through his eyes" (*W*, 61). On the other hand, his grandmother pretended to be indignant; she called her husband an "infidel" and a "heretic." But Sartre could tell she believed in nothing either. "Her skepticism alone kept her from being an atheist" (W, 61). In fact, the members of his family were always making fun of someone else's religion. "It was done without any meanness, a kind of family tradition. . . . My conclusion was that neither of the two confessions had any worth."[23] Sartre wryly observed that his mother and grandmother maintained a thin coating of religiosity, just deep enough to get them through an organ recital at Notre-Dame (W, 16).[24] The emotional kernel at the heart of Sartre's lifelong atheism, therefore, was neither theological nor ethical. It was the simple apathy that he had absorbed from his family. His whole family respectfully believed in God, of course, "as a matter of discretion" (W, 61). But this bourgeois religion was really more concerned with civility and good social etiquette than genuine or profound belief. Young Sartre felt bored by the whole business. "I was led to disbelief not by the conflict of dogmas but by my grandparents' indifference" (W, 63). As early as eight or nine years old, Sartre remembered, he had only "neighborly relations" with God. He courteously said his prayers every day, but inwardly he thought about God very little.

Thus Sartre's childhood experiences with religion offered him only a form of bad faith, a public demonstration of belief in something that was void of inner meaning. He followed his family's example all too well. "I maintained *public* relations with the Almighty. But *privately*, I ceased to associate with him" (W, 64; emphasis added). Sartre's realization that he had lost his faith came to him with only "polite surprise" (W, 157) rather than as a dramatic reconciliation of a "divided self." He recalled waiting for a bus when he was eleven or twelve, thinking about God to pass the time, and then simply saying to himself: "'You know what? God doesn't exist.' And that was that: faith left, and never came back" (SH, 16).[25] Of course, it is unlikely that Sartre's atheism really did take form so simply while he stood at the bus stop. He obviously preferred to attribute a conclusion that had been incubating in him for some time to a single dramatic moment. Nevertheless, he gave little indication of a genuine theological struggle in coming to this conclusion.

Throughout his autobiography Sartre complained that the emphasis in his childhood on putting on a good act in order to please others

23. Sartre, "To Show, To Demonstrate," *Yale French Studies* 30 (1962–63):40.
24. Simone de Beauvoir reports that Sartre's mother was vaguely deistic, but belonged to no religion, and did not want a church service when she died (*All Said and Done*, p. 105).
25. Sartre has recounted this anecdote several times in slightly different versions (W, 157; A, 380, 434).

eventually made him feel like an impostor, a fake. The world had been presented to him as a stage on which there were only roles and props, never real feelings or actions. In struggling to find some source of personal identity which was not contaminated by hypocritical playacting, Sartre came to reject all of the attitudes and values of the bourgeoisie as obstacles to authentic selfhood. Christian religion in particular became a target of considerable animus for him, since it, above all else, had been utterly compromised by the bourgeoisie and its facile hypocrisy.

In time, Sartre became well known as the major thinker behind the philosophical and cultural movement known as atheistic existentialism. Throughout his life, he never hesitated to declare the nonexistence of God, as well as the philosophical and ethical consequences of the absence of the divine. On one occasion, he is said to have gotten off a plane and greeted reporters with the simple statement, "God is dead." Such a bold public statement must have seemed totally disrespectful and testified to Sartre's desire to free himself from the social norms that had kept him from yelling "Boom" in church when he was a child. [26]

In *Being and Nothingness*, Sartre went so far as to present an ontological "proof" for the nonexistence of God. Like most proofs for God's existence or nonexistence, the plausibility of Sartre's "proof" rested primarily on one's prior acceptance not only of its conclusion but also of its author's definitions of the nature of God and certain central philosophical categories as well. Yet elsewhere Sartre contended that proofs and disproofs of God's existence were ultimately irrelevant to the existential struggle all people face in trying to act authentically (*EH*, 311). In an interview with Simone de Beauvoir near the end of his life, Sartre admitted that his argument against the existence of God in *Being and Nothingness* was not the real reason for his atheism. He was merely trying to present a philosophically respectable justification for a conclu-

---

26. Simone de Beauvoir's path to atheism was remarkably similar to Sartre's. As an adolescent, she, too, discovered her own atheism quite painlessly and with little surprise. "I was not denying Him in order to rid myself of a troublesome person: on the contrary, I realized that He was playing no further part in my life and so I concluded that he had ceased to exist for me" (*Memoirs of a Dutiful Daughter*, p. 137). Yet despite her lack of faith, she felt compelled for some time to continue attending church and receiving communion, i.e., to keep up respectable appearances. Bourgeois attitudes toward religion forced her to be an impostor. The result was that she had to live "a double life; there was no relationship between my true self and the self others saw" (ibid., p. 139). When she finally felt able to tell her mother that she had ceased to believe in God, her mother was crushed, but she was greatly relieved: "At last I would be able to live without a mask" (ibid., pp. 171–72).

sion he had drawn for much simpler reasons. The "real reasons" for his denial of God, he continued, were "more direct and childish—since I was only twelve—than theses on the impossibility of this reason or that for God's existence" (A, 438). Ultimately, one discovers that some of the deepest of Sartre's objections to religion were more sociological than philosophical in nature. They were rooted, first, in Sartre's childhood experience of the role of religion in his own family, and second, in a more or less Marxist analysis of the historically conservative function of religion in Western civilization.

When Beauvoir met Sartre in college she was delighted to find he was hostile to the same things she was hostile to: "The right, conventional thinking, religion."[27] For both of them, these three "enemies" were closely linked together. The problem with religion was not philosophical inconsistency or illogic as much as its embarrassing links with conventionality, ceremony, respectability, and conservativism.

Despite the fact that Sartre's "disproof" of the existence of God is both philosophically unexciting and relatively tangential to his real religious concerns, the central elements of his analysis can be reinterpreted from a more sociological perspective which will then illuminate certain polarized roles of religion in society. In other words, Sartre's conclusion that the concept of God is philosophically contradictory may have disguised his more profound sense of the opposing *social* functions of religion.

Sartre claimed the concept of God was contradictory and illusory because it required an impossible union of "being-for-itself" and "being-in-itself," the two central ontological categories of *Being and Nothingness*. He defined being-for-itself as the mode-of-being of consciousness. It represents the ability of consciousness to transcend any given situation, object, or fixed state of affairs and to freely posit possibilities for the future. Of course, this freedom of being-for-itself to transcend that which is given means that being-for-itself is perpetually denied any stable foundation in the present, fixed essence, or state of permanent identity with itself. Being-in-itself, on the other hand, refers to the mode-of-being of physical objects, or objects with a fixed permanent essence. Sartre argued that God could not logically exist, since the concept of God depends on a paradoxical union of that which is eternally fixed or immanent in its nature (being-in-itself) with that which is also transcendent and free (being-for-itself). God is only a

27. Beauvoir, *Force of Circumstance* (New York: Harper and Row, 1977), p. 645.

symbol, continued Sartre, of every person's desire both to be free to transcend his or her given situation through the power of consciousness and to find some permanent foundation for one's own being, some justification for one's existence.

These major ontological categories can also be used to represent Sartre's concern about two opposing types of religion and their underlying social perspectives. Being-in-itself can easily be compared to the "priestly" religious ideology which is firmly committed to the status quo and which attempts to provide sacral justification for the existing social structure. It is the religious embodiment of the judgment of the respectable Others. Being-for-itself, the transcendent power of consciousness to rise above any entanglement in present state of things, finds its ideological correlate in the "prophetic" dimension of religion which takes its stand apart from the status quo in order to criticize the deficiencies of the latter and to project possibilities for social change and reform.

Most of the time when Sartre discussed religion he was concerned with the first of these two dimensions of religion, and he openly expressed his serious reservation about it. There are scattered elements in Sartre's work, however, which would also seem to indicate a recognition of another, more socially positive, function for religion. Although this aspect of Sartre's thought remained largely undeveloped, it offers an important nuance to his otherwise vehement denunciation of religion, one which opens the possibility of a new way of thinking about relations with the Other. We will return to this other side of religion in the final chapter.

Sartre's criticism of religion must be situated within his specific cultural context. When he discussed the negative social consequences of religion in Western society, he was thinking primarily about the Roman Catholic church. In the case of the church, the main function of religion was to justify a hierarchical political and social structure. Acceptance of religion and acceptance of political authority went hand in hand. Religion thereby helped to preserve the status quo, and served the interests of the dominant or oppressive class of society.

Sartre's criticism of this aspect of the church was neither new nor very radical within French social thought. Indeed, there is a robust tradition of anticlericalism in France rooted mainly in the consistently antirevolutionary and reactionary political positions of the church in the period leading up to and following the revolutions of 1789 and 1848. The *philosophes* of the Enlightenment had been long concerned about the oppressive and excessive power of the Catholic church. They demanded only tolerance and freedom of conscience, freedom to practice religion or not. After the revolution, a movement of de-Christianization spread throughout Paris and the country. For a time, a new revolutionary religion based on liberty, equality, and fraternity was actively pursued. As a result, the power of the Catholic church was permanently diminished. The revolution made the church dependent on the state, which soon took control of both the clergy and education.

In the nineteenth century, as a result of certain excesses of the revolution as well as a desire to preserve the gains they had made from the revolution, there was some movement among the bourgeoisie back to the church, since the church presented an image of society as orderly, disciplined, and hierarchical. The bourgeoisie accepted the outward structure of Catholicism but was considerably less concerned with the church's spiritual teachings. Sartre observed, "The God of the bourgeois faithful . . . guarantees order, meaning real property" (FI, 1:499).

In a long digression in his very first book, *Imagination*, Sartre offered an interesting bit of his own sociology of knowledge to tie changes in social thought with developments in the philosophy of mind in the latter part of the nineteenth century. The rise of associationist psychology, which saw all mental syntheses as built up from individual parts, was a reflection of the attitude of many people about the relation of a person to society. Atomism in the realm of psychology was consistent with the ideology of individualism in general. Sartre pointed out that the philosophical reaction against associationism, and the idea that there had to be something that organizes and transcends individual images, also had political and social roots. In the social realm, individualism had come to be distrusted out of fear that it would lead to anarchy, materialism, and atheism.

> For there occurred in France at this time a strong conservative reaction. The notions of order and social hierarchy returned in full force. At the Versailles Assembly, censure was meted out to "radical thinkers . . . [who] do not believe in God, and in [whose] writings one finds definitions of man that degrade our species." . . . Frightened by the Commune, the conservative bourgeoisie turned again to Religion, as in the first part of the reign of Louis-Philippe. Hence the necessity for the incumbent intellectuals to combat in every quarter the analytical tendency of the eighteenth century. Above the individual must be posited synthetic realities, the family, the nation, the society. Above the individual image must be reasserted the existence of concepts, of thought. (IM, 26)

It was no accident that the major opposition to associationism came from conservative Catholicism. The church supported intellectual ideas that supported a hierarchical and corporate image of society. It opposed those ideas that threatened its power. Religion collectively congeals the image of society just as bad faith congeals the sense of individual self by favoring rules and order over freedom and movement.

It would be easy to argue that Sartre's own philosophy of mind likewise reflected a particular social and political ideology. In *The Transcendence of the Ego*, Sartre called the transcendental ego an unnecessary principle of unification. Other philosophers had posited a "transcendental ego" behind all consciousness at the "I" responsible for synthesizing the variety of an individual's experience. Sartre, however, acknowledged only that the ego was a *creation* of consciousness, not its director or unifier. He argued that consciousness is originally "pre-personal," and that one's sense of a transcendental ego only appeared in retrospect, as part of an ongoing synthesis within consciousness.

It is easy to see how Sartre's rejection of the transcendental ego was at the same time a kind of rejection of psychological "monarchism" in favor of a "democratic" gathering of the moments of consciousness. At each moment in a person's life, the ego or self is democratically "elected" by one's accumulated experience. This ego is neither permanent nor fixed, but rather constantly subject to change. Nor was dethroning the elusive transcendent ego as the synthesizer of consciousness unrelated to Sartre's rejection of both political authoritarianism and the idea of God as a supreme principle of synthesis or justification of what exists in the world. Each moment of consciousness creates its own synthesis without relying on any external entity, just as each human being creates meaning for himself without a transcendent deity to help. Thus, Sartre regarded as superfluous both the transcendental ego and the transcendental deity that claimed to provide the meaning of every moment of one's life.

The freedom of human consciousness to create its own meaning and essence requires freedom from external rules and traditional roles. The endless revolution within consciousness that Sartre described in *Being and Nothingness* was not unrelated to his ongoing revolt against bourgeois respectability. For Sartre, this freedom required liberation from the religion of respectability and the respectability of religion. The kind of religion that is preserved out of habit and respect for the past, and practiced for the sake of appearance and affiliation, was yet another of the multifarious forms of bad faith. Indeed, if God is "the concept of the Other pushed to the limit" (*BN*, 266), then perhaps religion is the bad faith of civility pushed to its limit.

To the extent that a civilized person discovers his or her essence by embodying rules of civility, he or she falls into *bad faith*, for civility is nothing other than bad faith made flesh. Sartre's atheism is thus a rejection of this bad faith as much as it is a rejection of God. He repudiates the inauthentic security of religion that masks the real struggle of existence. In this rejection Sartre was invigorated, for there he found the aliveness, the passion, and the vulgarity of freedom. His early view of consciousness as utterly severed from the influence of the past fit nicely with the need he felt to uproot himself from the hollow traditions he had been taught.

As for the ontological shame that arises with the realization of the Other's consciousness of one's being, the true issue may really be whether all persons and groups stand equally under the judgment of the Other. The person of civility may choose to trade shame for bad faith, and authenticity for acceptance. On the other hand, when shame loses its sting, the vulgar hero may choose to accept judgment as the price of authenticity.

# THREE

# The Ambivalence of Being Civilized

Not only each country but each city has its particular forms of civility, and so has each occupation. I was brought up in this carefully enough in my youth, and have lived in good enough company, not to be ignorant of the laws of our French civility; I could run a school of it. I like to follow these laws, but not so timidly that my life would remain constrained. They have some troublesome forms, which a man may forget, provided he does so by discretion and not by mistake, without losing grace by his behavior. I have often seen men uncivil by too much civility.

—Montaigne, "Ceremony of Interviews between Kings"

## Civility and Its Discontents

A large component of the process of "civilization" and a major function of specific conventions of "civility" consist of ways by which human-kind has achieved some limited victory or mastery over its own savage, coarse, and primitive side. In 1568, as a renaissance of culture broke through the darkness of the Middle Ages, the French first used the word *civiliser* to describe the successful transcendence of barbarism. What distinguishes a civilized human being from an uncivilized brute is the process that leads from the state of nature into the realm of culture. A person is said to become fully and authentically human only by rising above the level of instinctual need or desire, and by eschewing openly aggressive, embarrassing, or crude behavior.

Society facilitates this transcendence of the natural both prescrip-tively, by developing codes of manners and customary etiquette, and proscriptively, by controlling violations of civility with an internalized sense of shame and embarrassment in each individual. Manners tend to dignify or even spiritualize the inescapably natural, corporal aspects of life. Indeed, the major areas of human ceremonial behavior involve those areas where we confront the bodily nature of life; that is, activities related to sexuality, eating, and excretion. These activities are either secreted out of public view, disguised with social rituals, or both. A twentieth-century French etiquette manual explains that the effect of civilization is to sever the connection between the first appearance of primary human appetites and their satisfaction. It is a system of rules and practices that have progressively eliminated "the brutality, vulgarity, and animality of our ancestral instincts."[1]

On this side of the Atlantic, Ralph Waldo Emerson earlier praised the way in which social manners have elevated human beings above their original state. We rely on them to make ourselves endurable to each other. Manners serve, said Emerson,

> to get people out of the quadruped state; to get them washed, clothed, and set up on end; to slough their animal husks and habits; compel them to be clean; overawe their spite and meanness, teach them to stifle the base, and choose the generous expression, and make them know how much happier the generous behaviors are.

Our erect stature raises us higher from the ground and the world of nature that it represents. From this new elevation we can gaze down upon our animal past. We trade our naked, dirty, smelly bodies for neatly scrubbed and clothed little "machines" that do our work and interact politely with others. Emerson realized that civility was merely a thin layer over a core of animality, but it was the essence of what made human life special. Manners were a "rich varnish" which makes the routine of life shine. "If they are superficial, so are the dew-drops which give such a depth to the morning meadows."[2] Civility does not merely offer a means of transcending the physical body: it elevates social behavior above selfish instinct; it encourages generosity over spite. The rules it offers smooth any awkwardness in our relations with others.

The evolution of civilized behavior is, despite its accomplishments, a process that has produced deep-seated ambivalence. The social roles that civilized people must play can be seen as either a useful way for

1. L.-P. Renaud, *Notions pratiques de politesse, de tenue, et de savoir-vivre* (Paris: Charles-Lavauzelle & Co., 1952), p. 59.
2. "Behaviors," in *The Complete Works of Ralph Waldo Emerson*, vol. 6 (New York: Houghton, Mifflin, 1904), pp. 172, 169–70.

individuals in social groups to function, or as a shallow game. For some people, civilization exacts an unacceptable price. Indeed, some have questioned whether to be "civilized" is to be truly human. Rather, they regard civilization as a path of inauthenticity that leads inevitably to alienation and a tragic loss of genuine selfhood. Critics contend that the progressive cultivation and refinement of human beings can only culminate in a stifling, mechanical, lifeless atmosphere. To such people, concern for tradition, respectability, and conformity to social convention may only represent a headlong flight from true selfhood. The elements of civility do not always allow us to truly know other people or to be known by them. There are those who complain that civility produces a general level of sociability lacking the intensity and seriousness of one's deepest identity. Such a concern with ceremony and etiquette was disgusting to Flaubert, for example, since he thought that it produced, in Sartre's words, "an affective banality which momentarily masks the true color of feelings" (*FI*, 1:594).

This theatrical quality of civility was what disturbed Rousseau, who argued that the roles people play in society have no purpose other than gaining the applause of others by making one's own performance conform to theirs. In this sense, one's identity becomes little more than a mask, though a mask that might be confused with what lies beneath it.[3] Civility, therefore, teaches the skill of the actor and the art of self-alienation. It amounts to

> the art of counterfeiting himself, of putting on another character than his own, of appearing different than he is, of becoming passionate in cold blood, of saying what he does not think as naturally as if he really did think it, and finally, of forgetting his place by dint of taking another's.[4]

Those who see civility as a superficial, alienating, and inauthentic process rather than a humanizing and uplifting one, tend to focus on an idealized core of the self that is muted or compromised by the cheap veneer of civilization. This true self may be variously guided by unfettered passion, instinct, intuition, or intellect. In some cases, we are told to reject those formal, ceremonious social rules that thwart the natural power and development of our passions and bodily experiences.

Rousseau believed that only precivilized people knew how to maintain their personal autonomy. "The savage lives within himself; the sociable man knows how to live only in the opinion of others, and it is,

3. Richard Sennett, *The Psychology of Society* (New York: Vintage Books, 1977), p. 91.
4. Rousseau, quoted in ibid., p. 101.

so to speak, from their judgment alone that he draws the sentiment of his own being."[5] To be civil is to be sociable, and to be sociable is to be governed by others on whom one depends for a sense of self. Nietzsche, likewise, noted that when we refrain from expressing our passions and suppress coarse language and gestures, the passionate side of human life dries up, leaving in its place only "graceful, shallow, playful manners." The more civilized we become, the more our passion, the core of self, becomes conventionalized and routinized. Nietzsche looked forward to the return to passion, to a time when "our descendants will not only indulge in savage and unruly forms, but will be *really savage*."[6] The appeal of the savage and vulgar is that it reflects our own natural power and expresses it with refreshing honesty. Yet for most people, it would be hard to renounce the veneer of civility completely.

When Freud wrote his famous essay "Civilization and Its Discontents," he recognized both our resistance to being civilized, as well as the necessity for us to rise above our animal ancestors. Civilization has served us well by protecting us against nature and refining our relations with each other.[7] Civility erects an invisible wall to maintain distance between members of society, and between people and their natural instincts. Yet the memory of the suppressed instinctual self plagues the mind of the civilized person. While Freud looked at the role of civilization in making possible the earliest forms of social existence, the modern forms of civility are a response to changes in modern social existence. As the bonds of traditional or tribal society have broken down, systems of manners and politeness have become necessary to mediate between people who lack deep communal and emotional ties with one another. Ritual conventions and procedures, for example, can mask divisive private differences by maintaining proper, respectable social relations, and promoting a superficial solidarity among people. Conventions of etiquette are necessary to cushion us from both rudeness and unwanted intrusions into what we feel is private and intimate. Etiquette provides the oil of social life, lubricating the encounters of nonintimates.

This function has been a response to the progressive differentiation of what is public and private in modern society. The growing separation

---

5. *Second Discourse*, quoted by Lionel Trilling in *Sincerity and Authenticity* (Cambridge: Harvard University Press, 1972), p. 62.

6. Fredrich Nietzsche, *The Gay Science*, trans. Walter Kaufmann (New York: Random House, 1974), p. 112.

7. Sigmund Freud, *Civilization and Its Discontents* (New York: Norton and Co., 1962), p. 36.

between the home and the place of work, between church and state, and between ceremony and personal belief all reflected the widening distance between our *public* behavior, and the feelings we associate with our *private* selves. Urbanization and industrialization have both contributed to producing a public realm based on mastery of public social roles. For a person living in the modern world, the locus of individuality and of one's deepest sense of self has receded into the private realm. A life comprised exclusively of public civility appears empty and shallow.

Hannah Arendt has pointed to the importance of maintaining a realm of the private apart from public life. The private offers a depth that cannot thrive in the constant presence of others. Privacy clears a space where identity can develop separate from life in the community. It also protects certain natural parts of the life process from public exposure and shame. The civilizing process tends to stimulate a parallel growth in emphasis on the private, which may explain the contemporary preoccupation with issues of personal identity and consciousness of self.

Part of the widespread ambivalence regarding civility is captured in the German distinction between civilization and culture.[8] As early as Kant, the positive influence of art, morality, and science in *cultivating* members of society and producing virtuous people was contrasted with the notions of propriety, decency, and honor that succeed only in *civilizing* them, making *courteous* people of them. Norbert Elias saw this distinction between culture and civilization as in part a bourgeois polemic against aristocratic models of courtly behavior, the French model of civility. To the aristocratic class, "civilized" was the quality that distinguished *their* social manners from those of socially inferior people, an elitist view rejected by the bourgeoisie. Cultivating expresses the positive part of the process, while civilizing acknowledges the part of the process that may seem superficial and trivial.

The tradition of public ceremony and decorum in France was originally a product of the aristocratic court life—the realm of propertied, white Christian men—though it later was adopted by the more traditional of the bourgeoisie. This heritage has had a deep influence on French society. The French have a tradition of outlining the proper social conduct for all situations, even the most trivial. They have traditionally lived in a codified environment, where every situation was

8. Norbert Elias, *The History of Manners* (New York: Pantheon Books, 1978), Chapter 1.

either legislated or determined by usage. The result was that every aspect of life was transformed into a ceremony, an occasion of *savoir-vivre*. The French recognized that politeness is an artificial and contrived form of behavior, a gratuitous embellishment to ordinary behavior. It consists of a theatrical performance, hardly something that arises naturally. Yet it provides a sense of order and stability where religious institutions and social class no longer can.

With the revolutionary attack on the courtly tradition, good manners were denounced as a class weapon. There arose a countertradition of deliberate gruffness. Rudeness was a way for ordinary people to affirm their equality. In contemporary France, these two traditions coexist. The polite tradition is considered a rampart of French civilization, a code of behavior which makes life in society possible;[9] but it is simultaneously regarded with suspicion.

The ambivalence that permeates social thought concerning the tension between public civility and private feeling is clearly delineated in the work of a contemporary American theorist. Richard Sennett has presented a major critique of the modern move to elevate the realm of the private and to limit the allegedly artificial, constraining, and inauthentic conventions of civility. Sennett argued that cooperation for the public good does not require intimate revelations of private feeling. It was only in the nineteenth century that the ideals of sincerity and authenticity discredited the value of public roles. The new reigning ideology of intimacy totally reordered the priorities of public life. In modern society, psychological exposure of one's feelings is taken as a moral good. Cultural developments such as the human potential movement identify personal authenticity with revelation of the private self to others. Constraints on the self like civility, etiquette, or religion have been devalued in the name of liberation.

Sennett has described the goal of this modern obsession with intimate expression as one of "liberation of the self rather than liberation from the self."[10] He warns that a social model aiming at the liberation *of* one's feelings perpetuates or expands the situation of the family wherein children first experience their parent's adoration at their self-display. To be liberated *from* one's self and feelings, however, is the central purpose of civility in its best sense. It offers an impersonal experience of participating in collective models of behavior. In this sense, civility mirrors

9. Sanche de Gramont, *The French: Portrait of a People* (New York: Bantam Books, 1969), p. 290.
10. Richard Sennett, "Destructive Gemeinschaft," *Partisan Review* 43, no. 3 (1976): 358.

the child's early pleasure at playing games. Games offer the pleasure found in following a conventional form, and are not dependent on individual feeling. Sartre was clearly no fan of civility when it perpetuated a false sense of self. More likely, he sought a form of social existence that made possible this kind of liberation from such a self.

In Sartre's mind, literature was one of the foremost examples of culture's ability to take the wild and shapeless world of nature, and to give it a form; that is, to civilize and tame it. Art, he saw, could leave behind the material world and find a permanent existence beyond the ravages of decay and corruption in the natural world. Its achievement for human experience or thought is analogous to civility's attempt to structure the lawless impulses and vulgar instincts in human relations. Both literature and civility are ways of transcending everyday life and submitting it to the powerful molding effect of human consciousness.

Yet Sartre also realized early on in his childhood that both literature and civility could become roads to bad faith. In every society, certain values, symbols, beliefs, and behaviors are sacred because those in power have given them authority, and these values, symbols, and beliefs in turn give authority to those in power. What is defined as civility usually represents participation in this larger symbolic reality, for which writers are often enlisted to build support. When these values and symbols have been fully sacralized, people become so identified with them that they lose the ability to step outside them, to examine them from the point of view of the Other. And if the viewpoint of the Other, that is, of transcendence, is lost or suppressed, identity settles into a stagnant self-satisfaction.

Rousseau saw the corrupting influence of civilization in the way writers readily renounced their own personal authenticity in an effort to please other people and to gain their approval. The writer, said Rousseau, assumes a "uniform and false veil of politeness." Of course, such servile efforts to please are not the main goal or effect of great writers. As Lionel Trilling responded to Rousseau's critique, it is precisely the function of great literature to tear away the "false veil of politeness" and to reject "the compromises of urbanity."[11]

In both his personal life and his writing, Sartre struggled to avoid the pitfall about which Rousseau had warned. He realized that literature could *either* represent a way to master the wildness of experience, to rise above the superficiality of everyday life, and to penetrate the truth about

---

11. Quoted in Trilling, *Sincerity and Authenticity*, p. 61.

the world in a way that actually changed the world; *or* it could be a way of playing the role of the cultured person, participating in and supporting the existing structure of society, and allowing the transcendent quality of societal consciousness to collapse. In other words, to be a writer offers the choice of viewing society either from its stable, sacralized center, or from a more provocative stance at the vulgar margins where that central structure is questioned.

In *What is Literature?* Sartre presented his treatise on the committed or "engaged" writer. He proceeded to trace the role of the writer in European society at different periods of history as a way of clarifying his own sense of the function of the writer in the contemporary period. What he plotted was a progressive movement of the writer's concerns from support and legitimization of the dominant class of society and its code of civility to a more subversive concern with uncovering oppression as seen by the writer who stands outside of accepted conventions and values. In short, Sartre tried to explain his own position as a writer situated on the margins of the bourgeois worldview, whose writings would continually call that worldview into question.

Several years earlier, Sartre had analyzed the creatively destabilizing power of human consciousness in *Being and Nothingness*. Consciousness has the power to contest any situation in which one is located and to transcend any fixed attributes one might be tempted to assume as an identity. It offers an internal point of dialectical otherness within the self that melts the congealed identities into which people are tempted to flee. Now, in *What is Literature?* Sartre describes the ideal writer with the same kind of transcendent function in relation to his or her readers.

In earlier periods, literature had lacked authenticity, thought Sartre, because it failed to either hear or address the oppressed and vulgar masses, the Other that is necessary for transcendence. By ignoring the illiterate masses in their writings, the medieval clerics who were educated and able to write had chosen to produce only alienated writing. They sought only to preserve and transmit the Christian ideology. They described and focused on a fixed, eternal realm that existed apart from history, that is, one resistant to social change.

When one looks back at the seventeenth and early eighteenth centuries, one finds writers who were removed from their bourgeois origins and who had begun to identify themselves with the manners and style of the court, the classic locus for the tradition of courtesy. Writers and their patrons were both concerned with preserving their own world of privilege. The central values of this world included "faith, respect for the monarchy, passion, war, death, and courtesy" (WL, 87), all of which were seen as immutable parts of the world that were rooted in the distant past. "Good society" read books in order to see its own language, customs, and ceremonies tastefully and elegantly reflected back to it (WL, 82). The result was a literature of the elite. Its point of view was always that of the dominant tradition of civility. These writers saw their role as supporting the church and the monarchy by serving as an uncritical mirror of that world, or at least by accepting it implicitly. Thus, the writer was an accomplice of his audience—the elite—and provided it with the courtesy of a pleasant and familiar picture. The peasants, the true Other, were excluded from the audience. The world of these elite readers had not yet been "congealed into an object by the gaze of the Other, for neither the peasant nor the working-man has become the *Other* for it" (WL, 89). The latter are necessary to call into question the idleness and oppression on which the privileged class rested.

The bourgeois writer incarnated the dominant values in the bourgeois gentleman's relation to the world around him, and these values were repeatedly reincarnated in the books of the time. It was here that Sartre located a primary source of the kind of attitudes he described elsewhere as "bad faith." The bourgeois attitude toward human relations was to see them as an "art" with rules and methods that enabled one to please or intimidate other people as needed. "Ceremony, discipline, and courtesy ruled his behavior" (WL, 109), and much of the literature he read.

As the bourgeoisie assumed political and economic power during the nineteenth century, writers and intellectuals who still preserved vestiges of an aristocratic perspective began to express contempt for bourgeois materialism and vulgarity. Flaubert, for example, defined as bourgeois anyone who thought "basely," but that was an individual psychological description, not a real questioning of bourgeois ideology. Nineteenth-century writers who rejected the bourgeoisie could feel damned and misunderstood, but they expected their eventual glory and appreciation to come at some point in the future. Others, who were disgusted by bourgeois lack of taste and culture, cultivated a particularly refined sense of civility. They used clothes, food, conversation, and taste to separate themselves from the newly discovered vulgarity of the bourgeoisie, but they never really challenged the bourgeois world itself.

In contrast to the traditional bourgeois writer who disguised and legitimized existing power arrangements, Sartre believed that the challenge for the engaged writer is to present the world to his or her readers from the outside, as an Other, so that the readers may respond with "the astonished regard of unfamiliar minds (ethnic minorities, oppressed classes, etc.)" (WL, 85). For Sartre, the ideal writer embodied the consciousness of society. To the extent that human consciousness represented a transcendent uprooting from the givenness of existence, so, too, the committed writer transcended the assumptions and ideologies of his or her own society. The writer could then serve as the Other who enabled the reader to experience a different dimension of his or her identity and world. As a result, one might finally achieve a true experience of the real difference between various groups in the world. The writer is thus able to stimulate the guilty conscience of society (WL, 75), to be its principle of negation and disequilibrium. By remaining *at the margin* of the privileged class, the writer manages to contest rather than reflect society's dominant values.

Sartre thus demanded that writing be a way of revealing and changing the world. The engaged writer strips the innocence from the world and from the reader. The writer transcends the world toward the future, using words as "loaded pistols" aimed at targets that have not yet been named (WL, 18). He or she has given up the fruitless dream of giving an impartial picture of society and the human condition. Such a writer acts to indict those in power in society, to use writing to arouse the readers' indignation at social injustice. Sartre intoned, "The function of the writer is to act in such a way that nobody can be ignorant of the world and that nobody may say that he is innocent of what it's all about" (WL, 18). Only then can a writer avoid the condemnation of "bad faith." Sartre's goal was to redefine the writer's responsibility in a new revolutionary direction.

In Sartre's attitudes toward literature and civility, we seem to have a clear case of "ontogeny recapitulating phylogeny," or at least of Sartre describing the evolution of the bourgeois writer over several centuries in remarkably similar terms to his own evolution as a bourgeois writer. On the individual level, Sartre's road to freedom and to existential engagement passed through an early stage of pleasing others by mastering all the skills of civility. He found his meaning in reflecting back to his benefactors their own cultivated image of themselves. The library was young Sartre's temple where he communed with the saints of culture. As a typical bourgeois child, he incarnated the history of his class. Sartre saw that in each case—the individual and the collective—an identity of bourgeois civility was constructed on a hollow core that could be overcome only by stepping outside it and including the perspective of the margin, of the vulgar, of the Other.

## Distinction and Nature within Bourgeois Ideology

Of course, the role of the writer was merely a reflection of larger shifts in social ideology. Sartre's negative feelings about the civilizing process were closely tied to its relation to bourgeois ideology. In particular, he was struck by two interrelated elements of bourgeois thinking: its hostility toward nature and its desire for "distinction" (*IF* 3:245ff.; CDR, 770–74). In the latter half of the nineteenth century, a highly pessimistic view of nature developed among the bourgeoisie. Sartre described this ideology as a "black humanism" or "pessimistic naturalism" (*ST*, 93) in which nature in general and human nature in particular were regarded as evil, as that which drives people toward bestial and destructive acts. It was thought to be "only human" for people to act maliciously toward each other.

The bourgeoisie had special reasons for having reached an ideological position which altered the previous attitudes toward nature. For the earlier aristocracy, nature had been seen as good, since the aristocrat needed the justification of natural law to explain social inequality and hierarchical organization. Accordingly, the aristocracy could argue that both its social position and that of the peasants were rooted in the natural order of things. In short, nature guaranteed the privileges of the upper classes. After the fall of the aristocracy, nature remained good in the ideology of the revolutionaries, since their revolt itself was founded on, and justified by, the natural rights of all human beings. The human nature that was shared by all was good and noble.

The black humanism of the bourgeoisie emerged as the bourgeoisie became increasingly aware of and insistent on its differences from the working classes. Since the bourgeoisie had supported the revolutionary idea of natural rights and equality for all human beings, it could not base its own sense of superiority on the aristocratic claim of natural differences due to noble or ignoble birth. It needed to develop a different ideology to distinguish itself from the masses. The result was the ideology of "distinction," which rested simultaneously on an idealization of culture and civility and on a devaluation of nature. In the nineteenth century, the ideal of *distinction* or respectability represented something special that could only be acquired by individual effort, not by fact of birth. The respectable man distinguished himself simultaneously from natural human needs and from natural (i.e., vulgar) human beings. The bourgeoisie could claim it was different from the working classes because of its high level of cultural refinement, tact, and good taste in contrast to the unrefined vulgarity of the workers (*M*, 36–37). The lower classes were said to be driven only by "natural" needs; indeed, the only reason they worked was to satisfy their animal appetites (*IF*, 3:250). The kernel at the heart of the bourgeoisie's concept of culture was a negation of nature, a denial of the body's needs, and an "ostentatious refusal of human animality" (*IF*, 3:251; cf. *FI*, 3:338). The more cultivated the bourgeoisie became, moreover, the more it saw nature in a mediated way. The world of nature was not confronted directly, but encountered in the humanized form of manufactured goods that testified to the human meanings already inscribed on them.

Sartre argued that disdain for the worker became internalized within bourgeois consciousness in the form of a hatred of nature and the natural functions of the body. The final result was a puritanical philosophy based on the mastery of natural bodily needs and vital functions. The "distinguished" person "exercises a dictatorship over his body in the name of non-need; in other words, a dictatorship of culture over nature" (*CDR*, 771). This primacy of culture over nature is the bourgeoisie's means of purging itself of the animal nature it shares with the lower classes. Human nature may be common to all, but the goal of cultivation provides new criteria by which to set oneself apart. Nonetheless, as much as the bourgeoisie attempted to control the natural needs of the body, it could not remove them. Rather its obsession with doing so resulted in a greater attention to the body and thereby became "the vulgarity of distinction" (*FI*, 3:339).

The idea of *distinction* thus created the concept of *vulgarity* as its critical foil,[12] just as Saint Paul had said that it was law that made sin possible. The problem with nature was that it was common to all, absolutely democratic, hence absolutely vulgar. There exist no distinctions at the level of the natural. Sartre wrote of Baudelaire:

> When he felt nature—the nature which belonged to everyone—rising and taking possession of him like a flood, he went rigid and taut holding his head above the water. The great muddy wave was vulgarity itself. . . . He was irritated above all by the feeling that this soft, irresistible power wanted to make him compliant, make him "do the same as everybody else." For the

---

12. "Vulgarity and distinction . . . are two aspects of an identical reality" (*FI*, 3:338).

natural elements in us are the opposite of the rare and exquisite; they are everybody. How crazy to eat, sleep, and make love like everybody else. (*B*, 110)

To be natural was to be lost in the crowd. In the absence of religious belief, nature became a random, democratic leveling of all matter. Nature and Life were devalued in this ideology because "they smack of the rabble" (*M*, 40).

It is not hard to discern the classist origins and purpose of bourgeois antinaturalist ideology. "The denunciation of life as *vulgarity* is directed specifically at the disadvantaged classes" (*IF*, 3:249), noted Sartre. Oppressed groups within society are invariably associated with both nature and vulgarity, which are two common vehicles of otherness. The oppressed are devalued for lacking those qualities that lift one above the level of nature. The antinature bias in Baudelaire's ideal of the dandy, for example, was largely a function of social elitism. As the aristocracy collapsed following the French revolution, the ideal of the dandy emerged as a way to preserve refinement, elegance, and gentility, that is, "a new species of aristocracy." Baudelaire called the dandy "the last flare of heroism in a period of decadence."[13] Baudelaire's dandy disdained not merely nature, but also what he saw as the decline of culture: the mediocrity, uniformity, and above all vulgarity which accompanied a democracy of the masses. This was a question of taste rather than of morality, of etiquette, not ethics.

Such classist elements of hostility to nature were characteristic of the bourgeoisie in general. By constraining his body, the bourgeois denied his common humanity with the worker and refused to legitimate this vulgar other. If one could transcend or transform one's own hunger and fatigue, one could ignore the reality of the worker's struggle against hunger and fatigue. The idea of *mastery of natural needs* among the privileged class made it more comfortable to accept the *mastery of other people* in society who were associated with nature and natural needs. The bourgeoisie used the worker's gross animal appetites as justification for its own social position. Beneath the attitude that "needs are to be condemned," and "my body is simply one of my workers," lay the idea that "the needy are bad" and "each of my workers is no more than a body" (*ST*, 93; *CDR*, 775). The oppression of the worker by the employer was thereby both justified and disguised by an ideology advocating the oppression or suppression of nature by culture.

13. Charles Baudelaire, *Flowers of Evil and Other Works* (New York: Bantam Books, 1964), p. 197.

Sartre's description of the general bourgeois uneasiness with nature reached its logical extreme in his analysis of Baudelaire's "cult of frigidity," his preference for what was "sterile, gratuitous, and pure" over "the warm, soft, mucous life" (B, 117). Yet Baudelaire's hostility to the natural and his pretentious cultivation of the artificial were the subject of considerable ambivalence for Sartre himself. When we compare Sartre's analysis of Baudelaire with his own life, we discover an ambiguous combination of attraction and repulsion in relation to these values. For example, Sartre described Baudelaire's antipathy toward the fecundity of nature, his "horror of feeling this vast, soft, fecundity in himself" (B, 109), and his refusal to give in to the demands of nature. He noted that Baudelaire had been influenced by "the great anti-naturalist current" (B, 103) of the nineteenth century. The underlying ideal of this current had been "to inaugurate a human order which would be directly opposed to the errors, injustices and blind mechanical forces of the natural world" (B, 103). But Sartre himself frequently characterized human reality as specifically antinatural. What was unique about human consciousness was its capacity to rise above the contingencies of the physical world. In *Being and Nothingness*, we encounter the pureness of consciousness struggling to transcend the soft, slimy, engulfing power of being or nature. Sartre admitted, moreover, that the intrinsic value of nature and fertility were never of much interest to him (A, 316).

Baudelaire's fundamental attitude toward the world was based on an adamant refusal to be "natural." It was the principle of civility that distinguished the superior being. Nature, he said, did little for people other than drive them to satisfy their hunger, thirst, need for sleep and for shelter, and also to torture and murder their fellow human beings. "Crime, for which the human animal acquired a taste in his mother's womb, is in its origins natural. . . . We do evil without effort, *naturally*" (quoted in B, 101–2). In this respect, Baudelaire's view was not so different from that of Freud. For both, overcoming evil was not something that came naturally to human beings. "Virtue, on the contrary, is *artificial*. . . . Good is always the product of art" (B, 102). Baudelaire did not simply identify evil with nature, however, since he also saw that evil could be a product of deliberate artifice. But there was a difference between the two. Sartre observed, "If therefore there exists a distinguished and a vulgar evil, it was the vulgarity which must have shocked the poet and not the crime" (B, 102). Baudelaire himself said, "A dandy can never be a commonplace [*vulgaire*] person. If he committed a crime, he would not perhaps fall from his rank; but if the crime had come from a trivial source, his dishonor would be irreparable."[14] It was not the crime itself but vulgarity which brought dishonor.

Baudelaire's attitudes, of course, were only an extreme case of the overall concern with distinction among the bourgeoisie in the nineteenth century. What was essential to the bourgeoisie, said Sartre, was that private feelings be suppressed and the mastery of bodily needs be made public. The bourgeois gentleman was concerned above all with appearance. He paid special attention to politeness, good taste, and the impression he gave. For Baudelaire this meant avoiding any spontaneous feelings, thoughts, or actions. "From dawn till dusk, he never let himself go for a moment. His least desires, his most spontaneous *élans* were repressed, filtered, acted rather than lived; they were only allowed to pass when they had been duly transformed into something artificial" (B, 110). As a result, his relations with others were characterized by "an icy, ceremonious politeness" (B, 118). The poet Mallarmé was little different in Sartre's eyes: "He fears his own natural instincts as if they belonged to some sort of ape locked up inside him. Tightly buttoned up, starched and stiffened, he refuses to let go in any way" (M, 34).

Sartre understood most of Baudelaire's personal tastes to be expressions of "his horror of natural needs" (B, 113). Out of scorn for the demands of the body with its hungers and thirsts, Baudelaire tried to disguise the naturalness of hunger and food. His pretentious discussions about the "art" of cooking represented his effort to transform eating from a natural need into a kind of art appreciation. Sartre observed, "He ate in order to appreciate with his teeth, his tongue, and his palate a certain kind of poetic creation" (B, 113). Sartre even went on to theorize that Baudelaire preferred "meats cooked in sauces to grills, preserves to fresh vegetables," and "meat disguised, concealed by highly spiced sauces" (B, 113, 115). The reason, of course, was Baudelaire's desire to denature the natural by making it artificial or sophisticated. Human life may depend on the brutal fact of butchering and eating other forms of life, but even that harsh reality can be hidden beneath a tasty sauce.

Such remarks about Baudelaire's culinary preferences become particularly intriguing when they are juxtaposed with Sartre's own relationship to food. Sartre always insisted that beyond its nutritive value, all food also has a symbolic value (BN, 604; A, 332). "It is not a matter of indifference whether we like oysters or clams, snails or shrimp, if only we know how to unravel the existential significance of these foods" (BN,

14. Ibid., p. 195.

615). The symbolic meaning of his own favorite foods is not difficult to discern. Sartre had a particular dislike for shellfish, especially when they were served raw. Crabs and lobsters reminded him of insects, a symbol of the swarming life beyond the realm of the human, and he found the quality of flesh in shellfish viscous and disgusting.

Like Baudelaire, he preferred food that had been transformed to disguise its natural origins. Both men, moreover, saw deep significance in the methods of food preparation. Sartre also found raw vegetables and fruits basically unappealing. He found them "too natural" and disliked the fact that their texture and taste were purely contingent facts of nature. Raw food forces us to confront the world of nature, of vegetation. The fact that cultivating vegetables and fruits has already domesticated the plant world for human purposes was no consolation for Sartre. Only after raw food has been prepared or cooked does it lose its connection with nature. Vegetables cease to be vegetables after human intervention transforms them into puree or cooked salad.

Sartre was especially fond of cakes, tarts, and pastries, but not by reason of a sweet tooth. He saw them as objects that were entirely dependent on human effort. He explained: "The appearance, the putting together and even the taste have been thought out by man and made on purpose" (A, 333). They were wholly human objects. Bread, for example, requires that one crush, grind, knead, and bake the original natural grain in order eventually to produce something utterly new and different, a new substance that exists only thanks to that human labor. For the same reason, Sartre preferred prepared or delicatessen meats to steaks or roast beef. In a sausage or pâté, human effort has changed the meat into something new, whose shape and taste have been invented by human beings (A, 334). If human life rests inescapably on nature for its sustenance, the civilizing process can at least try to disguise the animal origins of our food.

It is not surprising that a person who avoids contemplating the naturalness of raw food might assume a similar attitude in other areas where the world of nature and the natural functions of the body are present. For Baudelaire, Sartre noted, this involved an avoidance of undisguised nakedness. His sexual desire seemed most excited by women who remained fully clothed. He preferred women's bodies when they were "veiled by furs or by theatrical costumes which still retained a breath of perfume or the gleam of the footlights" (B, 115). Baudelaire's meticulous use of cosmetics and dressing enabled him to transform the natural body into something artificial. Fashion, he said, is "a sublime deforming of nature, or rather . . . a permanent continuing reformation of nature."[15] When nature comes to represent a degrading of one's level of humanity, the obsessive struggle to disguise, master, or remold the natural functions of life becomes a daily battle for one's self.[16]

The ascendancy of culture over nature has traditionally been associated with the suppression of women by men. The highest levels of culture have usually been reserved for men and described in exclusively male terms. Women, on the other hand, have most often represented the link between mankind and nature. Unfortunately, Sartre remained oblivious to the way in which the idea of respectability has contributed to the oppression of women. Consider, for example, his description of the bourgeois suppression of nature: "His clothing is *constraining* (corsets, stiff collars, top hats, etc.); he advertises his *sobriety* (young ladies eat beforehand when they go out to dinner, so that they can fast in public), and his wife does not conceal *her frigidity*" (CDR, 771; cf. IF, 3:246). In each case, Sartre's parenthetical examples reveal the particular ways in which it was left to women to mold or disguise their natural appearance and needs. A woman's attire managed to alter her natural figure with the aid of a corset or simply hide it behind layers of fabric. It was the woman, moreover, who struggled to appear neither to require food nor to enjoy sex. Thus, the battlefield where man's fight with nature is waged often turns out to be women's bodies. In nineteenth-century poets like Mallarmé, disgust and horror over the "carnal reality" of women coexisted with respect for and imitation of "abstract femininity." Women represented both the problem and the solution.

Although Sartre himself was critical of the hypocrisy of bourgeois playacting, he shared the bourgeois reluctance to acknowledge his own natural needs. Simone de Beauvoir reported that during a serious attack of renal colic, Sartre confounded his doctor by denying that he was suffering. "Though the pain was such that it kept him pinned to his bed, he regarded it as a 'porous,' almost intangible entity."[17] Sartre felt that to give in to tears or nerves or seasickness was simply weakness. He wanted his body to submit to the will of his consciousness. Later in life, he treated the declines in his health as affronts to the authority of his consciousness as much as they were medical problems.

While it is certainly true that Sartre's uneasiness with the realm of nature and his ambivalence about his own body was a symptom of the

15. Ibid., p. 203.
16. For similarities in Sartre's own attitudes toward women, see Chapter 5.
17. Beauvoir, *The Prime of Life*, p. 107.

same bourgeois ideology he criticized in Baudelaire and others, he ultimately could find little of value in the bourgeois idea of distinction. The quest for distinction was nothing more than an alienation of one's own action or *praxis* (*CDR*, 772). It resulted in a kind of conformist other-directedness, an imitation of certain mechanical, preordained, prefabricated patterns of behavior calculated to maintain a certain public appearance (*FI*, 1:596). A person acted in a certain way because that was how "one" was supposed to behave. Sartre wrote: "*Respectability* as serial reason became the dictatorship of the Other. At first, *I* was oppressing *my* body; this became the oppression of my body by all the others. Free innovation solidified into cant once it was propagated and serialized by imitation" (*CDR*, 774). Distinction thus became a class inheritance rather than an individual choice. The gentleman's manners, clothes, and tastes were simply a symbol of his class. For this reason, the "dictatorship of the Other" implied in respectability refers to only a select group of others. It is the respectable Other of one's own class for whom one performs. Distinction in turn gives the bourgeoisie the security to engage in its own dictatorship over the vulgar Other who is lacking in distinction.

The longer such collective attitudes and practices persist, the more inauthentic they become. They acquire the unreflective and inert qualities of encrusted religious rituals still performed out of habit rather than out of conviction. The result is a highly "civilized" person who consists of merely an assemblage of public gestures. The older social conventions become, or the longer they persist, the "denser, thicker, more inert, more absurd" (*FI*, 1:595) they become. These are the kind of collective attitudes and practices that govern human society.

## Life in the City

It is perhaps no accident that Sartre preferred a physical and social setting for his life in which he could witness the efforts of civility to keep nature at bay, as well as the masses of naturally commonplace people who worried little about distinction and respectability and stood open to the real presence of nature. The urban landscape felt like home to Sartre for it represented a monument to the power of human action to mold nature. According to Simone de Beauvoir, when Sartre was not in a city, that is, not "in the heart of an artificial universe filled with man-made objects" (*WS*, 469), the only places that he could tolerate were "the level sea, the unbroken desert sand, or the mineral coolness of alpine peaks" (WS, 469). In other words, if he left the familiar world of the city, he looked for places with the appearance of sterility, devoid of vegetation and the power of fertility. These were also places where one's vision stretched to the horizon or to a peak, wonderfully symbolizing the farthest reaches of consciousness.

Like literature and culture, cities can provide a place of liberation or a home for bad faith. In *Nausea*, Roquentin describes much of Sartre's own ambivalence about the civilizing powers represented by the city. Shuttling back and forth between Paris and Bouville, he confesses:

> I am afraid of cities. But you mustn't leave them. If you go too far you come up against the Vegetation belt.[18] Vegetation has crawled for miles toward the cities. It is waiting. Once the city is dead, the vegetation will cover it, will climb over the stones, grip them, search them, make them burst with its long black pincers; it will blind the holes and let its green paws hang over everything. You must stay in the cities as long as they are alive; you must never penetrate alone this great mass of hair waiting at the gates; you must let it undulate and crack all by itself. In the cities, if you know how to take care of yourself, and choose the times when all the beasts are sleeping in their holes and digesting, behind the heaps of organic debris, you rarely come across anything more than minerals, the least frightening of all existents. (N, 208–9)

The city has often represented a refuge from the wildness of nature. Sartre himself had internalized a considerable amount of the bourgeois legacy in his attitudes toward Nature. In particular, he hated the country, with its swarming insects and teeming vegetation (WS, 469). In *Nausea*, Roquentin's voice is not far from Sartre's own when he expresses his fear of and disgust with the creeping power of nature. For both, nature stands as an enemy of the city and of civilized life. Nature outside the city is like a giant vagina, a hairy mass that may be penetrated, but will also destroy.[19] It is what will take over when the city dies. The death of civility will be followed by the return of nature, relentlessly engulfing all that had tried to rise above it.

But who really are the "beasts" who sleep and digest their food out of sight in their holes? When we ignore them, Roquentin says, we can contemplate the minerals—the stone and glass—that physically make

18. "Le cercle de la Végétation." Sartre's capitalizing of the word Vegetation suggests something symbolizing Nature itself.

19. One may recall Sartre's childhood relation to his mother and the twin beds they used. Sartre sensed nervously again the "hairy mass" of female sexuality. We will return to that issue in Chapter 5.

up the city. Perhaps the hidden allusion is to the beast of natural bodily functions that is hiding within every person. Clothes may hide the body, buildings may hide Vegetation, but we cannot eliminate our perpetual link to nature. Only when one sees the beast as totally other, epitomized by the nonurban, nonbourgeois, noncivilized Other can one create the illusion of control over it.

Mostly, Sartre found in the city a model of order and a refuge from the power of the organic world. It was a monument to the power of human consciousness to carve out an area of humanly significant space that held at bay the organic processes of nature. He loved to stroll through the twisting city streets of Europe, to discover the little secrets and mysteries of a city, and to observe the flow of life through the streets (*LPE*, 123).

And yet Sartre also noticed certain stifling qualities of European cities. Apparent salvation is sometimes only a disguised prison. Like the literature that defends the present state of being because it is based on the past, cities, too, can become stuck in the glorification of their pasts. People wander around in them as though they were museums for their ancestors (*LPE*, 131). The inhabitants develop unique neighborhoods where they feel a sense of communal belonging that makes this place home, but they may also become afflicted with a kind of existential nearsightedness (*LPE*, 127). The original layout of the city tends toward myopia, focusing inwardly on itself, surrounding itself with outer walls to conceal the presence of untamed Nature outside. "Once you are inside the city, you can no longer see beyond it," Sartre observed. This inward focus is not only a protection against nature, it may also be a form of insulation from others who are unlike you. "In France we are surrounded and protected by urban centers; the prosperous districts protect the rich from the poor, and the poor districts protect us from the disdain of the rich and similarly, the entire city protects us against Nature" (*LPE*, 127).[20]

Many people may look to the city, as to literature or culture, to be

20. When Sartre visited Naples in 1936 he had a very different experience. Beneath the appearance of a civilized city of palaces, villas, and casinos he discovered the Naples of the poor, where people had been swallowed up by their organic existence (*WS*, 2:60). In fact, he wrote to Simone de Beauvoir that he felt somewhat repulsed by the fact that people were so open, so animalistic. Little boys urinated in the street and mothers nursed their children openly without shame or modesty. He was especially struck by the sight of a five-year-old girl sitting on the stairs with a dozen flies on her naked genitals. "To this display of dirty flesh is joined a carnal naturalism, a peasant promiscuity which would perhaps be pleasant with clean healthy bodies, but which here is disturbing" (*LC*, 65–66).

comforted rather than disturbed. Those who dwell in the city of bad faith acquire a self-satisfied quality like those residents of Bouville who continually nauseate Roquentin. From the hilltop outside the city, he looks down on Bouville and the lives of its people.

> I feel so far away from them, on top of this hill. It seems as though I belong to another species. They come out of their offices after their day of work, and they look at the houses and the squares with satisfaction. They think it is *their* city, a good, solid bourgeois city. They aren't afraid, they feel at home. All they have ever seen is trained water running from taps, light which fills bulbs when you turn on the switch, half-breed, bastard trees held up by crutches. They have proof, a hundred times a day, that everything happens mechanically, that the world obeys fixed unchangeable laws. . . . Cities have only one day at their disposal and every morning it comes back exactly the same. . . . They make laws, they write popular novels, they get married, they are fools enough to have children. And all this time, great, vague nature has slipped into their city, it has infiltrated everywhere, in their house, in their office, in themselves. It doesn't move, it stays quietly and they are full of it inside, they breathe it, and they don't see it, they imagine it to be outside, twenty miles from the city. I *see* it, I *see* this nature. (N, 211–12)

The people of Bouville have tamed and mastered water, light, and trees. Their laws and customs have created a certain predictable yet mechanical way of life. What Roquentin sees in this city, however, is the underlying uncontrollable aspect of existence that will never be mastered. He senses a kind of Otherness that challenges, permeates, and invalidates the easy life they have chosen.

In the concluding pages of *Nausea*, Roquentin turns to the timeless quality of a jazz melody to find some relief from the overflowing superfluousness of existence. Yet in thinking about the song's birth, he begins to think of a different city from Bouville and a different kind of city-dweller. He imagines a Jewish songwriter sitting at a piano in a sweltering apartment on the twenty-first floor of a New York skyscraper, and he asks himself, Why couldn't that be me (N, 235). Indeed, it is in this image of a Jewish writer and a black female singer creating a jazz song that Sartre finds another kind of city, one inhabited by those who may seem vulgar and other to the residents of Bouville, but who confront the harshness of existence and find a way to survive. Roquentin leaves us with the thought that if he could only see himself as this kind of person he might be able to overcome his self-repugnance and come to accept himself. Surely, this was Sartre's quest as well, including the intuition that somewhere in Jews, blacks, and women might lie the secret to authenticity. At one time, both Roquentin and Sartre may have envied and believed in the sense of salvation and immortality to be found by creating a work of art or even a song. But the vocation of a creative artist may not be the only thing that Roquentin envies. Perhaps it is also the specific identities of these artists: "So the two of them are saved: the Jew and the Negress" (N, 236). Even when Sartre abandons cultural salvation as his goal, there may still be other ways in which he wanted to embody certain qualities of Jews, women, and blacks.

When Sartre actually visited New York City in the 1940s, he experienced his trip to the "new world" as a journey to the frontier of civilization. He was simultaneously disoriented, intimidated, and exhilarated by qualities of New York. Compared to Paris, New York seemed wild and untamed. The scale of Manhattan's streets and buildings was unfriendly and provided little protection from rain and hurricanes.

> Even in the depths of my apartment, I am open to attack from a mysterious and secretly hostile Nature. I feel as though I were camping in the heart of a jungle crawling with insects. There is the wailing of the wind, the electric shocks I get each time I touch a doorbell or shake a friend's hand, the cockroaches that scoot across my kitchen, the elevators that make me nauseous and the inextinguishable thirst that rages in me from morning till night. New York is a colonial city, an outpost. All the hostility and cruelty of Nature are present in this city. (LPE, 129–30)

Much of Sartre's reaction to New York will seem a bit off to others who are familiar with the city, either as it was then or now. From his descriptions, one could hardly tell that the climates of New York and Paris are relatively similar. Sartre presents a New York that is an outpost against the horrible powers of nature. It is flooded by storms; suffocating heat descends on it each May "like an atomic bomb"; it is an insect-infested jungle; dirt, nausea, thirst abound.

There was another dimension of nature beyond storms and cockroaches that Sartre also experienced in New York—its inhabitants. New York's diverse population and the absence of Parisian civility may initially have been unsettling to Sartre, since it left him exposed to other people as much as to the weather. But Sartre also loved the natural feeling of simply merging with a heterogeneous mass of people and being liberated from the distinctions that separate people in a more traditional society. Once acclimated to New York, Sartre reported, "there is no place in which I feel more free than in the New York crowds" (*LPE*, 131). A city that simply numbers its streets and avenues is saying that each place is like another (*LPE*, 129), and consequently, that each person is like the others. Freed from attachment to a street or neighborhood, he thought, a person in New York can experience "the simultaneity of human lives" (*LPE*, 131).

If New York seemed closer to the nature and vulgarity that perpetually contest the control of civility, it also was the home of the Jewish songwriter with thick brown eyebrows who sprang up in Roquentin's imagination. In some ways, New York itself had certain "Jewish" qualities. As Sartre described in *Antisemite and Jew* soon after his visit to New York, Jews displayed a refreshing spontaneity to him because they were unencumbered by the layers of tradition and culture that molded Christian behavior. New York, too, seemed free of such cultural encrustation in Sartre's eyes. As a result, though it lacked the mystery of European cities, it made up for this by its feeling of freedom.

A city is a society's self-incarnation in physical form. Its structure, therefore, parallels cultural attitudes of individuals toward their bodies. In *Antisemite and Jew*, Sartre contrasted the Gentile attitude toward the body—which focused on gracefulness and disguise of natural function—with what he called the Jewish attitude, which took a rationalized view of the body as a mechanism to express human meaning. In this sense, New York is more Jewish than Gentile in its style. It is a logical, rational city without pretense or mystery. Its streets are straight and reveal themselves immediately. They carry one's vision outside the city, where one can confront the reality of nature and sense the presence of immense space surrounding the city (*LPE*, 123). New York is a city for the "farsighted." The open horizon of America appealed to Sartre's thirst for transcendence. The feeling he discovered in American cities was that of being temporary and unfinished; they offered a perfect image of freedom. "The cities are open, open to the world, and to the future. This is what gives them their adventurous look and, even in their ugliness and disorder, a touching beauty" (*LPE*, 125). The New York skyscrapers make the sky seem very high above. They symbolized to Sartre the unlimited individualism that grows out of the conformist foundation of America (*LPE*, 113).

Sartre must have been struck by the lack of social elitism and *distinction* that he witnessed in New York. He found himself intrigued by the process of Americanization, which sought to "melt down" the individual differences of Europeans and others. A Frenchman he met shortly after arriving in New York had already taken on "a deliberately vulgar accent" (*LPE*, 105). To Sartre, American life had subtle yet powerful forces that slowly transformed alien elements into Americans like "an Ovidian metamorphosis" (*LPE*, 105).

Indeed, it was the conformism of Americans that replaced any idea of distinction. Sartre observed, "It is when he is acting like everyone else that he feels most reasonable and most American; it is in displaying his conformism that he feels freest" (*LPE*, 108). In the absence of a tradition of *distinction*, American civility shows up in its own unique way. The American personality is reflected in the mass-produced quality of American manufactured goods. Manufactured goods have a universalizing effect: "The American uses his mechanical corkscrew, his refrigerator or his automobile in the same way and at the same time as all other Americans" (*LPE*, 109). Mechanical conformism in New York is no different from that in Bouville or Paris. In this respect, Americans let go of individuality in order to participate in the sense of being like everyone else. Sartre's first impression was that New Yorkers were free to do whatever they liked, but that public opinion kept them fairly uniform. They "conform through freedom" (*LPE*, 109). But Sartre also noticed American individualism linked with conformism. While he saw a conformist element in the physical layout of the city's geometrical grid of numbered streets, he found individualism in an architecture of creative chaos, which linked traditional and modern, skyscraper and low-rise buildings. The relation between conformism and individuality is thereby revealed in three dimensions. Despite a surface layout based on conformism, skyscrapers can symbolize each person's accompanying aspiration to rise above all the others. So Sartre does see some principle of distinction in the American society, but it is built on a foundation of conformity. The worker is first organized and integrated into the community. Then he can distinguish himself by his initiative and creativity (*LPE*, 113).

The messianic power of culture to redeem nature continually collided in Sartre's thought with the shallow hypocrisy of civilized conventions. In the abstract, Sartre enlisted in the crusade for culture's triumph over nature, flesh, and instinct. But he also saw that those who put on the armor of culture were interested not just in rising above nature *per se*, but also in creating divisions within humanity itself to reflect the two sides of human reality. Once civility and culture are claimed as the unique possession of a single class of people, they no longer represent the highest achievement of human consciousness, but rather a profoundly polarized state of self-alienation. Indeed, Sartre would need to turn to the Other to begin to reclaim part of what he felt had been lost to his bourgeois consciousness.

Sartre rarely saw the bourgeoisie's culture as an advantage over the masses. Instead, he inverted the relationship that the ideology of *distinction* presupposed. Distinction was not a liberating transcendence of nature after all. The natural qualities of the masses offered a refreshing escape from the suffocating blanket of civility in which the bourgeoisie wrapped itself. In the vulgar masses, Sartre saw those who truly embodied the impetus for revolutionary change in society. They were the margin of otherness necessary to throw the established structure of society into question.

PART 2

EMBODIMENTS OF OTHERNESS
AND THE REJECTION OF CIVILITY

# FOUR

## Strangers on the Train: Jewish Marginality and the Rejection of Civility

While I believed that I was describing the Jew in *Anti-Semite and Jew*, I was describing myself, a guy who had nothing, owned no land, and was an intellectual.[1]

—Jean-Paul Sartre

Sartre's discomfort and embarrassment regarding his own bourgeois background led him to idealize marginal groups and others who are seen as outside the normative model of selfhood. He identified part of his own self, moreover, with the situation of such classic outsiders as Jews, women, homosexuals, blacks, and other groups. But it was the Jews in particular who represented the clearest embodiment of *otherness* for Sartre. They were the consummate pariahs, wanderers in a society that often regarded them as illegitimate, unjustifiable, un-Christian, and vulgar.

Throughout his life, Sartre was intrigued by the situation of the Jews. The reasons for this lifelong attraction to the Jewish people are complex, involving both personal and ideological considerations. Whereas Sartre had intimate friendships with a number of intellectual Jews during his life, "the Jew" also served as a kind of ideal type or symbol for him. His adopted daughter Arlette remarked that there was something special and palpable about Sartre's fascination with the fact of being Jewish that made him respond to Jews differently than to other op-

1. Sartre quoted from an unpublished interview in Benny Lévy, "Sartre et la Judéité," *Études Sartriennes II–III, Cahiers de sémiotique textuelle* 5-6 (1986):141 (my translation).

pressed groups. To a certain extent, his ideas about Jews reflected his own mythology of the Other. They reveal more about Sartre's attitude toward his own background than they do about his knowledge of Jews and Judaism. Sartre's "fantasy of the Jew"[2] stood between him and any real Jews. Indeed, in the early part of his life, Sartre had contact only with assimilated Jewish intellectuals, and he was profoundly ignorant of Judaism and Jewish history per se.[3] What appealed to Sartre about the Jews had little to do with any particular set of beliefs or observances they maintained, but rather concerned their position in society. To a great extent, the precariousness of being Jewish represented the epitome of the human condition for him. He regarded Jewishness as a kind of contingency that one must accept and live as one's fate.[4] Above all else, "the Jew" represented for Sartre *the negation and subversion of the central values of bourgeois society* that he, too, had rejected. The Jews' marginality, Sartre suggested, had both given them a special sensibility and presented them with a greater opportunity for existential authenticity.

Since Sartre associated the normative tradition of his society with irremediable hypocrisy, he concluded that those who were denied or who refused membership in this group were those who were most likely to live "authentic" lives. Accordingly, he approached the social predicament of the Jews not only with great empathy but also with a peculiar sort of envy. In his *War Diaries*, he described his memories of wandering around the Jewish quarter of Paris, Rue des Rosiers, where his Jewish friend Peter had actually *lived*. Though Sartre was a mere "tourist" there, Peter had lived in that neighborhood as "a Jew among Jews, a hoodlum among all those other little hoodlums" (*WD*, 120). When he later wrote his screenplay about Freud's early life, he imagined the small crowded Jewish ghetto that Freud called home. To belong in either of these places, of course, would mean to be outside the respectable society in which Sartre had been raised and where he legitimately belonged. Nonetheless, Sartre felt that he had much in common with the Jews, and he frequently attributed the same kinds of qualities to both Jews and himself.

We can begin to appreciate the special closeness Sartre felt toward the Jews and his identification with their existential situation by considering some of the dominant metaphors that emerge from Sartre's description

2. Ibid.

3. See Stuart Charmé, "From Maoism to the Talmud (With Sartre Along the Way): An Interview with Benny Lévy," *Commentary* 78, no. 6 (December 1984):52–53.

4. Stuart Charmé, "Sartre's Jewish Daughter: An Interview," *Midstream* 32, no. 8 (1986): 26.

of himself. In his autobiography, *The Words*, Sartre used the image of travelling on a train without a ticket as the major metaphor for his own life and as a frame for the narrative. In the first part of *The Words*, Sartre used this image to characterize the quality of his existence as a seven-year-old child. Later, he concluded the book by returning to the same image to describe himself in the present, as the middle-aged narrator of the book. On the surface, this image of being caught without a "ticket to ride" expressed Sartre's uncomfortable existential intuition that his life lacked any metaphysical justification, purpose, or destination. This *philosophical* dilemma, to which he believed every person was condemned, was also in part the result of a particular *social* dilemma with which Sartre continually struggled.

To understand Sartre's sense of himself as a ticketless traveller, it is necessary first to recall the thematic focus of *The Words*. The impression Sartre left us of his childhood was of its overwhelming theatricality. His grandfather had been an old-fashioned bourgeois gentleman who was concerned above all with maintaining proper public appearances. He was a consummate performer from whom the impressionable young Sartre learned not sincerity, but rather posing and "impression management." Sartre played the part of the "good child" and defined himself solely by the approval of his audience. However, in becoming completely an object for others, in striving solely to please them, Sartre discovered that he had sacrificed an inner sense of self. He had become an impostor whose public role only disguised his inner emptiness. At this point in his recollections, Sartre introduced the image of the ticketless rider:

I had sneaked onto the train and had fallen asleep, and when the ticket-collector shook me and asked for my ticket, I had to admit that I had none. Nor did I have the money with which to pay my fare on the spot. I began by pleading guilty. I had left my identity card at home, I no longer even remembered how I had gotten by the ticket-puncher, but I admitted that I had sneaked on to the train. Far from challenging the authority of the ticket-collector, I loudly proclaimed my respect for his functions and complied in advance with his decision. At that extreme degree of humility, the only way I could save myself was by reversing the situation: I therefore revealed that I had to be in Dijon for important and secret reasons, reasons that concerned France and perhaps all mankind. If things were viewed in this new light, it would be apparent that no one in the entire train had as much right as I to occupy a seat. Of course, this involved a higher law which conflicted with the regulations, but if the ticket-taker took it upon himself to interrupt my journey, he would cause grave complications, the consequences of which would be his responsibility. I urged him to think it over: was it reasonable to doom the entire species to disorder under the pretext of maintaining order in a train? Such is pride: the plea of the wretched. Only passengers with tickets have the right to be modest. I never knew whether I won my case. The ticket-collector remained silent. I repeated my arguments. So long as I spoke, I was sure he wouldn't make me get off. We remained face to face, one mute, and the other inexhaustible, in the train that was taking us to Dijon. The train, the ticket-collector, and the delinquent were myself. (W, 70)

Within European society, certain groups of people had amassed power, respectability, and a sense of justification for their way of life and its prerogatives. As a white, male Christian born within a solidly bourgeois and highly cultured family, Sartre already had received his admission "ticket" to respectable society. His seat had already been reserved on the train, so to speak. Why then was it so important for him to make himself into a "delinquent"?

The answer to this question may become clearer if we consider the importance the figure of the Jew assumed in Sartre's thought. The ways in which he felt his situation in the world was both similar to and different from that of the Jew reveal several important elements of modern Jewish identity. A good example of some of the major issues in Jewish identity can be seen in the life of one famous Jew who had much to say about the nature of identity—Sigmund Freud. Not long before working on the self-analysis that led to his autobiography, Sartre had accepted a proposal from film director John Huston to write a screenplay on the early life of Freud. Here Sartré found a perfect example of many of the difficulties in being a Jew that he had described fifteen years earlier in *Anti-Semite and Jew*. Immersing himself in the life of Freud also gave him some clues to understanding his own life and identity. To be sure, Sartre began his thinking about the world from a very different location from someone like Freud, for whom complete admission into the world of bourgeois civility was a lifelong and ultimately unattainable goal. Sartre imagined what may have gone through Freud's head when he saw a respected Gentile academician go by:

And I wanted to work my way up: student, Privatdozent, Professor. When they'd given me their title, I thought they'd accept me. What gullibility! Those people keep us in quarantine, they'll always do so. . . .

Christians have the right to be commonplace: the whole world belongs to them. And what do they have to prove: they *are* Humanity. At any rate, they think they are. How supremely comforting! I shall never be *that*: I *cannot*. It took two thousand years of Christianity to produce that bloodless bigwig. . . .

He's a goy: the goys honour him because he reflects their own mediocrity. But me they wouldn't accept. I'd go to their homes, in my carriage with its two horses, they'd be all smiles, and when I'd left them they'd say to each other: "For a Jew, he's not too bad."

To be like everybody else; sometimes that's my dream. Ruled out! Everybody else—that means the goys. (*FS*, 399–401)

Yet this world into which Freud struggled to be accepted was the same one from which Sartre strove to escape. Sartre may have had a reserved seat on the train, but he came to regard his ticket as invalid. He wanted to throw his ticket out the window and get off the train.

Having found bourgeois society and its values so fraught with bad faith and inauthenticity, Sartre's greatest desire was to disengage and dissociate himself from it. Although he had been born at the very center of respectable society, Sartre came to believe that the ongoing price of social respectability was too great. Bourgeois respectability could only be purchased at the expense of existential authenticity. Unlike those newly emancipated European Jews who wanted nothing more than to "pass" in Gentile society, Sartre found himself deliberately trying *not* to "pass" as what he already was. He felt compelled, moreover, not only to reject his bourgeois Christian background but also deliberately to scandalize the sensibilities of the respectable. In effect, Sartre's effort to escape his bourgeois background was a labor of *déclassement*, the reverse movement of "passing." He would have loved to have been "thrown off the train." But that could never really happen because the train was also in some way himself.

Thus when Sartre described his "ticketless" existential condition, he sounded somewhat like a millionaire describing the underlying unreality or evil of all material goods. His alienation sprouted on the soil of the unwanted privilege and power to which he had been born. Sartre realized the difficulty of his task. He and Freud were looking at society through opposite ends of the same binoculars. He wondered, "How can I reasonably think that a member of society's elite would be able to lower himself—if it can be called lowering himself—to the level of the oppressed and exploited people and to consider *with the eyes of the people* the crushing pedestals on which the bourgeois hierarchy sits?" (*LS*, 197).

## Civility and the Jew: The Shaping of Personal Identity

Although Freud and Sartre came out of radically different religious and cultural traditions, their individual backgrounds forced each of them to confront a disturbing dilemma: how to relate to the demands and limitations imposed by bourgeois civility, those conventions and customs which govern proper public behavior and determine membership in "respectable" society. Freud and Sartre present an intriguing contrast in the opposing yet interrelated ways in which they responded to their respective backgrounds. In both cases, the resolution of a sense of conflict over bourgeois civility produced profound reverberations in each one's sense of personal identity.

Curiously, the same image of travel by train that Sartre used to describe his sense of identity can be found in various dreams, anecdotes, and jokes sprinkled throughout Freud's work. In the *Freud Scenario*, Sartre took note of Freud's fear of railway stations and trains (*FS*, 203). One way of interpreting this image has been to see it as a metaphor for the social situation of the European Jew in Freud's time. Although legal emancipation had been extended to the Jews throughout most of Europe during the nineteenth century, their social integration and acceptance were much slower in coming. If we consider a train as a symbol of passing freely throughout society, the ticket that permits this passage is mastery of the rules of civility, or possession of—to use a French word for ticket—the appropriate *étiquette*. Too often the Jew remained a stranger on the train, a ticketless traveller whose progress came into doubt every time his ticket (or etiquette) was inspected.

Living at a time when conversion to Christianity was a common means of transportation into respectable society for Jews, Freud showed a certain amount of ambivalence about his own Jewish identity. While he resented the social barriers that hindered Jews from "passing" comfortably within Gentile society, he never made any attempt to disguise his Jewish background. In his *Autobiographical Study*, Freud observed matter-of-factly, "My parents were Jews, and I have remained a Jew myself."[5] Clearly, Freud suffered no doubts about his sense of identity. His father had left him (and the Gentile world around him) with little question as to who he was. He knew he was a Jew.[6] If he desired to surpass his father, it may have been due to an unconscious wish to

---

5. Sigmund Freud, *Autobiographical Study* (New York: Norton, 1963), p. 13.
6. Interpreters of Freud in the past two decades have become increasingly attentive to the influence of Freud's *Jewish* identity on all his theories. Indeed, the development of psychoanalysis itself has been convincingly interpreted in part as a response to this social dilemma. Elliot Oring's *The Jokes of Sigmund Freud: A Study in Humor and Jewish Identity* (Philadelphia: University of Pennsylvania Press, 1984); Marthe Robert's *From Oedipus to Moses: Freud's Jewish Identity* (Garden City, N.Y.: Anchor Books, 1976); and John Murray Cuddihy's *The Ordeal of Civility: Freud, Marx, Lévi-Strauss and the Jewish Struggle with Modernity*, among others, have discussed this issue.

escape the identity he had received, an identity which had made him heir to antisemitic hostility and which stood in the way of his admission to respectable society. Sartre's scenario brilliantly conveys Freud's ambivalence toward his father, and recognizes the centrality of Jakob Freud in the foundation of his son's identity. Sartre sees Freud as a model of Jewish authenticity. He neither denied his Jewishness nor was daunted by the antisemitism that was behind the initial rejection of his theories. "Running away, retreating, I can't accept that. Especially from a Jew" (*FS*, 215), Sartre had him saying defiantly.

Conversely, Sartre actively rejected his own bourgeois background, for it had resulted in a certain instability in his own sense of identity and left him in a chronic state of identity crisis. If psychoanalysis is marked by Freud's Jewish experience, then much of Sartre's existential philosophy can likewise be seen at least *in part* as a response to his unhappy experience as a fatherless bourgeois child.

The theme of travel by train in Freud's dreams and memories was also related to his deep desire to visit Rome. Rome and, to a lesser extent, Paris were favored, yet elusive, destinations for Freud. He recognized that in his dreams, his wish to go to Rome had become "a cloak and symbol for a number of other passionate wishes." Rome symbolized the Gentile world of culture and respectability from which he felt excluded because of his Jewishness. Freud related his feelings about Rome to the experience of his own otherness, his recognition of "what it meant to belong to an alien race," and his experience of antisemitism among other boys in school.[7] Early in Sartre's screenplay, Freud encounters vendors hawking vile pamphlets like the *Protocols of the Elders of Zion*, "The Jew and the Pig," and "The Child Eaten by a Rabbi." Back in the safety of their own neighborhood, Freud tells his wife, Martha,

> When I was that kid's age, I used to call the goys Romans; we, the Jews, were Carthaginians. There was a picture in a prize-book. I tore it out of the book and kept it. Hamilcar, the great man of Carthage, was making his son Hannibal swear to wreak vengeance upon Rome. Hannibal was me. (*FS*, 32)

For Sartre, too, Rome was a symbol of civilized respectability, a world from which Jews were effectively isolated. In *Bariona*, a play Sartre wrote as a prisoner of war (using the Romans to represent the Germans), a Roman official of the first century points out that most Jews are "real savages" who tend, apparently, to prefer messiahs who are

7. Sigmund Freud, *The Interpretation of Dreams* (New York: Avon Books, 1970), p. 229.

lacking in breeding and respectability. This same Roman is very pleased to find a Jew with refined "manners" who has studied in Rome. He suggests that the Roman government would be willing to accept a Jewish messiah if he were "appropriate," that is, if he "came from an old Jewish family, had studied in our country, and would offer guarantees of his respectability" (WS, 2:76). The only kind of Jews that are acceptable to Gentile society, Sartre thus suggests, are Jews who have assimilated Gentile culture and in some way been de-Judaized. The first-century Romans in Sartre's play are not very different from modern Europeans who expected the Jews to be refined before they could be fully accepted.

In *The Interpretation of Dreams*, Freud recounted a number of his own dreams and memories dealing with train travel and Rome. In one of his dreams he was only able to see Rome at a distance from the window of a train. In another dream, he realized that he had reached Rome, but he still needed to ask a Herr Zucker for the way to the city. Freud's associations to this dream led him to recall two very telling Jewish anecdotes. The first one he called "the 'constitution' story":

> An impecunious Jew had stowed himself away without a ticket in the fast train to Karlsbad. He was caught, and each time tickets were inspected he was taken out off the train and treated more and more severely. At one of the stations on his *via dolorosa* he met an acquaintance, who asked him where he was travelling to. "To Karlsbad," was his reply, "if my constitution can stand it."[8]

Here we have a perfect example of the Jew as a traveller without a ticket, who suffers every time that tickets are inspected. The newly emancipated Jew found himself travelling in a society whose "étiquette" he did not possess. The poor Jew's destination in the anecdote is also interesting. Freud associated the remark "to Karlsbad, if my constitution can stand it" with the fact that he prescribed treatment there for those with the "constitutional" disease diabetes. Perhaps, we can see this particular association in relation to the social dilemma of the Jew. A "constitution" which cannot tolerate sugar—diabetes—might be considered as a symbol of the Jews' failure in etiquette, the "sweet" coating of everyday life.[9] As Marthe Robert puts it, Jewishness for Freud seemed like a hereditary and incurable disease that prevented him from reaching his destination, and he either refused or was unable to pay the price of the

8. Ibid., pp. 227–28.
9. Oring points out that diabetes was seen as a particularly Jewish disease in Freud's time. *The Jokes of Sigmund Freud*, p. 60. In Freud's dream, he had to ask a Herr Zucker (Mr. Sugar) for directions to get to Rome.

ticket. [10] Elliot Oring notes that Freud associated Karlsbad with Rome on several occasions, Rome being a symbol for him of Christian civilization. [11] Curiously, in Freud's retelling of this anecdote, he linked the train stations on the way to Karlsbad with stations of a very different sort, the "stations of the cross" (*via dolorosa*) of Jesus. Such an analogy compares the Jew to the founder of Christianity itself, yet simultaneously alludes to the most famous humiliation of a Jew at the hands of the Romans, the crucifixion.

The second anecdote that Freud recalled concerned "a Jew who could not speak French and had been told when he was in Paris, to ask the way to rue Richelieu." [12] Paris, like Rome, was a place Freud had wanted to visit for many years. To go to Paris, a traditional symbol of highly civilized society, but to be unable to speak French, the language of cultivated society and etiquette, would be quite comparable to travelling on a train without a ticket. This sense of being out of place is apparent in the letters Freud wrote to his wife while he was studying with Charcot in Paris. He complained about the superficial charm of the French and noted that other foreigners shared his feelings about "the so-called civility of the French." [13] He was struck simultaneously by the politeness and the vulgarity of the Parisians. On some level, Freud always felt like an outsider in both Paris and Rome.

Sartre, on the other hand, had every reason to feel at home in both Paris and Rome (and the cultural traditions they represented). Unfortunately, this fact was nothing about which he felt very happy or proud. The more comfortable he felt in either place, the more he felt the difference between someone like Freud and himself.

In his book on jokes, Freud once again returned to the dilemmas of Jews travelling by train. He recounted the joke about a Galician Jew who had made himself comfortable in a train compartment by unbuttoning his coat and putting his feet up on the seat. When a well-dressed gentleman entered the compartment "the Jew promptly pulled himself together and took up a proper pose." After checking his notebook, the stranger suddenly asked the Jew the date of Yom Kippur. "'Oho,' said the Jew, and put his feet up on the seat again before answering." The fact that the Jew could abandon his "decent" behavior when he realized he was in the presence of another Jew represented, according to Freud,

10. Robert, *From Oedipus to Moses*, pp. 108–9.

11. Oring, *The Jokes of Sigmund Freud*, p. 61.

12. Freud, *The Interpretation of Dreams*, p. 228.

13. *Letters of Sigmund Freud*, ed. by Ernst L. Freud (New York: Basic Books, 1975), p. 182.

"the democratic mode of thinking of the Jews, which recognizes no distinction between lords and serfs, but also, alas, upsets discipline and cooperation."[14] Perhaps Freud meant that the Jews recognize no distinctions *among themselves*, since the Galician Jew did indeed recognize not only a distinction between Jews and non-Jews but also his need to behave differently (artificially) in the presence of the latter. Freud, too, recognized this distinction, and was infuriated by the social hierarchy that gave special privileges to counts, officials, aristocratic couples, and others. Legal entitlement to a place on the train by the purchase of a full-fare ticket did not eliminate the kind of "insults and humiliations"[15] that Freud experienced, any more than legal emancipation brought smooth social assimilation.

In the *Freud Scenario*, as in his own autobiography, Sartre created two important train scenes to express the changes taking place in Freud. In the first, Freud dozes off and imagines that the three cardplayers in his compartment are his three intellectual or spiritual "fathers": Meynert, Breuer, and Fliess. They ask him to play, but when the ticket-collector comes, there are only empty places. The ticket-collector is Freud's father, who says of the three men, "They had no tickets: that's why they're dead." He continues, "My job is to check tickets, so I'll help you. I'll help you. I'll help you. Your ticket!" (*FS*, 280). As Freud gives up his teachers, he realizes how much his father has helped him to reach his destination. His fame and success have been a way of avenging his father's humiliation at the hands of antisemites. In Sartre's final scene, Freud explains to Fliess that he has cured his anxiety about trains, having realized that his first train was "the train of exile and rupture" that took his family from an easy life in Freiburg to poverty in Vienna. Trains had come to mean the passage from prosperity to poverty. Now, as Freud has begun to achieve fame, a young admirer asks if he may join Freud on the train to Vienna. Freud accepts, boards the train, and says, "I was forty-one. It was my turn to play the role of father" (*FS*, 539). At last, Freud had earned his place on the train, yet without having compromised himself to do so.

When one examines the relationship of these various train and ticket metaphors to Sartre's social background, a number of interesting links to Freud's experience emerge. Sartre implicitly or explicitly compared his own existential plight to that of the Jews. There was obviously a great

---

14. Freud, *Jokes and Their Relation to the Unconscious*, pp. 80, 112.
15. Freud, *The Interpretation of Dreams*, p. 494.

difference between what being without a ticket meant to Sartre and what it meant to Freud. For Freud, the Jew was a stowaway on the train *of* and *to* Gentile civility. As a Jew, Freud had no doubts about who he really was inside. But staying on the Gentile's train to its ultimate destination required passing as something he was not. The ticket-collector, the other passengers (for the most part), and the train itself all represented the world of the Other, a world, moreover, that branded the Jew as the archetypal Other in return. On the other hand, the train was also a metaphor for the difficult path the Jew had to travel, a path that began in humiliation and deprivation because of antisemitism, but culminated in a triumphant return to Vienna, not unlike Hannibal's entrance into Rome.

The most intriguing part of Sartre's own parable of ticketlessness was its concluding line. Unlike the Jewish stowaway Freud, Sartre felt that he was *not only* the delinquent, *but also* the ticket-collector *and* the train. At the same time that he felt like a stowaway, he realized it was his own train that he had been riding. And who was it who really had caught him? Himself! What for Freud was a social confrontation with a world to which he did not quite belong, was for Sartre a confrontation within himself and within his own world. Sartre envied Freud's firm sense of self, since beneath his own "civilized" playacting he did not really know who he was. The missing ticket might have told him the reason or justification for his life. Unlike Freud's dilemma, the place where he discovered that something was missing was not an alien world; it was in his own home. Sartre's childhood world *was* the world of bourgeois civility. It was in that world, or on that train, that he had fallen asleep, lulled by the pleasant game of meaningless role-playing. However, all was not well; he was not completely taken in by his act. Hence, he had also become his own accuser.

In his parable, Sartre told the ticket-taker that he had left his identity papers at home. In reality, it was not true that his sense of identity was any more secure at home or that he even had a home of his own. Indeed, part of Sartre's childhood confusion came from his sense of always being in someone else's home, where it was especially important for him to watch his behavior. He remembers that as a child, "My mother would whisper to me: 'Be careful! We're not in our own home!' We were never in our own home, neither on the rue le Goff nor later when my mother remarried" (W, 55).

Sartre's sense of homelessness was one thing that may have given him an insight into the predicament of the Jews, or at least may have contributed to his sense of identification with Jews and led him to see them as symbols of a universal kind of existential homelessness. Throughout most of European history, the Jews have lived in other people's "homes." They were seldom fully at ease in their host countries. People who are never at home can never stop performing. They cannot put their feet up on the furniture. They are always "on stage." In his analysis of the Jewish predicament, Sartre emphasized the awkward situation created by the attempts of some Jews to play a certain role in society that only alienated them from themselves.

In both his philosophy and his autobiography, Sartre removed these experiences of homelessness, exile, and dispersion from the social arena and made them into global existential themes. The fundamental structure of human consciousness and the self had a parallel in Jewish reality. Indeed, Sartre described the structure of the "for-itself" as "diasporatic" after the notion of Diaspora that refers to "the profound cohesion and dispersion of the Jewish people" (BN, 136). The mystery that holds together a people without a land provides a metaphor for a view of consciousness as lacking any firm or fixed foundation of its own. It is no wonder, in turn, that Sartre could not give any concrete sense to the meaning of Jewishness. It, like consciousness itself, was a form of transcendent "nothingness" to him. Just as Freud universalized his own particular social predicament as a Jew by incorporating it into a general theory of the structure of the psyche, Sartre transformed his unique childhood situation into a microcosm of the human condition that was somehow parallel to Jewish experience. [16]

If the problem of personal identity continually plagued Sartre, it was not nearly so problematic for Freud. For Freud, the nature of his personal identity was rooted first of all in the fact of his Jewish identity. In his well-known address to the B'nai B'rith, Freud explained:

> What bound me to Jewry was (I am ashamed to admit) neither faith nor national pride, for I have always been an unbeliever and was brought up

16. It would be fascinating to explore similar intersecting themes in the life and work of Derrida. Derrida's childhood experience with antisemitism left him feeling out of place both in the insular Jewish community and the hostile non-Jewish world. Much like Freud, he was left with "the desire to be integrated into the non-Jewish community, a fascinated but painful and distrustful desire, one with nervous vigilance, a painstaking attitude to discern signs of racism in its most discreet formations or in its loudest denials. Symmetrically, oftentimes, I felt an impatient distance with regard to various Jewish communities, when I have the impression that they close in upon themselves, when they pose themselves as such. From all of which comes a feeling of non-belonging that I have doubtless transposed. . . . [Interviewer: "In Philosophy?"] Everywhere." "An Interview with Derrida," in David Wood and Robert Bernasconi, eds., *Derrida and Differance* (Evanston, Ill.: Northwestern University Press, 1988), p. 75.

without any religion though not without a respect for what are called the "ethical" standards of human civilization. . . . But plenty of other things remained over to make the attraction of Jewry and Jews irresistible—many obscure emotional forces, which were the more powerful the less they could be expressed in words, as well as *a clear consciousness of inner identity*, the safe privacy of a common mental construction. And beyond this there was a perception that it was to my Jewish nature alone that I owed two characteristics that had become indispensable to me in the difficult course of my life. Because I was a Jew I found myself free from many prejudices which restricted others in the use of their intellect; and as a Jew I was prepared to join the Opposition and to do without agreement with the "compact majority."[17]

In short, Freud credited his Jewishness with anchoring his identity, freeing him of intellectual narrowness, and preparing him to face the opposition of the majority. Considering Jews like Freud led Sartre to the conclusion that Jews were bound together, in the final analysis, less by their common interests, beliefs, or practices and more by their situation of being identified as Jews in a world of non-Jews. Sartre argued that a Jew's identity is created in large measure by the hostility and disdain of others. It was the antisemitism of Vienna that forced Freud to become intellectually aggressive (*ST*, 131). Despite what Jewish religious law may say about the singular importance of a Jewish birth-mother, Sartre countered that *Jews are made, not born*. It is the outside world that says, in effect, "You are a Jew." In this respect, neither Freud nor Sartre understood Jewish identity to stem from some inherent spiritual message in Judaism. They both focused mainly on the consequences of antisemitism on the Jewish character. For Sartre, Jewishness was, therefore, not only a metaphor for the diasporatic nature of consciousness, but also the starkest example of the power of the Other's "look": "To recognize others and, if I am a Jew, to assume my being-a-Jew are one and the same thing" (*BN*, 527). All people monitor to some extent what they are to the Other. Jews do this both as Jews and as individuals. "It amounts in a sense to a doubling of the fundamental relationship with the Other" (*AJ*, 79).

There are several reasons why Sartre gave little attention to Jewishness as a coherent religious system. First, he had difficulty recognizing religion of any kind as anything other than shallow, social convention. He insisted that adherence to religious practice was largely a matter of

17. Freud, "Address to the Society of B'nai B'rith," in *The Standard Edition of The Complete Psychological Works of Sigmund Freud*, trans. James Strachey (London: Hogarth Press, 1959), 20:273–74 (emphasis added).

polite, ceremonial behavior rather than intellectual conviction. Early on, a child learns that religious practice is a way of pleasing one's parents and of being respectable in the eyes of friends and neighbors. It is the "right thing to do," not in a moral sense, but in terms of civility— that is, it is the socially right thing to do. To the extent that Jews were actually observant at all, said Sartre, they were not very different from the kind of bourgeois Christians who kept their religion for the sake of appearance. Accordingly, Sartre observed that "the Jews who surround us today have only a ceremonial and polite contact with their religion" (AJ, 65). He regarded observance of Jewish religious rituals such as circumcision as purely a question of social convention, like the Jew who had his son circumcised "because it pleased my mother, and because it's the right thing to do," while his mother held to tradition "because of her friends and neighbors" (AJ, 65). While this is obviously a very limited view of the function of religious practice and ritual, Sartre had difficulty seeing beyond his own experience of a lifeless, though socially appropriate, form of religion.

Second, Sartre argued that Jews maintained their religion only because antisemitism excluded them from the national traditions of the places where they lived. Failing to appreciate the intrinsic value of religious ritual in general and Jewish religious observance in particular, Sartre explained the latter behavior as mainly a response to the "homelessness" of the Jews, a symptom of the Jewish sense of rootlessness. The real reason for Jewish religious ceremony, he said, was "a secret and deep-seated need to attach oneself to tradition and, in default of a national past, to give oneself roots in a past of rites and customs" (AJ, 65). He implied that if the Jews were ever able truly to assimilate and be accepted as Frenchmen, their allegiance to Jewish practice would evaporate, since the reason for it would also have disappeared. This reasoning has been aptly criticized by Harold Rosenberg, who notes how Sartre privileged French national identity over Jewish identity and failed to see that the desire for assimilation is itself a response to prejudice. A society without prejudice would offer little incentive to assimilate.[18]

Third, Sartre denied that theological commitment was the link that bound Jews together. He found it hard to respect any genuine religious commitment to Judaism, since he was convinced that the critical outlook and rationalism of the Enlightenment had made all religious

18. Harold Rosenberg, "Does the Jew Exist?" *Commentary* 7 (January 1949): 9–10.

commitment suspect. Thus, he rejected Judaism as a religion on the same grounds that he had rejected Christianity.

Though Sartre's analysis of Jewish commitment has a number of serious weaknesses and limitations, such conclusions were understandable in light of the kind of contact he had with Jews throughout most of his life. Sartre did not know any religiously committed Jews at the time his ideas about Jews were being formed. Moreover, atheism was common among the Jewish intellectuals he did know. While it is true that Jews played a considerable role in the cultural life of France in the early part of the twentieth century, most of the prominent Jewish intellectuals, artists, and radicals were only marginally Jewish. They were neither affiliated with the organized Jewish community nor took much part in Jewish activities. These assimilated, acculturated, deracinated Jews provided Sartre with a skewed picture of Jewish identity. For most of them, Jewishness was merely a matter of origin.[19] A good example might be Sartre's college classmate Raymond Aron, who had no formal Jewish education and no desire to identify as a Jew. Only "the shock of Hitler" and the 1967 Arab-Israeli War were finally able to revive his sense of Jewishness. Sartre's premise that the Jew is defined by the Other, Aron admitted, applied quite well to Jews like him: "de-Judaized, an unbeliever, non-practicing, of French culture, with no Jewish culture."[20] As Sartre's adopted Jewish daughter noted:

> There were always a fair number of Jews around Sartre and they could explain to him the problems caused by persecution, how their families had been persecuted and what that meant to them. But these Jews—this is not to excuse Sartre—were intellectual Jews who didn't have the inner sense of what it meant to be Jewish in a positive sense any more.[21]

In Sartre's thought, what the Jew most represented was an archetypically marginal person whose lack of acceptance in respectable society provided the opportunity for achieving authentic existence. The particular social position or status of the Jew, like that of women, created a sensitivity in the Jew which Sartre found very attractive. He denied that this "Jewish sensibility" was due to any peculiar qualities of Jewish culture. Indeed, Sartre insisted that the "peculiar characteristics" of the

19. Paula Hyman, *From Dreyfus to Vichy: The Remaking of French Jewry, 1906–1939* (New York: Columbia University Press, 1979), p. 21.

20. Raymond Aron, *Memoirs* (New York: Holmes and Meier, 1990), pp. 335–36, 351, 446.

21. Charmé, "Sartre's Jewish Daughter," p. 25.

Jew "are neither ethnic nor physiological nor religious," but almost exclusively a function of antisemitism (AJ, 145).[22]

The contrast between Sartre's attitudes toward the Jew and the antisemite is a reflection of the dual nature of identity. Identity is something that one creates, but it is also something to which one is condemned by others. More than any other recent thinker, Sartre emphasized the immense freedom of all human beings to determine and construct the meaning of their own identities. At the same time, however, he recognized the reality of a person's "being-for-others," that is, the fact that a portion of every person's identity is determined by the way he or she is perceived by other people, and that one must accept responsibility for that portion.

The difference between the antisemite and the Jew is also paradigmatic of the connection between identity and social position. The proportion of one's identity that one personally creates and the proportion of identity to which one is condemned by others may vary in different groups of people. A greater amount of freedom to create one's identity is to some extent a privilege of the dominant class or group in a society. For Sartre, this greater freedom also produced a greater sense of insecurity and anxiety about the issue of identity. For Jews, women, blacks, and other oppressed groups, however, a larger proportion of their identity is determined for them by others. Ironically, the imposition of a devalued identity on the oppressed Other often insulated them from certain temptations to bad faith, and gave them a more secure sense of who they were.

Unlike Freud, who gave his father credit for an identity that left him "ticketless" in an antisemitic world, Sartre did not hold his father responsible for his own existential "ticketlessness." Rather, the culprit was *the absence* of his father. By dying shortly after his son's birth, Sartre's father had deprived him of an existential patrimony. Freud's father had propelled his son forward with an oath of vengeance to fulfill. Sartre imagined, moreover, that Jakob Freud might have told young Sigmund, "If I'd done nothing else but bring a man of genius into the world, I wouldn't have wasted my life" (FS, 339). Sartre's father, however, bequeathed him neither a ticket nor a destination. "If Jean-Baptiste Sartre had ever known my destination, he had taken the secret with him" (W, 55). Sartre continued,

22. Sartre regrettably accepted certain common racist ideas about Jews, including the belief that there is a Jewish "race" in the sense that Jews in France have "certain inherited physical conformations" such as hooked noses, protruding ears, and thick lips (AJ, 60–61, 62, 101–2, 118).

Nobody, beginning with me, knew why the hell I had been born. Had he left me property, my childhood would have been changed. . . . House and field reflect back to the young heir a stable image of himself. He touches himself on his gravel, on the diamond-shaped panes of his veranda, and makes of their inertia the deathless substance of his soul. . . . Worldly possessions reflect to their owner what he is; they taught me what I was not. *I was not* substantial or permanent. *I was not* the future continuer of my father's work, *I was not* necessary to the production of steel. In short, I had no soul. (W, 55)

For his own reasons, Sartre thus adopted a fundamental characteristic of groups who have been declared *other*—a negative identity. He defined himself in terms of what he was *not*, that is, as a negation of the work of his father, of property, economic power, and a secure place in the universe. His identity represented a dismantling of these dominant forms of culturally approved identity. Yet it is hard to believe that Sartre really wished that he had inherited house, land, or factory; or that they would really have given him a firm sense of identity. On the contrary, Sartre thought that those who identify with their land and property were guilty of bad faith. It was a bogus source of identity. In Sartre's case, paradoxically, it was the son who justified his father's existence. Certainly, Jean-Baptist Sartre's most notable act was fathering Jean-Paul.

Although Sartre suggested that his own family and social situation had produced his feeling of ontological insecurity, when he analyzed a similar aspect in the social situation of the Jew—whose identity was likewise severed from a relation to land and property—he saw the same negative identity, but not the same insecurity. Certainly Jews suffered from a basic "uneasiness" due to their tenuous position in European society, but antisemitism provided the kind of opposition in relation to which the Jews could define themselves.

## The Identity of the Antisemite

In 1946, in the wake of the Nazi genocide and the shame of French collaboration, Jean-Paul Sartre published his now classic *Réflexions sur la question juive,*[23] a "phenomenological description" (WS, 143) of antisemitism and Jewish identity. As was often the case with Sartre, he dashed headlong into a controversial issue. Only much later did he admit that he had done no research regarding either Jewish history or antisemitism before writing the essay, and that if he were to redo it, he

23. Translated as *Anti-Semite and Jew* (New York: Schocken Books, 1965).

would need to include historical and economic analysis (WS, 143). Sartre was praised for confronting the problem of antisemitism when few others were willing to do so, but he was likewise criticized for ignoring the religious and ethnic aspects of Jewish identity, as well as the historical roots of antisemitism. To a great extent, however, the apparent weaknesses of Sartre's essay may stem from a misreading of its underlying purpose. There was little reason for Sartre to do much historical research, since he was less interested in the actual historical analysis of the "Jewish question" than in developing an outline of two paradigmatic types of identity: the antisemite and the Jew. If Sartre did not provide a historical approach to the relations between Jews and non-Jews, it may have been partly because Jew and non-Jew were archetypes within a mythology of the Other that he had elaborated throughout his work, and through which he understood himself and his own social background.

Sartre saw the antisemites' identity as indicative of a comprehensive conception of the world and their own relation to it, rather than just an isolated set of nasty opinions about Jews (AJ, 17). Perhaps the most striking aspect about Sartre's description of the antisemitic mentality is its similarity to the kind of identity found in primitive tribes. Although he provided no references, Sartre's essay obviously borrowed several central categories from the work of French Jewish sociologist Lévy-Bruhl on primitive mental functioning. [24] It is true that Lévy-Bruhl's work has been criticized by subsequent sociologists and anthropologists for overdramatizing the difference between "primitive" and "civilized" mental functioning, but for Sartre it provided a helpful model for another dualism he had detected in certain types of modern identities.

One possible purpose in this type of approach may have been to show that the antisemitic worldview is not only socially destructive and based on "bad faith," but that it is also an anomalous throwback to "primitive" thinking. [25] Not only is the antisemitic identity type contrary to the type of rationality of civilized society, but its continued existence today reveals the fragility and vulnerability of that civilized rationality.

One of Lévy-Bruhl's main points about primitive peoples concerned

24. Lévy-Bruhl was professor of the history of modern philosophy at the Ecole Normale during the time that Sartre was a student there. Although Sartre rarely made explicit reference to Lévy-Bruhl in his work, there is at least one reference to Lévy-Bruhl made around the time *Anti-Semite and Jew* was written (see CPM, 369). In an interview near the end of his life, Sartre reported that his unfinished work on ethics was to have included a critique of the ethical perspectives of Lévy-Bruhl and Lévi-Strauss. "Jean-Paul Sartre et Michel Sicard: Entretien," *Obliques*, nos. 18–19 (1979):14.
25. Sartre domesticated prelogical mentality, says Howard Davies, and incorporated it, like the unconscious, as a part of bad faith. See *Sartre and 'Les Temps Modernes'* (Cambridge: Cambridge University Press, 1987), pp. 10–11, 23.

their "prelogical" and "mystical" way of thought. Primitive thought, he argued, does not follow the ordinary rules of logic of modern "civilized" societies. Causal connections and facts are irrelevant to the primitive's sense of the world. The mystical element of primitive thought comes from its belief in occult and invisible forces that link persons and things together and are manifest through them.

According to Lévy-Bruhl, the primitive does not differentiate individual beings from the essence or idea of the species that they express. The primitive, therefore, spoke about a whole species in the singular. "The real individual is not such and such a stag or such and such a whale, but *the* Stag, *the* Whale. . . . A very close connection unites animals of the same species. Their individuality is but relative, and they are actually only multiple and transient expressions of a single and imperishable homogenous essence." Lévy-Bruhl himself recognized the similarity between this phenomenon and modern stereotypes. "It is somewhat analogous to the way in which, during the Great War, many people would talk of 'the Boche,' and as many colonists in Algeria talk of 'the Arab,' or many Americans of 'the black man.' It denotes a kind of essence or type, too general to be an image, and too emotional to be a concept."[26]

Sartre understood the mental life of the antisemite in a similar way. The antisemite can only relate to an individual Jew as an example of "the Jew," that is, a kind of universal essence. Whatever the underlying economic or political causes of antisemitism that Sartre ignored, he accurately saw that the antisemite's reaction to the Jew was informed by neither reason nor experience. Like members of primitive tribes, antisemites inhabit a religiously valorized world, one in which their fight against the Jews has become a holy war. To the antisemite, the Jew represents what is beyond the boundary of acceptable difference. This gives the Jew the forbidden sacred quality one might associate in tribal societies with religious taboos.

Sartre used Lévy-Bruhl's work to uncover within antisemitism a desire to return to a preurban, premodern form of communal life in which one feels integrated into nature. The antisemite's response to the uprootedness of modern life is to seek refuge in a sense of identity based on what Lévy-Bruhl called "mystical participation." In contrast to the Jew, the antisemite's identity is rooted in a sense of tradition, relation to the land, custom, and a premodern conception of property and possession. The antisemite only understands

26. Lucien Lévy-Bruhl, *The 'Soul' of the Primitive* (New York: Frederick A. Praeger, 1966), pp. 61, 59.

a type of primitive ownership of land based on a veritable magical rapport, in which the thing possessed and its possessor are united by a bond of mystical participation. . . . To put it in another way, the principle underlying antisemitism is that the concrete possession of a particular object gives as if by magic the meaning of that object. (*AJ*, 23–24; cf. 148, 150)

Obviously, Sartre was not talking about ownership of land in the sense of a paid-off mortgage and a clear title; rather it is ownership by means of a mystical link. The antisemite feels secure about his identity and his place in world, since he sees "the bond that unites him to his country as *natural*" (*AJ*, 133). Antisemitism is a safe haven where the crises of identity brought on by modern society cannot be felt. It is a regression to the security of childhood, like the child who feels linked to his mother by a "primitive mystical participation" (*B*, 16).[27]

For Lucien Fleurier, the antisemitic character in "The Childhood of a Leader," antisemitism meant trading in one kind of "dirt" for another, that is, learning to understand himself in terms of the "unconscious reeking of the *soil*" rather than the "*filthy*, lascivious images of Freud" (*CL*, 143). The earth is a nourishing soil when it is seen as the source of natural power, uncontaminated by civilization, but it becomes filthy and defiling when it is negatively associated with sexuality, disease, decay, and death. Lucien longed for the former and expressed a *mystical* sense of the region of his birth. In the soil and subsoil of Férolles, he could find a kind of life-energy "stretched in the woods, the springs, and the grass like nourishing humous from which he could draw the strength to become a leader" (*CL*, 143). His health and strength were rooted in the land, while self-contemplation now seemed "sterile and dangerous" to him. Lucien hated the urban setting of Paris, the natural habitat of Jews, and remembered with nostalgia how "the soft countryside enveloped him in its discreet caresses" (*CL*, 143). Thus, his mystical relation to the land could restore and replace some primal maternal bond, while at the same time he could displace onto Jews his disgust with the dirt and corruption of the modern city, his terror of his own dark instincts, and the threatening forms of nature.

European racist theories often appealed to the mystical link between a people and its land, a link not unlike the one Lévy-Bruhl described in the primitive's sense of the land: "The land . . . belongs—and this in the fullest sense of the word—to the social group in its entirety, that is, to the living and dead collectively."[28] When this type of thinking is applied

---

27. "*Participation primitive et mystique*" (translation changed).
28. Lévy-Bruhl, *The 'Soul' of the Primitive*, p. 107.

to modern society by the antisemite, Sartre noted, the implications are obvious. Since true "possession" cannot be acquired or purchased, the antisemite denies that the Jew can ever really possess anything: "All that he [the Jew] touches, all that he acquires becomes devaluated in his hands; the goods of the earth, the true goods are always those which he has not" (*AJ*, 83). The Jew is thereby denied the firm sense of self that is built on a particular relation to land and property. In France, the Jews cannot feel the same ease of identity, since the antisemite had denied them any roots in the land.

Thus the Jew became "antinatural" in relation to the "natural" identity of those people who were tied to land, property, race, and nonrational instincts and emotions. The Jews' exclusion from the land, their intellectual cultivation, and their urban history set them at odds with a certain sense of the "natural." In this respect, Sartre saw his own identity as closer to that of the uneasy Jew than the naturally secure Aryan. His father's early death had spared him the kind of stable identity that the antisemite achieved through primitive thinking. The situation of the Jews reminded him of his own childhood experience and the way in which the lack of property and possessions had undermined his sense of self, that is, until he realized that identity could never really be based on such things.

Both the primitive's identity as a member of his tribe and the antisemite's "natural" sense of security and superiority are based on birth rather than merit. Therefore, it cannot be acquired by those who lack it, or lost by those who have it. "It is given once and for all" (*AJ*, 26–27). From this point of view, the French antisemite would never acknowledge the Jew as a natural or real Frenchman. To be French had nothing to do with legal rights (or "tickets"). "Paying full fare" would never be enough. Despite the fact that the Jew may be legally accepted or that he "joins the game and conforms to all the ceremonies, dancing with the others the dance of respectability," he is never accepted by the "real" society that is "amorphous, diffused, and omnipresent" (*AJ*, 80). To the antisemite, the Jew can never share the French sense of values. To be a "true" Frenchman "is above all to have the use and the sense of these values" (*AJ*, 80). Even if the Jews seemed to share French values and customs, they could never know, said the antisemite, "the true sense of things . . . the *genuine* France, with its *genuine* values, its *genuine* tact, its *genuine* morality" (*AJ*, 82). This privilege belonged only to those born with a natural intuition of it. The implication was that the extension of civil rights to the Jews would not make them just like other French people. Such identity is inherited, not acquired by legislative decree. What the Gentile had and what the Jew would always lack, were precisely the qualities associated with ethnic civility. In the eyes of the antisemite, Jewish vulgarity was incurable.

Sartre was not dealing here with ethical values as much as "the collective currents, the styles, the customs" that emerge in a traditionalist society and which give a person a sense of belonging to society. These shared values, precisely the elements which constitute a society's idea of civility, remove each individual's sense of contingency, and replace it with a sense of justification for his or her existence. The antisemites avoid the anxiety of existence by persuading themselves that they have a fixed place in the world and "tradition gives [them] the right to occupy it" (*AJ*, 54). This sense of certainty about one's place in the world is associated by Sartre with the inauthentic attitudes of respectability and distinction. "Antisemitism is *distinguished* as are all the manifestations of a collective and irrational soul which seek to create an occult and conservative France" (*AJ*, 51).

The antisemite has chosen for himself a fixed identity (as someone who does not like Jews) that has "the permanence and impenetrability of stone" (*AJ*, 53), rather than accepted reality as indefinite, ambiguous, and tentative. Thus, Sartre saw antisemitism as "fear of the human condition" (*AJ*, 43), that is to say, a refusal to confront the existential anxieties of a world without fixed boundaries and qualities. In some ways the antisemite's fear resembled the primitive sense of the world and its resistance to what Mircea Eliade called "the terror of history."[29] As Sartre was later to recognize, Judaism was founded on a very strong sense of the dialectical movement of history. The antisemite prefers the timeless qualities that he claims for himself, rather than the terror of an uncertain and ever-changing history.

Of course, Sartre rejected the idea that a person's identity could be grounded in a fixed essence—as the antisemite claimed—as an illusion of the highest order. Intoxicated by this illusion, the inauthentic person might avoid confronting his or her own individual freedom to create an identity. In "The Childhood of a Leader," Sartre described the metamorphosis of Lucien into an antisemite as a kind of self-deception in the quest for identity. Lucien felt purified by his antisemitism. He knew at last who he was: "I am Lucien! Someone who can't stand Jews" (*CL*, 156). As a symbol of otherness, the Jew helps the non-Jew to define himself. Lucien was afraid of examining his own self, for he found

29. Mircea Eliade, *Cosmos and History* (New York: Harper, 1959).

nothing there that was permanent, that was not a matter of chance, or that set him apart from others. He escaped by seeing the world as a place in which he had certain sacred rights and a preordained destiny to fulfill. The Jew is thus a projection of the existential rootlessness the antisemite fears most.

Sartre reinforced his picture of the primitive quality of the antisemitic mentality by describing it as a kind of "mechanical solidarity" in the heart of an "organized society" (*AJ*, 29). The antisemite is "incapable of understanding modern social organization" and has "nostalgia for periods of crisis in which the primitive community will suddenly reappear and attain its temperature of fusion. He wants his personality to melt suddenly into the group and be carried away by the collective torrent" (*AJ*, 30). Antisemitism expresses "a primitive society that, though secret and diffused, remains latent in the legal collectivity" (*AJ*, 69). Thus the antisemite's understanding of the world is the primitive type characteristic of irrational mobs and primitive tribes. The "mechanical solidarity" to which Sartre referred was Durkheim's term to describe the structure of traditional societies. In a society of mechanical solidarity, each person is a microcosm of the collectivity, each member being interchangeable with any other. There is little individuation or particular personality characteristics. Modern social organization, Durkheim said, was based on "organic solidarity," where individuals are more differentiated and linked in interdependent but not interchangeable ways.

In a bourgeois society, Sartre observed, where hostile groups such as rich and poor, workers and capitalists, city-dwellers and country-dwellers could easily fragment society, antisemitism offers a "loose solidarity" by suppressing social and economic differences through emphasis on the distinction between Jew and non-Jew. The antisemite simply collapses all other social tensions and differences between groups into this primordial category of difference.

Various people have observed the ambivalent or protean nature of Jewish stereotypes, a kind of antisemitic version of "Heads I win, tails you lose." Because the Jew is the marker of otherness or difference for the non-Jew, the Jew becomes the incarnation of the dangers of both too much and too little civility. On the one hand, Jews are seen as under-civilized: dirty, uncultured, philistine, backward, superstitious, carnally driven, and bestial in sexuality. But on the other hand, they are also overcivilized: overly cultured, cosmopolitan, decadent, degenerate, too progressive, too successful, too modern, too urban, deviant and diseased in sexuality. Like depictions of other groups branded as

"Other," the antisemite's image of the Jew is an imaginary projection of what threatens the social norms of propriety, decency, conventionality, and health.[30]

Philo-semitic Sartre acknowledged this Jewish otherness but chose to regard it as an *antidote to* rather than a *violation of* civility. To the extent that the Jews are "undercivilized," they offer fresh, spontaneous, uninhibited perspectives that are uncorrupted by the hypocrisy of civility; to the extent that they are "overcivilized" the Jews represent the avantgarde, the highly creative, the catalyst for cultural evolution.

Sartre could not help noticing that the same kind of bourgeois concern with preserving tradition, ceremony, and distinction that produced hypocritical religion also could be found in the antisemite. The French church in particular often found itself allied with the supporters of antisemitism. Antisemitic leaders were often Catholics. They were threatened by the same values that were most attractive to Jews, namely the ideals of the revolution: justice, equality, progress, freedom of religion.

## The Nature of Nature

For the most part, Sartre identified with the Jewish lack of connection with the rhythms of nature. He especially appreciated both Jews' bookishness and their transcendent relation to nature. Throughout his work, Sartre had expressed great fear of being engulfed by the powers of nature. In *The Words* he noted,

> I later heard anti-Semites reproach Jews any number of times with not knowing the lessons and silences of nature; I would answer: "In that case, I'm more Jewish than they." In vain would I seek within me the prickly memories and sweet unreason of a country childhood. I never tilled the soil or hunted for nests. I did not gather herbs or throw stones at birds. But books were my birds and my nests, my household pets, my barn and my countryside. The library was the world caught in a mirror. (W, 30–31)

Sartre liked Jews because their exclusion from a deep tie to the land paralleled his own lack of territorial roots. Yet the urgency of Sartre's comparison should not be missed. He insisted on being even *more Jewish* than the Jews. Here again he presents an identity of negation, an "I" defined by being what it is not and not being what it is.

---

30. See Barry D. Adam, *The Survival of Domination: Inferiorization and Everyday Life* (New York: Elsevier, 1978), p. 42.

Sartre was attracted to the Jews not only because of their lack of a "natural" identity, but also because of their exclusion from an unnatural identity. If bourgeois civility is a way of refining and disguising certain natural parts of human existence (e.g., bodily functions) then the Jew was *very natural*, uncompromised by the unnaturalness of Christian respectability. This Jewish naturalness accounts for the spontaneity of the Jew that Sartre sensed. While Jewish naturalness or vulgarity was something that the antisemite saw as incurable, it was also something that Sartre treated as a badge of authenticity. The social curse of the Jews, the exclusion from bourgeois circles of civility, was also in some sense the means of their redemption.[31]

Ironically, the Jews' most important characteristic for Sartre had less to do with what they *were* than with what they *were not*. A Jew was *not* a "respectable" member of the bourgeoisie. The positive characteristics of the Jews were all a result of this negative characteristic. In Sartre's view, the involuntary segregation of the Jew from the artificiality of bourgeois culture marked the Jew more than any alleged ethnic, racial, or religious factors. He argued that exclusion from the compromising and inauthenticating conventions of bourgeois society was responsible for the qualities of "gentleness, humanism, endurance, and sharp intelligence" (SG, 203n) that he found prevalent in Jews. Indeed, Sartre indirectly suggested that the complete assimilation and acceptance of the Jew, like the complete liberation of women, might result in the loss of the special qualities that made him prefer the company of women and Jews to others. "What I particularly appreciate in my Jewish friends is a gentleness and subtlety that is certainly an outcome of antisemitism" (PB2, 76). He observed that Jewish feelings had a "disarming freshness and uncultivated spontaneity" (AJ, 131), and that "there is a sincerity, a youth, a warmth in the manifestation of friendship of a Jew that one will rarely find in a Christian, hardened as the latter is by tradition and ceremony" (AJ, 132). In contrast, the "cultivated" feelings and sense of self of the non-Jew were based on "a profound traditionalism, a taste for the particular and the irrational . . . the tranquil enjoyment of deserved privileges: all these the principles of

---

31. Jewish otherness was also a source of fascination and attraction within European society. The rise of colonial empires gave rise to an interest in what was different and strange. While the savage or native often appealed as a contrast to the superficial sophistication of civilized life, Jews were a kind of homegrown yet exotic species. Jews represented the exotic and abnormal to outside society, and along with homosexuals, enjoyed periods of being fashionable to have as friends in bourgeois society.

an aristocratic sensibility" (AJ, 132). Sartre feared that the cultivation of this kind of sensibility was also a move toward artificiality. The Jew was his symbol of the kind of identity that avoided such inauthenticity.

Sartre's analogy between the antisemite and the primitive has an ironic twist within his analysis. It is a common position of antisemitic thinking to look upon the Jews as a more primitive group of people than "civilized" Christians. Yet in Sartre's analysis, it is the Jews who embody the major qualities of modernity and the antisemites who are the "uncivilized" primitives. Or to put it slightly differently, the antisemite embodies the qualities of civility that Sartre identifies with superficial pretense and convention. Conversely, the sense of civility that appeals to Sartre, namely, the transcendence of nature and irrational intuition, is what the antisemite rejects. At this level, it is the Jew who is most civilized and may be held up as a civilizing force on the uncivilized masses of humanity. In this respect, Sartre's social mythology about the Jews parallels the way women came to be seen in the nineteenth century, that is, as a civilizing force for brutish men.

What is also at stake is the different senses of civility that are embodied by the Jew and non-Jew. Bourgeois Christian civility derives from traditions of medieval chivalry. Chivalry includes the idea of social interaction and life itself as a game with specific rules to be followed. Even aggression is "civilized" when it is transformed into a game, a good, fair, clean fight. The model person is the graceful and gracious gentleman who fights, and even kills, for the sake of honor.[32] Although he had been attracted to such knightly ideals as a child, Sartre ultimately found such notions very shallow.

Jewish civility, on the other hand, does not derive from knightly traditions, since Jews were excluded from participation in them. Jewish civility is associated with intellectual critique and moral fervor. The aggressive qualities of the knightly code found no equivalents in Jewish tradition, unless it was the intellectual swordsmanship of the Talmudic rabbis. Sartre was dismayed by those Jews who attempted to exchange Jewish civility for the kind with which he had grown up.

How is it that centuries of persecution have managed to produce in Jews the kind of human qualities that Sartre most preferred? Primarily, it is because the historical experience of European Jews has caused them to develop a suspicion and distrust regarding the Gentile world and the ideological positions of bourgeois society. Indeed, Jewish mar-

---

32. Maurice Samuel, *The Gentleman and the Jew* (New York: Alfred A. Knopf, 1952).

ginality in relation to the governing assumptions of society contributed to the intellectual revolutions led by Jewish intellectuals of the nineteenth and twentieth centuries.[33]

Sartre admired the Jew's intellectual freedom from the conventional thinking of society at large and from the specific presuppositions and prejudices of Christian culture. Certainly, someone like Freud believed that being a Jew had enabled him to propose unpopular ideas and to be persistent in the face of powerful opposition. Freud saw the opposition he received to psychoanalysis as analogous to the opposition Jews have grown accustomed to experiencing from a largely hostile and unfriendly world.

Sartre's idea that the Jew is created by the antisemites' insecurity about their own place in the world was developed at a time when Sartre had little knowledge of, or interest in, Judaism as an autonomous religious perspective. It was only toward the end of his life that he began to appreciate the prophetic elements in Judaism, especially its moral critique of the existing structures of society. In rabbinic Judaism, moreover, Sartre would find a religious tradition of deliberate distance from political power and the status quo.[34] The exclusion of the Jews from genuine political power throughout European history enabled Judaism to maintain its moral independence with less danger of compromise.

## "Jew or Aryan, Spiritual, Vulgar, or Distinguished"

In *Being and Nothingness*, Sartre discussed the way in which the existence of the Other creates limits to our own freedom. Thus, we all discover that we are certain things for the Other despite the fact that we have not chosen them ourselves. These qualities are not merely a matter of the Other's opinion, but of "objective characteristics which define me in my being-for-others" (*BN*, 524). In discussing this topic, Sartre gave a number of telling examples of the kinds of characteristics we can have in the eyes of others. He wrote, "Here I am—Jew or Aryan, handsome or ugly, one-armed, etc." (*BN*, 523). Or later, "How

33. See Cuddihy, *The Ordeal of Civility.*
34. The Talmud counsels caution about getting too close to the ruling powers: "Beware of the ruling powers! For they do not befriend a person except for their own needs: they seem like friends when it is to their advantage, but they do not stand by a man when he is hard-pressed." "Even when you have to have dealings with the ruling powers, for communal purposes . . . beware of their smiling faces and honeyed words! Let them not seduce you into revealing to them the secrets in your heart." *The Living Talmud: The Wisdom of the Fathers* (New York: New American Library, 1957), p. 84.

then shall I experience the objective limits of my being: Jew, Aryan, ugly, handsome, king, civil servant, untouchable, etc." (*BN*, 527). And again, "For myself I am not a professor or a waiter in a cafe, nor am I handsome or ugly, Jew or Aryan, spiritual, vulgar, or distinguished" (*BN*, 527). In each of these examples, Sartre included two different types of qualities. Some were clearly associated with social acceptance, power, and respectability (e.g., Aryan, handsome, king, spiritual, distinguished) while others pointed to social outcasts and marginal types (e.g., Jew, ugly, untouchable, vulgar).

Embedded in Sartre's general ontological category of being-for-others is a sociological polarity. These two different sets of qualities are not at all equivalent, however, in their relationship to identity and authenticity. Authenticity for a "distinguished," "bourgeois," "Aryan" person requires *not* taking comfort or feeling security in who one is. Sartre felt that the dominant (or oppressing) class of society (into which he had been born, much to his embarrassment) could find authenticity only by *transcending* its class benefits, and recognizing the equality of all human beings. Accordingly, Sartre wanted to see himself as—in the concluding phrase of *The Words*—"A whole man, composed of all men and as good as all of them and no better than any" (*W*, 160). Sartre also suggested that a bourgeois like himself might try *not* to act like a bourgeois, to identify with the characteristics of an oppressed group, and to ally himself with their struggle.

For marginal or oppressed members of society such as Jews, however, Sartre felt authenticity required accepting who one is, affirming the label others attribute to one, and not escaping from it into universalized humanistic categories.[35] *Jewish* authenticity lay in renouncing the

---

35. Recognizing how antisemitism made the lives of her Jewish friends different from her own, Simone de Beauvoir remarked, "I remembered how once I had said to Olga that there was no such thing as 'a Jew'; there were only human beings: how head-in-the-clouds I had been" (*The Prime of Life*, p. 366). The implication of Jewish identity became especially clear to Beauvoir in her relation with Claude Lanzmann, for whom Jewishness was the most salient part of his identity. Beauvoir recalled, "To define himself, he said first of all: I'm a Jew. I knew the weight of those words; but none of my Jewish friends had ever made me fully understand their meaning. They let their situation as Jews pass without comment—at least in their relations with me. Lanzmann insisted that his be recognized. It was the ruling force of his life" (*Force of Circumstance*, p. 282). Although Lanzmann initially felt pride at being a Jew, his discovery of antisemitism when he was an adolescent was a serious trauma. To the extent that antisemitism reduced him to an abstraction, a "Jew," a rift opened in his identity. He felt alienated, "expelled from his own being." "Rejected because of this difference at the age when all children want most to conform, his exile left its mark on him for good" (p. 282). In *Saint Genet*, Sartre described how Genet had responded to being called a thief by actively accepting this identity. In the same way, Lanzmann responded to his "exile" for being a Jew by actively willing it and affirming his identity as a Jew. Lanzmann's

liberal idea of universal humanity, accepting the pariah status of the Jew and feeling a sense of solidarity with all other Jews.

> Jewish authenticity consists in choosing oneself as a Jew—that is, in realizing one's Jewish condition. The authentic Jew abandons the myth of the universal man; he knows himself and wills himself into history as a historic and damned creature; he ceases to run away from himself and to be ashamed of his own kind. He knows that society is bad; for the naive monism of the inauthentic Jew he substitutes a social pluralism. He knows that he is one who stands apart, untouchable, scorned, proscribed—and it is *as such* that he asserts his being. (*AJ*, 136–37)

## Assimilation and Authenticity

Present-day society continues to condemn the Jew to social marginality, observed Sartre. Despite all efforts to merge with the rest of society, "the Jew remains the stranger, the intruder, the unassimilated at the very heart of our society" (*AJ*, 83). Sartre was doubtful that Jewish attempts at assimilation could ever succeed, since the Jew is "never accepted as *a* man, but always and everywhere as *the* Jew" (*AJ*, 100). Although some might point to a relatively high degree of acceptance of Jews today, especially in places like the United States, it is uncertain that Sartre would have considered such acceptance a wise objective to begin with. In a world where antisemitism still exists, it is bad faith for the Jew to expect to be recognized simply as a person, "'a man,' nothing but a man, a man like all other men" (*AJ*, 97–98). No person behaves just as an abstract human being.

Indeed, Sartre spoke strongly *against* the idea of Jewish assimilation. He regarded it as a sign of inauthenticity for Jews to try to "pass," to conceal or ignore their Jewishness rather than affirm it. He compared their situation to that of workers who similarly had to liberate themselves "as workers," and not deny their condition by acting like the bourgeoisie. This analogy is flawed, however, since Jews are in a very different situation than workers. The liberation of the proletariat will only come where there is a revolutionary reordering of bourgeois so-

---

dilemma, as Beauvoir saw it, was that which confronts every Jew. If he affirmed himself as an individual, he renounced his Jewishness, whereas to affirm his Jewishness was to compromise his individuality. In Lanzmann's case, the result was that "when he said *I* he always felt like an impostor" (p. 284). Nevertheless, in some ways this situation created in Lanzmann a more open expression of his emotions and desires, in contrast to Beauvoir, Sartre, and their friends, who were "puritans" and "kept [their] reactions under control and externalized [their] emotions very little" (p. 284). Beauvoir found Lanzmann's spontaneity very alien.

ciety. It is highly unlikely that Jews could ever mount a revolt against an antisemitic society that would be capable of producing an equivalent restructuring of society.[36] In addition, workers are workers by virtue of what they *do*, whereas Jews are Jews regardless of what they do. If Sartre denied ethnicity or religion as a genuine basis of Jewishness, what then were the characteristics of the Jews that he was encouraging them to affirm? It is difficult to *affirm* a characteristic that exists *solely* in the eyes of others, except if it is *otherness* itself that one is affirming.

In short, Sartre's prognosis for Jewish identity is not simply a complaint about social injustice and a failure in society's commitment to embrace the Jew. Without a total transformation of society, the Jews will remain unassimilated strangers or intruders in society, regardless of their efforts to disguise their identity. In the absence of this transformed society, Sartre held on to "the Jew" as the primary symbol of the transcendent power of Otherness, a symbol of some point outside the accepted ideas and values of society.

Although Sartre believed that all people should be treated as individuals, he recognized that neither antisemites nor the Jews themselves saw Jews in that way. In an interview in 1939 on the "Jewish question" he addressed the issue of the Jewish contribution to culture and civilization. Here he is considerably more tentative about the existence and source of any unique Jewish characteristics.

> To me it seems dangerous to talk about a specific Jewish temperament. In doing so, one saddles the Jew with a prosemitic, antisemitic argument about the good or bad effects of his peculiar mentality. Of course, if it were established that Jews do have a specific temperament, then in spite of everything, we would have to accept this postulate in the interest of the truth. But it is not. . . . Jews undoubtedly have their distinguishing characteristics. But we are unable to establish them because it is impossible to determine the extent to which they are attributable to the times, living conditions, or ethnic origin. And every attempt to isolate and define these characteristics is a concession to antisemitism. Personally, I can find no particular distinguishing characteristics common to the Jews I know. I think then when we do find them, it's because we put them there ourselves. . . . I have reasons for being opposed to antisemitism. I am suspicious of an "anti-antisemitism" based on "the spirit of tolerance" and "broadmindedness." (WS, 175–76)

Paradoxically, Sartre refused to oppose antisemitism in the name of humanistic tolerance, if that meant ignoring the Jews' uniqueness. And

---

36. See Lévy, "Sartre et la Judéité."

yet he later concluded that any Jewish uniqueness was itself a reaction to antisemitism in the first place. Probably, Sartre was more insightful than he himself realized when he noted that the qualities attributed to the Jew—whether by antisemites *or* prosemites—say as much about the non-Jewish Other as they do about the Jew.

And yet Sartre did not want to erase the category of Jew as a mere fantasy. A Jew must be accepted and must accept himself "with his character, his customs, his tastes, his religion if he has one, his name and his physical traits" (*AJ*, 147). Shortly after the publication of *Anti-semite and Jew*, Sartre said in a letter to the Hillel organization: "It is as a Jew and not just as a man (that is, insofar as this age-old situation had led to your culture, your own conception of the world, and your own particular virtues) that you should claim your absolute equality with non-Jews" (*WS*, 145). Whatever uniqueness there may be within Jewish customs, culture, or worldview, Sartre remained convinced that all of these were merely responses to the piercing look of the non-Jew who labelled the Jew as different. Twenty years later, Sartre reaffirmed (while noting historical and economic flaws in his earlier analysis in *Anti-semite and Jew*) that "Being authentic [for a Jew] does not necessarily mean committing oneself to Israel: a Jew is authentic when he has become conscious of his Jewish condition and feels solidarity with all other Jews" (*WS*, 143–44). Jewishness remains a *condition* that the authentic Jew accepts.

Sartre's portrait of the *inauthentic* Jew focused on the attempts of some Jews to be accepted simply as persons rather than as Jews. The inauthentic Jews play at not being Jews, which condemns them to a continual struggle of "impression management." They "cultivate [themselves] in order to destroy the Jew in [themselves]" (*AJ*, 98). The "Jew" in them is thus an uncultivated kernel that must be extirpated before a "ticket" to bourgeois society can be granted. Consequently, assimilation constitutes a denial of their real selves. "Cultivation" equals alienation, to become like the Other, and other than oneself. The Jews who study the behavior of the non-Jews in order to learn the proper behavior of civilized society are reduced to constant role-playing. Their fear of "acting like Jews" produced intense introspection and self-consciousness about social behavior, since they try to see themselves from the outside, to detach themselves from themselves in order to assume the viewpoint of the Other (*AJ*, 97, 104–5). They may feel contempt for "other Jews" who act too much "like Jews" and who pursue the servile emulation of the majority. Yet the more Jews monitor their own or other Jews' behavior for telltale Jewish qualities, the more they reinforce the "mystical and carnal participation in the Jewish reality" (AJ, 107). That is, the more they are obsessed with Jewishness.

This form of self-alienation results when a Jew's identity has been poisoned by the Christian majority's definition of what is acceptable, good, and civilized. By trying to change him or herself rather than the sources of oppression, the Jew as pariah trades active rebellion for dignified passivity and thereby loses all claims to authenticity (cf. SG, 54–55; AJ, 108). Either to deny one's Jewishness in the name of universalism or to sink into a passive acceptance of one's Jewishness without freedom are the distortions formed by an inauthentic identity" (AJ, 109).

Albert Memmi, whose analysis of the Jewish situation was deeply influenced by Sartre, pointed to the temptation of oppressed persons to deny their difference from their oppressors:

> He insists that he does not see what separates him from his oppressor. That is the best way he can find to draw closer to his oppressor, to lighten his oppression. To that end he is ready for any sacrifice, even to repudiating himself for the benefit of his oppressor, whose person and values are held up to him as superior and steadfast, a height to which the oppressed aspires. To me there is nothing more intolerable, more humiliating than the memory of certain Jewish appeals to non-Jews: "We are all alike, aren't we?" On the lips of the oppressed that statement of equality and brotherhood always has the same note, humble, unconvinced and desperate. . . . True justice, true tolerance, universal brotherhood do not demand negation of differences between men, but a recognition and perhaps an appreciation of them. . . . "In the nineteenth century," Nahum Goldmann, a Jewish leader, recently said, "we had to fight for the right to be equal; in the twentieth century we have to fight for the right to be different."[37]

This fear of being different lies behind Maurice Samuel's scathing description of the theory of "niceness," that is, the way some Jews hope to evade antisemitism by trying to fit in and imitate non-Jews. If Jews acted "nice," attended to their manners, were inconspicuous and reticent about their Jewishness, were not radical in their causes, then they would have no problems. However, there is a high price behind this kind of attempt.

> The nice Jew is like the diplomat who does not say what he means, but has come to mean what he says. He has taken the gesture seriously and talked himself out of his soul. Nothing remains for a man in this desperate position

37. Albert Memmi, *Portrait of a Jew* (New York: The Orion Press, 1962).

but to surrender his identity too; and, consciously or unconsciously, this is the intention behind the theory of niceness.[38]

The type of Jews that Sartre knew had long since migrated from the traditional religious life of the village to the cities where they could be tempted by a double imposture. At the same time that Jewish observance became emptied of conviction, the effort to be like the Gentiles presented the constant need to play a role. If Jews studied the behavior of the non-Jew in order to learn the proper behavior of civilized society, they were no different from the waiter described by Sartre in *Being and Nothingness* whose conformity to a role kept him in bad faith, or from a young Jean-Paul who had constantly tried to act the way adults expected him to.

The road to tolerance is not to obliterate one's differences from the majority, but to affirm them. In the *Freud Scenario*, Sartre presents a Freud who asserts his Jewish authenticity in the face of antisemitism by refusing to be "a good Jew, an honorary goy" (*FS*, 401). Clearly, the social situation of the Jew was a metaphor for Sartre for the authentic existential situation of all human beings: the condition of unjustified existence, contingency, and homelessness. Assimilation would offer no solution to these existential issues, but would only serve to plunge the Jews in the kind of bad faith from which they had been spared. The Jews' dilemma is to be caught between an attraction to a liberal humanism that would erase their otherness, and a deep-seated suspicion of those others who see the Jew as Other. This is why a Jewish man, Sartre believed, could not love a non-Jewish woman in the same way he would a Jewish woman (*AJ*, 130), and why all a Jew's emotions change slightly when they are directed to a Christian rather than a Jew. What Sartre seems to be claiming is that as a Jew tries to act like a non-Jew, to relate to non-Jews on their own terms, the Jew becomes alienated from who he or she authentically is.

Sartre did not describe the Jew's attempt at assimilating as inauthentic simply because assimilation appeared futile in a world where antisemitic thinking is so deeply entrenched. A deeper reason why he insisted that Jews maintain an identity of otherness was his fear that assimilation would result in the loss of the positive qualities that oppression had developed in Jews. The Jews' detachment from standard social roles gives them the freedom to pursue new ideas, and to debunk old ones.

The "inauthentic" Jew who tries to assimilate is inauthentic not only

38. Maurice Samuel, *Jews on Approval* (New York: Liveright, Inc., 1932), p. 11.

because of the kind of social identity he wants to deny or leave behind, but also primarily because of the new kind of social identity he wants to acquire in the process. Sartre regarded respectable bourgeois society itself as so hopelessly inauthentic that those who would seek to join it would only be infected with its inauthenticity. As a member by birth of this bourgeois society, Sartre sought to escape any association with it at all cost. He likely gave little encouragement to those who, being socially excluded from it to begin with, tried to force their way in.

## The Mythology of the Jew

Since Sartre found in the Jew a central symbol or model of identity, he could not logically criticize antisemitism for imagining a difference between Jews and non-Jews that was purely fanciful, even if he had claimed that it was only antisemitism that created the Jew. Rather, he needed to maintain the difference between Jew and non-Jew. He did not, therefore, plead that all people are indistinguishable in their common humanity. On the contrary, when Sartre analyzed a number of qualities traditionally attributed to the Jew by antisemitic mythology, his approach was to affirm the accuracy of such antisemitic stereotypes. Nonetheless, he did so in two different ways that were at odds with each other. First, he said that these traits were only characteristic of "inauthentic" Jews. This implied that it would be illegitimate to apply such qualities to Jews in general. However, one quickly learns that Sartre's "authentic" Jew is more of an ideal type, rarely achieved in reality. If it is true that the Jew represented the promise of authenticity to Sartre, it would be odd for him to depict most Jews as inauthentic. So he offered a second avenue of response. Once again he affirmed the accuracy of certain stereotypical Jewish traits, but he did not simply condemn them as inauthentic. On the contrary, he insisted not only that there were good reasons for these qualities, but also that they were really worthwhile traits after all.

Sartre's two types of responses were constantly in tension in his discussion. On the one hand, the so-called Jewish traits are bad faith responses to antisemitism, but on the other hand, they are also rejections of bourgeois, Christian, or Aryan inauthenticity, and thus the path to authenticity. In short, there *is* a distinct Jewish sensibility, and it is the product of the social situation of the Jews.

Denying the existence of an *innate* or *culturally autonomous* Jewish mentality, Sartre located the sources for most Jewish traits in the need for Jews to find ways to respond to antisemitism. In other words, he believed that Jews use the antisemite's attitudes to determine their own sense of identity. Because Sartre could not conceive of Jewish life without reference to the ideas of antisemitism, he ended up indirectly endorsing the antisemite's image of the Jew.[39] The antisemites were right in their "mythology"; their error was merely in reversing the chicken and the egg. Antisemitism is not a response to annoying "Jewish" qualities; rather these qualities are the Jews' response to the pain of antisemitism. It might be true that the Jews were attracted to money, and that they were shameless and tactless, Sartre allowed, but given their situation, these were understandable, possibly even desirable, ways to behave.

In the case of each "Jewish" trait that Sartre discussed, the underlying attitudes producing the trait were manifestations of the kind of identity that Sartre himself preferred. We should all be more like the Jew. For example, Sartre claimed that Jews have developed special feelings about money as a means to counteract the antisemite's claims of mystical ownership. Money represents the power to purchase and own property without regard to the background or identity of the purchaser. It facilitates the exchange of property in an abstract, rational, universally accessible process, in contrast to the antisemite's appeal to "irrational ownership by participation" (*AJ*, 127). Thus, the Jews' attraction to money is a way of contesting the antisemite's exclusionary claim to property.

Perhaps the antisemite's simultaneous identification of the Jew with both capitalism and communism could be discussed in this light. Both capitalism and communism disrupt, albeit in radically different ways, the mystical possession of property experienced by the primitive and the antisemite. Sartre cared little for the historical and cultural factors that pushed Jews into both banking and revolutionary movements. In either case, the Jews symbolized a different form of identity.

Other major qualities of antisemitic mythology that Sartre described were directly related to the civility of the non-Jew and the vulgarity of the Jew. In particular, the antisemite reproaches Jews for their *lack of shame* and their *lack of tact*. Sartre seemed to accept the validity of these descriptions as his premise, but then offered his own explanation for the presence of such qualities in Jews.

39. See Elaine Marks, "The Limits of Ideology and Sensibility: J. P. Sartre's *Réflexions sur la question juive* and E. M. Cioran's *Un Peuple de solitaires*," *French Review* 45, no. 4 (March 1972):784.

The issue of shame reflected the differences between Christians and Jews in their attitudes toward the body. Sartre claimed that the Christians or "Aryans" of France have an idealized relation to their bodies. They see the body as "a fruit of the French soil; they possess it by that same profound and magical participation which assures them the enjoyment of their land and their culture" (AJ, 119). They disguise their disdain for certain lower functions of the real body with codes of behavior and feelings about the body (e.g., modesty) that idealize the body as an object of veneration. "The body is hidden in its sanctuary of clothing like an object of adoration" (AJ, 120). They are concerned with certain ideal values such as elegance, nobility, virtue, taste, grace, honor, and style which express "the aristocracy of the body" (AJ, 120).

Since Jews were denied real access to these ideal values, they responded by taking a universal and rationalized attitude toward their bodies. They regarded the body as merely an instrument. The "shamelessness" of the Jews was "primarily an effort to treat the body rationally" (AJ, 121). They did not share the Christians' ascetic disdain for the body nor did they establish the hierarchy of natural functions that the Christians did. Jews did not try to master or control their bodies. Rather, they cared for their bodies as though they were machines—"without joy, without love, and without shame" (AJ, 122). They felt no need to hide their bodily functions. This was why Jews were seen as "shameless" and lacking in the "nobility and grace" of body that Christians claim for themselves (AJ, 121). This openness about bodily functions was obviously related to the antisemites' sexualized image of the Jew, and their fear and disgust at the Jews' purported "carnality."

It would clearly require a great deal of evidence to establish the accuracy of this account of Jewish and non-Jewish attitudes toward the body. For Sartre, however, the special symbolic function of the Jews was more important than the results of such empirical analysis. Even if individual Jews are not noticeably more shameless than other people, perhaps they *should* be. They should enjoy and celebrate their exclusion from the non-Jew's bad faith. Their attitudes toward the body should reveal their rejection, like Sartre's own, of certain dominant attitudes.

In this discussion, it should be further noted that Sartre has contrasted the "Jewish" attitude toward the body with that of the "Christian," not specifically the "antisemite." Even if one grants the deep Christian roots of so much antisemitism, it would still be unfairly misleading to use the labels "Christian" and "antisemite" interchangeably in such comparisons. Yet it is clear that for Sartre the terms

"Christian," "antisemite," and "Aryan" could all be used to represent a special model of identity, while "Jew" described the opposite or negation of each element in that type of identity.

Sartre turned to another quality the antisemite ridiculed in the Jews: the Jews' exaggerated gestures in their conversations. Again, he did not question whether or not this characterization was true. Instead he defended it in a novel way. Jewish gesticulating was not a graceless use of the body as the antisemites claimed, but an effort to use the whole body to express one's feelings. The Jew has "a desire to be totally meaningful, to feel the organism as a medium in the service of an idea, to transcend the body that weighs him down and go beyond it toward objects or truths susceptible to reason" (*AJ*, 123). This was preferable to the grace and style of the non-Jew, which only disguised feelings.

Sartre also offered an explanation for the alleged Jewish "lack of tact" (*AJ*, 124). He defined tact as the ability to appreciate intuitively a situation with one's feelings rather than analyzing it and "to direct one's conduct by reference to a multitude of indistinct principles, of which some concern vital values and others express ceremonies and traditions of politeness that are altogether irrational" (*AJ*, 124). Tact, of course, is a major component of civility, a way of relating to the world based not on critical reason, but on tradition, ritual, the common ideas, mores, and customs of a community (from which the Jew is excluded). "The Jew has as much natural tact as anybody, if by that is understood a basic comprehension of others, but he doesn't *seek* to have it" (*AJ*, 124). Being a victim of the irrational, magical opinions of others, the Jew uses reason as a guide in human relations, rather than obscure opinions or powers of intuition.

In all these examples, Sartre ingeniously preserved the Jews' symbolic function as a foil to the corrupt identity that he himself had inherited. Paradoxically, his observation about the Jew's role in the antisemite's worldview—"If the Jew did not exist, the antisemite would invent him" (*AJ*, 13)—was probably true of Sartre himself. Sartre's solidarity with the Jew who was ill-mannered enabled him to reject civility and all that it represents. This "Jew," no less than the antisemite's, was in large part a projection of his own idealized model of modern identity.

## Identity Lost and Found

Ironically, the Jews' situation could give them a certainty of self that forever eluded Sartre. Even if Freud lacked house and field to give himself an identity, he was able to make an affirmation about himself that Sartre could not. Freud had said, "My parents were Jews, and I have remained a Jew myself." The hostility of antisemitism, Sartre suggested, told Freud who he was. He was actively affirming what in any event he already was in the eyes of the Christian world.

Sartre often regretted his own lack of a source of opposition that would have helped him to define himself. He mused that his father's early death had spared him an Oedipal complex and superego, but it also had meant that he knew nothing of aggressiveness, violence, hatred, or jealousy. "Not having been bruised by its sharp angles, I knew reality only by its bright unsubstantiality. Against whom, against what, would I have rebelled? Never had someone else's whims claimed to be my law" (W, 16).[40] Later, he went on to lament, "If one is defined only by opposition, I was the undefined in person" (W, 25). If being subjected to the whims of others furthers the process of self-definition by giving one something to oppose, then the Jews' historical experience left no doubts in their minds about their identity.

But just how seriously should we take Sartre's lament over the absence of aggressiveness, violence, hatred, and jealousy in his childhood? If indeed this was a problem for him, it was not just due to his father's premature death. It was also rooted in bourgeois class consciousness itself. Sartre believed this absence of real opposition was one of the causes for the bourgeois concern with trivialities. "In that period, the Western world was choking to death: that is what was called 'the sweetness of living.' For want of visible enemies, the bourgeoisie took pleasure in being scared of its own shadow" (W, 92).

As for himself, the young Sartre solved his identity problem by imagining a secret mission he had for mankind that justified his presence on the train. Later, he would describe his fantasies of becoming a cultural savior. The destination of his life was something crucial to mankind. Artistic creation would be the antidote to his sense of insubstantiality. "Depicting real objects with real words that were penned with a real pen. I'd be hanged if I didn't become real myself! In short, I knew once and for all what to answer the ticket-collectors who asked me for my ticket" (W, 99).

During the period of what Sartre called his "neurosis" of literature, he felt he had a ticket, a justification for his life based on his role as a creator of culture. But by the end of *The Words* Sartre confessed that he no longer believed writing could save or justify one's life. Here again, he returned to the image of ticketlessness.

40. Cf. "One rebels against an oppressor and I had only benefactors" (W, 70).

I've again become the traveller without a ticket that I was at the age of seven: the ticket-collector has entered my compartment, he looks at me, less severely than in the past; in fact, all he wants is to go away, to let me finish the trip in peace; he'll be satisfied with a valid excuse, any excuse. Unfortunately, I can't think of any; and besides, I don't feel like trying to find one. We remain there looking at each other, feeling uncomfortable, until the train gets to Dijon where I know very well that no one is waiting for me. (W, 159)

What had changed for Sartre from his first metaphoric train trip to his second one? If the ticket-collector was still Sartre himself, his greater indulgence toward the stowaway may have been because Sartre had accepted his lack of a ticket. He was no longer even interested in finding an excuse for himself. If no one was waiting for him in Dijon, it was because he had relinquished his illusions of literary immortality.

But what may also be true, albeit unspoken, is that Sartre simply accepted the ticket he had always possessed. Perhaps, by the end of his life, he was finally able to accept his own social background. He acknowledged: "That old, crumbling structure, my imposture, is also my character: one gets rid of a neurosis, one doesn't get cured of oneself" (W, 159). Despite Sartre's early conviction that all human beings possess total freedom to create their own lives, to escape their own backgrounds, and to make something completely new of themselves, he was gradually forced to acknowledge the limitation of human freedom and the fact that our social experience leaves indelible marks on our characters regardless of the efforts we make to fight it. As Sartre realized near the end of his life: "Even people who try and deny their roots and background, as many do today, are nonetheless victims of both. And that background will assert itself in the very manner by which they try and deny it" (SH, 59).

Although this last remark was not intended primarily as an autobiographical reflection, it does point to a chronic dilemma for Sartre. On the one hand, he could say in 1950: "I swore to the bourgeoisie a hatred which would only die with me" (S, 198). Or in 1955: "As far as I am concerned, I now have nothing more to say to the bourgeois" (ST, 50). But by the 1970s Sartre had to admit that despite his hatred of the bourgeoisie, his works were "addressed to them, in their language and—at least in the earliest ones—there are elitist elements which are not hard to find" (SH, 4). Thus Sartre knew he could not escape being a bourgeois writer and intellectual, or the special temptation to bad faith, inauthenticity, and cooptation that such a social position entails. He hoped, nonetheless, that his constant questioning of his position, his refusal to be "an elitist writer who takes himself seriously," evidenced by his perpetual struggle against the bourgeoisie, explained and legitimized his feelings of solidarity with the workers, Jews, blacks, and other oppressed groups.

Obviously Sartre was never a victim of antisemitism or anything remotely resembling it. The fact that both Sartre the bourgeois "Christian" and Freud the Jew ultimately—perhaps reluctantly—accepted their given social identities should not obscure the differences in how these identities functioned for them. Sartre's problem was not that society had denied him a favorable social identity. Rather, the positive social identity that was so readily available to him created a crisis of authenticity in him. His "ticketlessness" was a response to the lack of substance he detected in that identity. He understood such "metaphysical uneasiness" as "the special privilege of the Aryan governing classes," or at least of those who are "sure of their rights and firmly rooted in the world . . . free of the fears that each day assail the oppressed minorities or classes" (AJ, 133). Sartre remedied his sense of lack in two ways: by asserting an autonomous region of existential freedom independent of his social identity, and by identifying himself with an oppressed social group like the Jews who were genuinely ticketless at the level of social status and respectability.

# FIVE

## Woman Real and Imagined: The Female Other

I've always been very fond of women. They have always been at the center of my thoughts. Without any doubt, it is women I have thought the most about, as a child, as an adult and as an old man. Even when I think about subjects that are not directly related to women, I am still thinking about women. (*PBI*, 103)

—Jean-Paul Sartre

Sartre was repeatedly asked during his life about his attitudes toward women. While he admitted to certain elements of male chauvinism, he also considered himself a feminist—at least to the extent he thought it possible for a man—and he counted prominent feminists among his friends.[1] Nonetheless, Sartre's attitude toward women was riddled with a profound ambivalence that could be seen both in his concrete relations with women throughout his life as well as in the symbolic associations he made to women and the feminine as a general category. If it is true that Sartre was thinking of women even when he was working on other subjects, we might legitimately wonder how his feelings about women influenced his ideas on many subjects not directly related to women. Conversely, we might also consider how Sartre's specific thoughts about women were influenced by his thoughts about other subjects.

At first glance, we discover a major difference between Sartre's warm

---

1. "La Gauche, le désespoir, et l'espoir: Entretien avec Jean-Paul Sartre," *Le Matin* (supplement), no. 843, 10–11 Nov. 1979, p. 5.

feelings about specific women in his life and his more troublesome characterization of qualities he called "female." In other words, it appears that the lifelong companion of Simone de Beauvoir, the mother of modern feminism, allowed indisputably sexist ideas to pollute his theoretical work. In the late 1940s, at about the same time that Beauvoir was preparing her classic study of women, *The Second Sex*, Sartre remarked in his own *Cahiers pour une morale*,

> Woman is the Other in a pure sense, the Other of whom I will never be able to say that from a certain point of view she is the same as me (same body, same activities, same love-making role). Her body is mysterious and inspires horror at the same time that it attracts. (*CPM*, 393; my translation)

In this case, the "I" in the text is as much that of Sartre himself as it is that of a random male reader. Beauvoir proceeded to demonstrate the extent to which woman has been an embodiment of otherness for men and the target of a deep cultural ambivalence regarding the meaning of this otherness.

> Man seeks in woman the Other as nature and as his fellow being. But we know what ambivalent feelings nature inspires in man. He exploits her, but she crushes him, he is born of her and dies in her; she is the source of his being and the realm that he subjugates to his will; nature is a vein of gross material in which the soul is imprisoned, and she is the supreme reality; she is contingence and idea, the finite and the whole; she is what opposes the spirit, and the spirit itself. Now ally, now enemy, she appears as the dark chaos from whence life wells up, as this life itself, and as the over-yonder toward which life tends. Woman sums up nature as mother, wife, and idea; these forms now mingle and now conflict, and each of them wears a double visage. [2]

Beauvoir had no farther to look than the philosopher in bed beside her to discover a man simultaneously attracted to and horrified by the dualistic qualities in his own image of women.

## The Link between Women and Nature

Much of Sartre's original existentialism was based on a refusal to use the term "nature" to describe anything human. He defined human reality as a fundamental transcendence of all forms of nature. On the one hand, if the concept of nature referred to an essential quality of a thing, Sartre denied that this concept could be applied to human beings. The

2. Beauvoir, *The Second Sex* (New York: Bantam, 1970), p. 133.

only constant truth about human "nature" is that there is no common essence shared by all human beings. Human beings create their own "nature" through the freedom of their actions and thoughts. On the other hand, if by nature one means the biological and physical processes on which all forms of life depend, it would be difficult to ignore the deep connection between human beings and nature. Indeed, Sartre devoted considerable attention to the consequences of having a body with specific biological needs, and he reluctantly acknowledged how nature delimited the transcendent qualities of human consciousness.

Unfortunately, Sartre's analysis of "human nature" in this second sense was weighed down by the deeply rooted dualistic categories of Western civilization. He presented the two halves of the term "human nature" as constantly at war with each other, the "human" constantly trying to rip itself out of "nature," "nature" continually humbling the "human" with simple animal demands. Sartre followed in the steps of Saint Paul and those other Greek and Christian thinkers who experienced a great uneasiness with the natural processes of life and the physical body. Like them, he characterized the physical world as something that had to be transcended. Where religious thinkers had pondered the struggle of the spirit to escape the bonds of the flesh, a secularized version of this conflict survived in Sartre's depiction of human consciousness floating lightly across the surface of the physical world and its demands. On the scales of social evolution, civilized life represented the movement away from the body and its concessions to nature toward the artificial constructions of human culture.

The tension between spirit and flesh, consciousness and body, civilized and vulgar has traditionally had rather different implications for the major groups that comprise humanity. What begins as a microcosmic conflict within every individual ends up being projected into a macrocosmic model of humanity. Those groups with the power to define social categories have usually identified themselves with the transcendent qualities of the human, while they equate those groups that they have defined as Other with the immanent qualities of nature. It is, for example, always the Other who threatens to undermine the values of society by his or her uncontrollable sexual instincts, deviant habits, and vulgar behavior.

Unlike his depiction of other groups that embodied otherness, Sartre's treatment of women contained as much that was negative as positive, reflecting his own ambivalent relation to the world of nature. Sartre characterized both women and blacks as closer to instinct, sexuality, and fertility than bourgeois men like himself. Yet curiously, while he found these qualities very attractive in the black man and black woman, he reacted with considerable hesitation when he dealt with woman in general. He could see the blacks in Africa as representing a kind of prelapsarian instinctual innocence, while at the same time he saw woman as tainted by the corrupting influence of the body.

As Simone de Beauvoir made clear in *The Second Sex*, culturally accepted polarities like that of "human" and "nature," "self" and "other," "good" and "evil" have produced a corresponding polarity in our conceptions of male and female. Within Christian tradition and elsewhere, men have often defined the realm of the spiritual, the intellectual, the rational, and the civilized as a primarily, if not exclusively, male territory: whereas the realm of the physical, natural, and instinctual has been the province of women. The accepted ascendancy of culture over nature has consistently been associated with the suppression of women, who have most often represented the realm of the physical, the natural, and the instinctual.[3]

Although the universal cultural tendency to associate the world of nature with woman underlies many common expressions and patterns of thought, in Sartre's work this linkage was dramatically drawn in powerful images laden with elements of fear and disgust. Maurice Cranston noted something sickening about almost all the women in Sartre's plays and stories.[4] Sartre himself admitted that the female characters in his literary works, with rare exception, are not very pleasant. "Indeed, women do not have a very important role in my stories," he said.[5] His female characters are either ruled by instinctual desires or are submissive and conventional. Margery Collins and Christine Pierce justifiably have labelled Sartre a "traditional sexist," since he seemed to attribute a fixed nature to women on the basis of their sexual anatomy.[6]

In *Being and Nothingness*, Sartre tried to explain philosophically the basis for certain obsessive images that had already emerged in his novel *Nausea*. He had described the physical world as heavy, impure, soft,

3. Even Beauvoir identified woman with nature and immanence. Like Sartre, she saw this immanence in contrast to all that transcended nature, all that was civilized and worthwhile. Civilization was essentially male; to the extent that women were admitted into the realm of transcendence and civilization, they had to shuck off their female identities.

4. Maurice Cranston, *Jean-Paul Sartre* (New York: Grove Press, 1962), p. 111.

5. "Interférences: Entretien avec Simone de Beauvoir et Jean-Paul Sartre," *Obliques*, nos. 18–19 (1978), p. 328.

6. Margery L. Collins and Christine Pierce, "Holes and Slime: Sexism in Sartre's Psychoanalysis," *Philosophical Forum* 5 (Fall/Winter 1973):112–27.

slimy, viscous, nauseating, inert, obscene—qualities which could all be summarized by a single word—*female* (*BN*, 609). Like nature itself, femaleness is a treacherous swamp in which the sharp, hard, light consciousness (which Sartre unconsciously associated with maleness) could become entrapped and inundated. In *Nausea*, Roquentin's disgust at the contingency of the physical world (especially in the experience of the chestnut tree root) is mirrored in the images of crawling insects, overgrown plants, and vomit that are evoked by a sexual encounter with a woman (*N*, 82–83). Sartre regularly depicted female sexuality and fertility in either frightening or nauseating terms.[7] In *No Exit*, Garcin compares a woman's romantic overtures to the threat of an octopus or a quagmire. The world of nature, the lush vegetation that overruns everything, female fecundity—all these endanger the tenuous control of civilization and male transcendence. Sartre himself was a perfect example of "the horror of his own carnal contingence" that men have traditionally projected onto women.[8]

On a personal as well as a theoretical level, something about female sexuality deeply troubled Sartre. When he was nearly seventy years old, he told Simone de Beauvoir that sexual relations with women had generally been a matter of indifference for him during his life and that raw sexual desire never figured into his affection for women (*A*, 302).[9] To caress a woman appealed to him far more than to sleep with her. Sartre observed, "I was more a masturbator of women than a copulator" (*A*, 302). In other words, he was content to stimulate women's bodies as a way to arouse desire in them, but without allowing himself to be drawn into the heat of passion. In this way, he duplicated in his relationships the uneasy alliance of consciousness and body that he had spoken of in *Being and Nothingness* (see *BN*, 388–90). When consciousness gives in to desire, it becomes clogged, sticky, ensnared, and sucked into the body.

Even though Sartre claimed to have enjoyed seeing his lovers naked, in the images of them which he preserved in his memory they were always fully dressed (*A*, 303). It is as though he preferred the distance and safety preserved by clothing. Clothing hides the reality of flesh as such. In disrobing, one leaves behind not only one's clothes, but also civilization itself, moving ever closer to the world of nature. Desire

7. See Leak, *The Perverted Consciousness: Sexuality and Sartre*, pp. 24ff.
8. See Beauvoir, *The Second Sex*, p. 138.
9. Of course, it is possible that Sartre downplayed his sexuality with other women in conversations with Beauvoir as a way to spare her feelings over his lifelong sexual infidelities.

continues the decivilizing process. "Desire," Sartre noted, "is an attempt to strip the body of its movements as of its clothing and to make it exist as pure flesh" (*BN*, 389). Flesh is what remains when cosmetics, clothing, movements, and consciousness itself are stripped away from the body. The caress is a way of compelling another person to feel his or her own flesh. Sartre preferred to do this to others, rather than have it done to him.

## Women and the Sliminess of the Other

The concluding pages of *Being and Nothingness* are devoted to a discussion of a quality Sartre described as "slimy" or "viscous" (*le visqueux*). Sartre believed that sliminess produces a primordial sense of repulsion in most people which makes it a perfect symbol for the "sticky baseness" of certain individuals. Of course, it is easy to understand the annoyance one feels at stepping in soft tar or getting glue on oneself, but the intensely negative response to this quality that Sartre described was tied to a more cosmic sense of the meaning of viscosity. He was determined to show that the moral qualities associated with sliminess were not merely projections of feelings onto a neutral physical quality. If we can apprehend a certain sliminess in a person's base behavior, he insisted, we must also recognize a certain baseness about sliminess itself (*BN*, 604–5).

This very strange discussion of sliminess might not be worthy of much attention were it not for the fact that Sartre's train of associations quickly led him from the sliminess of honey and tar to that of the female body in general and female genitals in particular. One major conclusion of the analysis was Sartre's apprehension of a dangerous feminine quality of reality. He saw something disturbingly feminine about sliminess, and something distinctly slimy about women's bodies.

For Sartre, sliminess symbolizes an ontological struggle between the eternal change and flow of consciousness represented by liquidity, and the inert, solid quality of the material world. In slime the free-flowing quality of liquid has become thick and sticky. Thus, sliminess embodies "a dawning triumph of the solid over the liquid" (*BN*, 607). To illustrate this process, Sartre described what happens when honey drips off a spoon back into the jar. The process of its merging back with the whole is a "deflation" and a "display" (*BN*, 608). Sartre then made a startling leap by comparing this process to "the flattening out of the full breasts of a woman who is lying on her back" (*BN*, 608). After all, he suggested, a woman's breasts in this situation cannot hold their shape, nor does the woman have voluntary control over them. They are simply pure flesh that melts into the rest of her body just as the drop of honey is "sucked into" the slimy substance. In this sense, Sartre would likely have regarded female breasts as "obscene" (just like the buttocks) and a reminder to a woman of her fleshiness.

A slimy substance has several other characteristics. Sartre emphasized its softness as it yields to the touch. Yet if I try to grasp it, I discover that it has really taken hold of me. I cannot let go of it. It sticks to my hands and clothes, stains them, and clings to me like a leech sucking (*BN*, 606, 608). "To touch the slimy is to risk being dissolved into sliminess" (*BN*, 610). Sartre saw an image of destruction and creation in this aspect of the slimy. Ordinarily, if I were to take some object in my hands and mold it, its shape would manifest my total creative power over it. When I grasp something slimy, however, the situation is reversed and I find myself "compromised" (*BN*, 609). Underneath the soft docility of the slimy is a "poisonous possession" (*BN*, 609). I start by *possessing it*, and end up *possessed by it*. This revenge of what is Other, which ends by possessing the one who tries to possess, is also the original structure of male-female relations, according to Sartre. In primitive society, the woman is *possessed* by men, either by her father, her husband, or her brother. Yet this possessing of women is merely a futile attempt to master corporeal otherness, and to disguise the fact that this otherness really possesses those who try to possess it. Sartre explained:

> That which is possessed is the Other in the tribe. And the Other, possessed, alienates in turn. It inspires fear and is magical, and is of the same sex as the mother goddess who is held in awe. Possessed, the Other possesses. One possesses it because it is Other; it's a certain way of reacting to Otherness. But because it is Other possessed, it possesses in turn. There is at the heart of this oppression which at first appears unilateral, a reciprocal tie of alienation. And yet it is necessary to state here that this alienation has a character of inequality in the reciprocity, since it is man who decides he is alienated by woman. (*CPM*, 393; my translation)

Obviously, there is something more at stake in the idea of sliminess than being left with honey on my fingers. Sartre was disturbed by the way the passive, yielding material (female) world had found a way to trap the transcendent creative (male) power of consciousness.

Sartre might have seen the slimy as a symbol of the coming into being of new form or the pregnancy of possibility. Its shapelessness and shifting between liquid and solid could evoke images of the primordial chaos out of which the world is born according to the cosmogonic myths of many cultures. In these myths, the original, shapeless matter out of which the world is constructed is often seen as a great mother. The linguistic links between "matter" and "mother" (*mater*) still exist. As one commentator put it, sliminess involves "the consistency of matter that promotes growth."

> This is the moist, formless consistency of lush tropical earth; of mold, moss, and fungus; of billions of larvae floating on the surface of a stagnant pool; of teeming cultures in a test tube; of the afterbirth; of sweat and spermatozoa; of mucous secretions; of sap, slugs, and plankton. This, in short, is the substance of nature making doubly sure, always in stubborn, swelling superfluity, and it is, for Sartre, entirely obscene. Fertility in all its forms is revolting because it *is* life, because it perpetuates existence for which there is no reason. The female creature bears this stigma of fertility and nauseates even as she attracts.[10]

Sartre was only able to focus on the fearsome destructive nature of this shapeless mass and its constant threat to engulf all that it touches. In terms of their symbolism, Sartre's reactions were much closer to the familiar cosmogonic themes of patriarchal religions, which saw the original chaos as dangerous or threatening, needing to be conquered and molded by the mind or spirit of a male deity. Just as this mythic system of religion is accompanied by fear and suppression of the feminine, it is likewise no surprise to find that Sartre repeatedly identified the danger of slime as distinctly feminine.

Sartre's remarks about the contaminating or compromising quality of sliminess also resemble magical notions of pollution that one finds in primitive cultures. Like sliminess, pollution (e.g., from a menstruating woman) overpowers all that it contacts. What is often regarded as polluting is uncontrolled nature, those places where culture reaches the limits of its ability to "purify" or "domesticate" natural bodily processes. The sources of pollution are far more frequently attributed to women, since women represent the border between the instinctual and the human, between matter and consciousness, between nature and man.[11] Just as consciousness must transcend the slimy, so man feels a need to surpass, or at least disguise, the body and the humbling demands it makes, especially those represented by woman. This kind of fear of

---

10. Margaret Walker, "The Nausea of Sartre," *Yale Review* 42 (Winter 1953):253–54.
11. See Sherry Ortner, "Is Female to Male as Nature Is to Culture?," in M. Rosaldo and L. Lamphere, eds., *Woman, Culture, and Society* (Stanford: Stanford University Press, 1974).

pollution became specifically associated with women in nineteenth-century European thinking where the prostitute became a symbol of *both* female sexuality *and* disease.[12]

In short, the issue of sliminess involves more than honey or tar. It implies a view of the entire natural world seen as a seductive, treacherous woman. The slimy "is a soft, yielding action, a moist and *feminine* sucking, it lives obscurely under my fingers, and I sense it like a dizziness; it draws me to it as the bottom of a precipice might draw me" (*BN*, 609; emphasis added). The slimy is a trap which invites me to it, seems to give in to me, but quickly turns against me. Sartre's example of honey is not accidental, since sweetness is another aspect of the slimy. He described sliminess as "a sickly-sweet, feminine revenge" into which consciousness is swallowed "like the wasp which sinks into the jam and drowns in it" (*BN*, 609). Is sweetness itself yet another manifestation of the dangerous female qualities of the slimy?

It was certainly not without significance that Sartre moved from a discussion of the slimy, gluey, and sticky aspects of reality to the meaning that holes have for human beings from childhood on. What a hole represented, Sartre said, was not something sexual, but rather "a nothingness" to be filled by my own flesh. "The hole is bound up with refusal, with negation, and with nothingness. The hole is first and foremost *what is not.*" To call someone an "asshole with no buttocks," he noted, is to call them a nothing, a zero (*WD*, 150). All human beings have a tendency to want to fill holes, to create symbolically such a fullness. "All holes plead obscurely to be filled, they are appeals: to fill = triumph of the full over the empty, of existence over nothingness" (*WD*, 151). If I squeeze myself tightly into a hole, I sacrifice my body in order to create a totality or fullness of being. A child sucks its thumb, Sartre hypothesized in total seriousness, in order to plug the hole in his or her face. Similarly, the ontological significance of the process of eating is that it seals one's mouth and fills one up (*BN*, 613). Holes attract us because they express the lure of annihilation and engulfment. Holes, moreover, can produce repulsion and anguish. They have a nocturnal, mysterious quality; they conceal. In describing a story that had frightened Simone de Beauvoir, Sartre explained:

> Isn't it the very essence of *hole*, that dark orifice which is violated, and which yields at first, and which is nothingness and night, and which then closes slowly like a mouth or sphincter, and which contains something at the

12. Gilman, *Difference and Pathology*, p. 94.

bottom of itself, conceals—what?—*another* hole endowed with devouring and annihilating power: a boa. (WD, 152)

Sartre rejected the entire instinctual and sensual side of sexuality, offering fascinating, though hardly convincing, ontological interpretations of erogenous experience. Sexuality, he insisted, had nothing to do with the appeal of holes. Rather it was the nature of the hole that gave special meaning to sexual holes like the vagina, mouth, or anus. Nonetheless, there is something more specifically masculine about the "ontological" desire to fill holes that Sartre proposed. Consider the following imagery:

> The hole is often resistance. It must be forced, in order to pass through. Thereby, it is already feminine. It is resistance by Nothingness, in other words, modesty. . . . The hole—nocturnal female organ of nature, skylight to Nothingness, symbol of chaste and violated refusals, mouth of shadow which engulfs and assimilates—reflects back to man the human image of his own possibilities, like sliminess or flakiness. (WD, 151–52)

Holes resemble the power of sliminess because in plugging a hole, one becomes one with the material one plugs. A child who sticks his finger into a hole in the ground becomes one with the ground, transformed through his finger.

Regardless of what we make of Sartre's obscure ontological interpretations of holes in general, we cannot easily dismiss the misogyny that emerged when he turned to sexuality. To Sartre, female sexuality is determined by the fact that women's bodies are essentially just holes looking to be filled up. He saw a woman's body as the determining factor in her ontological relations to the world. In other words, anatomy is ontological destiny. By focusing on women fundamentally as holes, Sartre could only see them as incomplete. As such, their goal is to fill this lack with a man's flesh and to dissolve his flesh into themselves, just as the slimy engulfs and absorbs.

Female sexual anatomy inspired both fear and disgust in Sartre. He explained: "The obscenity of the feminine sex [genitals] is that of everything which 'gapes open'" (BN, 613). It is not at all clear, however, just what is "obscene" about female genitals, in what sense they "gape open," or why it is obscene to gape open. Do they gape like a wound, the vagina being compared to a kind of injury? Female genitalia have often been characterized as both damaged and damaging.[13] Or do they gape open like a chasm, representing the vertiginous prospect of

13. Ibid., p. 116.

falling in? Is woman's body obscene because it reduces man to a piece of flesh? In many cases the obscene refers to the exposure of what should be hidden. But if that were the case, we could also say that it is the man whose sex is hanging open obscenely, while the woman's is discreetly hidden. Perhaps, the vagina seemed obscene to Sartre because he saw it as passive flesh in contrast to the active flesh of the penis. A man can feel in control of his penis, since his desire gives it life, whereas a woman's genitals are less clearly under her control.

Sartre's imagery throughout his discussion is reminiscent of the classic male nightmare of the *vagina dentata* ("vagina with teeth"), of woman's body as a supreme castrating danger: "Beyond any doubt her sex is a mouth and a voracious mouth which devours the penis—a fact which can easily lead to the idea of castration. The amorous act is the castration of the man; but this is above all because [her] sex is a hole" (*BN*, 614). Indeed, the deflation of the man's penis after climaxing could easily be seen as a dissolving of his flesh upon contact with the slimy. In Sartre's story "The Childhood of a Leader," the homosexual Bergère ridiculed the idea that only women were appropriate objects of sexual desire, merely because they had a hole between their legs. He showed Lucien obscene pictures of whores whose vaginas resembled mouths. "Lucien gazed on horrible naked whores, laughing with toothless mouths, spreading their legs like lips and darting between their thighs something like a mossy tongue" (*CL*, 115). In all this, Sartre's language implies that male attraction to women is like the force that draws one to look over the edge of a cliff. We are interested in surveying from above the view below, but we also realize the danger of falling off as we grow closer to the edge.

## Sliding versus Rooting

For Sartre, to be rooted in and nourished by the natural world, especially that represented by woman, was to compromise one's autonomy. His goal was to maintain mastery over nature without becoming entangled in it. Elsewhere in *Being and Nothingness*, he offered an antidote to the danger of being sucked down and devoured by the "slimy" aspects of nature. "Sliding" offered the image of a safer method of mastering the material world without being engulfed by it (*BN*, 584). Sliding is the opposite of rooting.

> The root is already half assimilated into the earth which nourishes it; it is a living concretion of the earth; it can utilize the earth only by making itself

earth; that is, by submitting itself, in a sense, to the matter which it wishes to utilize. Sliding, on the contrary, realizes a material unity in depth without penetrating farther than the surface; it is like the dreaded master who does not need to insist nor to raise his voice in order to be obeyed. An admirable picture of power. From this comes that famous advice: "Slide, mortals, don't bear down!" This does not mean "Stay on the surface, don't go deeply into things," but on the contrary, "Realize syntheses in depth without compromising yourself." (*BN*, 584)[14]

Sartre's deep discomfort at being rooted in nature had already inspired the dramatic turning point of *Nausea*, when Roquentin confronted the root of a chestnut tree in the park. In that scene, Roquentin glimpsed beneath the surface of the words, categories, and uses of human consciousness, and he discovered the overpowering existence of the material world. Human systems of categorization melted before his eyes leaving only "soft, monstrous masses, all in disorder—naked, in a frightful, obscene nakedness" (*N*, 172). He described the root in terms reminiscent of the ambiguous state of sliminess, the triumph of the solid over the liquid, and of nature over consciousness. "This root, with its congealed movement, was . . . below all explanation. Each of its qualities escaped it a little, flowed out of it, half solidified, almost became a thing" (*N*, 174). The existence of the world itself seems to Roquentin like something "all soft, sticky, soiling everything, all thick, a jelly . . . filling everything with its gelatinous slither" (*N*, 180).

It is not difficult to perceive the hints of female sexuality behind Sartre's description of the oozing fecundity of nature. Clearly, he felt that to penetrate the sliminess of women was compromising in some primal sense. One can imagine how sexual intercourse itself must have aroused in him the conflict between sliding and rooting, and between the pleasure of a hard male body sliding through a woman's body and the fear of being assimilated into it like a root into the earth.

The idea of sliding raises another suspicion in regard to Sartre's feelings about women and sexuality. The most perfect sliding in Sartre's eyes was that which did not leave a trace. Water-skiing or motorboating were ideal from this point of view.[15] To leave tracks behind after sliding seemed both to compromise the slider and spoil the material. Ideally, sliding preserved the virgin purity of matter. Why should Sartre have felt disappointed when he looked back and saw the tracks of his skis in

14. Compare how Sartre's grandmother used this phrase in *The Words*, pp. 7, 160.
15. See *The Words*, where Sartre refers to a motorboat's power of *uprooting* as a satisfying image (p. 145).

the snow or the scratches of his skates on the ice, if not because it amounted to a deflowering of virgin terrain? Skiing would be far better, Sartre mused, if the snow reformed after we had passed over it (*BN*, 584).[16] He very likely felt that the sliding of a man's penis into a woman's virgin body also left analogous traces of its presence on her body that compromised them both.

The implicit sexual innuendos of Sartre's discussion of sliding became explicit when he compared skiing to fondling a woman's body. A skier relates to snow, he noted, the way a man relates to "the naked body of the woman, which the caress leaves intact and troubled in its inmost depths" (*BN*, 585). This image of sliding on the surface rather than penetrating suggests masturbation more than intercourse,[17] consistent with Sartre's view of himself as a masturbator of women rather than a copulator. To Sartre, a woman's body, like the skier's snow, lies passive, inert, and docile, adapting itself to the man's touch that gives birth to certain changes within it.

There are several disturbing implications of this comparison between skiing and caressing. First, sex is portrayed as male sport, with women's bodies being little different than ski slopes. Part of the "sport" in the various kinds of skiing or sliding, moreover, lies in conquering the resistance of seemingly indomitable masses of water, snow, or earth, and establishing a master/slave relation with it (*BN*, 585). A skier affirms his "right" over the snow in the act of skiing: "It is my field of snow; I have traversed it a hundred times, . . . it is mine" (*BN*, 585). If caressing is a way to "ski" across a woman's body, then the woman, too, becomes an object to be overcome and mastered. To what extent could Sartre have been suggesting a parallel male right to appropriate and possess a woman's body through the act of sex?[18] Not only did Sartre offer this troubling and dangerous analogy for sexual relations with a woman, but he also transferred the language of creation and birth that would normally be associated with nature or woman to the active role of the skier (and male). He wrote: "Sliding appears as identical with a continuous creation." "While it exists, it effects in the material the birth of a deep quality which lives only so long as the speed exists" (*BN*, 584).

16. This image has its sexual counterpart in the Muslim traditions of the heavenly *huris* who cater to man's sexual pleasures and whose virginity is restored after each encounter.

17. Leak, *The Perverted Consciousness*, p. 18.

18. Curiously, Sartre avoided mention of one of the most obvious qualities of snow when he discussed the symbolism of skiing. That is its coldness. This cold surface that must be brought to life by the swift movements of the male may be connected to Sartre's occasional references to the frigidity of women.

"The skier makes it produce what it can produce" (*BN*, 585). This time when the skiing analogy is extended to the seduction of women, we find that any female creative power has now been appropriated by the male, and the woman has been reduced to passive matter.

On the personal level, Sartre acknowledged that the initial stages of a relation with a woman were a matter of male conquest. "Indeed, it was a question of overcoming a woman in almost the same way that one overcame a wild animal, but by wiles, smiles and ingenuity; to force her out of the wild state into one of equality with man," he admitted to an interviewer. After a relationship had been formed, however, he insisted it was always one of equality. "It was as if I had tamed a tigress that, once tamed, became my equal" (*PBI*, 104). Sartre displaced the "problem" of uncontrolled animal instinct onto the Other; in this case, woman as sexual tigress. Woman's body represented the mysterious and dangerous power of nature which must be either avoided or controlled. [19]

Sartre repeatedly emphasized that the purpose of his discussions of activities like skiing was to demonstrate different relationships between consciousness and being. In all probability, he would have insisted that the "philosophical" references he made to women and the feminine were merely metaphorical and did not reflect his own relationships with real women. Nevertheless, it would be difficult to deny that these kinds of objectionable images cast a shadow over much of his philosophical enterprise, or that his relations with women were more often paternalistic than egalitarian.

## Femininity and Women's Sensitivity

Although Sartre tended to treat woman in general as a symbol of the fearful corporal aspect of existence, his tone changed considerably when he described his personal relations with women. [20] As companions, he neither feared nor disliked women; indeed, he much preferred their company to that of men. Spending time with men bored him, since their identities were too bound up with their work and their conversations too much focused on "shop talk" (*SH*, 91). Male sen-

19. In his 1926 essay on lay analysis, Freud referred to lack of knowledge about female sexuality as the "dark continent" of psychology, thus tying female sexuality to the colonialist's image of the uncontrolled, uncivilized "native," and to the exoticism and pathology of the Other as well. See Gilman, *Difference and Pathology*, p. 107.

20. Simone de Beauvoir mentions the odd combination of Sartre's sexual coldness and enormous attraction to women (*A*, 302).

sibilities, Sartre regretted, lacked finesse; they tended to be either too pragmatic or too conventional. Men talked mainly about abstract issues of politics and morality, and they seldom strayed from the social roles they played (*SH*, 91). At one point he wrote in his journal that he had little desire to get to know most men: "I don't like men—I mean the males of the species" (*WD*, 278). To be sure, Sartre had close male friendships, but he did feel that too much tenderness from other men made him uncomfortable, perhaps, he thought, as a result of repressed homosexuality.

> As soon as relations with a man are no longer just superficially cordial, it embarrasses me. I neither like confiding, nor being confided in by him. A man's moral or physical nakedness shocks me to the highest degree. . . . Perhaps tenderness is so clearly sexual with me—as intimacy is, too—that I can't conceive of being tender with a man without at once feeling something like a brief surge of sexuality, which finds no outlet and at once repels and embarrasses me. (*WD*, 275–76)

At times Sartre enjoyed the coarse, crude part of himself that men brought out, and he did not want to confuse it with his way of reacting to women. At other times, he complained that this element of coarseness in men prevented real intimacy.

> Relations with boys meant a friendly exchange of fists, and nothing else. No tenderness. What I found among little girls was the sentiment and intimacy that I'd been given from the very start in my family by my mother, my grandmother, and their women friends. This sentimentality that blossomed forth with the girls was, for me, the essential factor in sex. (*PBI*, 104)

With women, therefore, he felt an emotional closeness that was generally absent from his relations with men. At the age of thirty-five, he noted that the only male friends he had were "women-men: an extremely rare species, standing out from the rest thanks to their physical charm or sometimes beauty, and to a host of inner riches which the common run of men know nothing of" (*WD*, 277). Since he himself was a "woman-man [*homme-femme*]," he believed that women treated him as one of their own and were able to laugh at men *with him* (*WD*, 278).

Sartre could afford to be highly critical of the sensibilities of men without implicating himself in any self-criticism, since he mentally separated himself from the average man and presented himself as a kind of androgynous ideal. He claimed a kind of female sensitivity in himself which he thought might have accounted for why women were comfortable with him and liked to spend time with him (*PB1*, 239; *WD*, 278). He confessed, "I have always believed that there was some sort of woman inside me" (*LS*, 93). It is not surprising that Sartre wanted to believe that women related to him as they would to another woman, since only in that way could he gain access to the powerful connection he observed in women's friendships and found lacking in relations with men. The same man whose astonishing images of the "female" danger which can clog or ensnare the freedom of consciousness have already been enumerated, could also say in an interview late in his life that "transparency" and "subjectivity" "belong much more to women than to men."[21] He further implied that philosophers who truly understood subjectivity, such as Descartes and himself, did so only by virtue of their identities as "women-men." But Sartre was always more than a woman, since he also saw in himself rational, intellectual skills that he considered masculine.

Sartre repeatedly referred to the special sensitivity that he found to be common in women, but generally lacking in men. He considered women's psychological insights more subtle and accurate than men's. In his experience,

> A woman always sees things and people better. She notices right away a certain manner, a certain gesture that characterizes someone, that reveals something about him; and she's capable of expressing it. You would never have that in a conversation with a man. . . . I love their sensitivity, their way of being. I love the profoundness of their conversation. (*PB1*, 239)

Of course, there were social and economic factors, Sartre realized, for the differences he noticed between men and women. Because women have traditionally been excluded from the world of business and politics, their views of the world are fresh, not colored by virtue of a particular job or profession (*PB1*, 239). Their oppression as women has spared them from the values and concerns of men in power, and enabled them to preserve a different type of response to the world, the viewpoint of the marginal, of the Other.

Sartre suggested several ways of understanding the differences between men and women's sensitivities. As we have already seen, he equated the transcendence of the female by the male with the transcendence of nature by consciousness. Although he considered this latter movement to be the essential factor characterizing human reality and the necessary basis of culture, he also implied that something gets lost in

21. "La Gauche, le désespoir, et l'espoir: Entretien avec Jean-Paul Sartre," p. 5.

this civilizing process. Women reminded Sartre of the kind of emotional reaction to the world that is left behind when young males are "civilized." Women's responses retained a childlike quality not as common in fully civilized adults.

Sartre denied that women's emotional side was inferior to the rational side of men, or that women were not capable of developing their reason. Clearly, however, there was a touch of condescension in his focus on women's sensitivities, insofar as this sensitivity represented an earlier stage of development and thereby attested to the lower intellectual development of women. Sartre explained that women's development is generally arrested at a stage of emotional sensitivity, because society has not encouraged, supported, or allowed them to develop their rational, intellectual sides. Men, on the contrary, tend to be more intelligent than women in general, since that rationality and intellectuality have been nurtured in them. They go beyond the "female" stage in their development. By developing their intellectual side, however, men lose the original sensitivity they shared with women, and subsequently they must rely on women to reveal it to them.

In children, Sartre contended, sensitivity and intelligence were both present in an undifferentiated way. "The task of childhood and adolescence was to cause this sensitivity to become abstract, comprehensive, and enquiring, so that is should gradually turn into a man's reason, an intelligence working upon problems of an experimental nature" (A, 299). Of course, men retain some of this sensitivity, but it usually remains unimproved, rough, and unpolished, while their intelligence develops. Although women, too, could develop their sensitivity in a rational direction, they tend to retain more of its emotional components, particularly an understanding of other people.

Sartre himself was grateful for his relations with women because women showed him emotional interpretations of issues that he had only approached intellectually. What he looked for in women was never sexuality *per se*, but rather "an atmosphere of feeling, of sentiment . . . with a sexual background" (A, 298). Sartre thought that in persuading a woman to love him he gained possession of her affective sensibility and thereby filled a lack in his own personality (A, 298–99). This position reflects the common idea that men have lost something in their progress toward domination and that women still possess that lost quality. Sartre could remedy his own sense of incompleteness through his relations with women. He explained:

> It could almost be said that as man has contrived to lose part of his sensibility
> in order to develop his intelligence, so he has been led to call for the other's,

for the woman's, sensibility—that is, to possess sensitive, percipient women so that his might become a woman's sensibility. (A, 302)

Women can reverse men's alienation from the emotional, natural side of human life. They are the antidote to too much civility and reminders of what has been lost to men in the act of making women into the Other.

## The Duality of Female Otherness

Sartre's praise of women's sensitivity and physical beauty might seem to contradict his warning about the dangers of feminine "sliminess." The link between these positions is the fact that each represents a different way in which women have traditionally been used to embody *otherness*. Sartre's ambivalence toward female reality demonstrates the dual functions of woman in his mythology of the Other. Women served as markers of both biological and social otherness for him. As we have already seen, on the biological level women represented the threatening power of nature to overwhelm the transcendence of consciousness. In this context, "civilized" existence was manifest in heroically resisting natural demands or in "sliding" on their surface as sport. At the same time, Sartre implied a more benign nurturing side of nature which, in conjunction with the position of women in society, produced the special female sensitivity that he enjoyed so much. In this case, women represented refuge from the overdevelopment of civilized rationality, and in them was preserved the other side of human experience.[22]

In particular, Sartre's remarks about women's sensitivity must be examined in the context of certain nineteenth-century bourgeois myths about femininity and "true womanhood." Throughout the nineteenth and early twentieth centuries, it was not at all uncommon to find praise of woman's special sensitivity and superior spiritual nature. Sartre was apparently indifferent to, or ignorant of, the fact that this attribution of greater sensitivity to women had traditionally served as an ideology of oppression. The rhetoric of feminine sensitivity and emotionality has often been used to preserve the subordinate social role of women. Women were described during this period as more evolved and refined in morals and sensibility, and therefore most suited to guide men in the development of character. Women's energy was to be diverted away

22. For a slightly different treatment of the dual qualities of women in Sartre's work, see Leak, *The Perverted Consciousness*, pp. 31–35.

from "coarse" politics and economics into housework, childrearing, religion, and etiquette. Among the middle classes, the model of the genteel woman was perfected.

Sartre's portrait of female personality was a diluted version of these bourgeois ideals of "true womanhood." In the face of turbulent changes brought about by the industrial revolution, the ideal of true womanhood provided a response to the disturbing process of secularization and social change, and the threats of industrialization to traditional values. Women represented the reverse image of industrial society. Their emotionality, sensitivity, intimacy, and intuitive wisdom compensated for the ascendancy of unfeeling, impersonal, and competitive technological rationality and materialism. Home became a privatized, female realm of intensive personal life.[23]

Accordingly, Sartre's complaints about men's "shop talk" in their conversation, and the exercise of power or violence as the main currency of male relations must be understood in the context of the changes in male and female roles after the industrial revolution. Bourgeois liberalism was dependent on a particular vision of the private world in which women played the role of softeners and civilizers for men.[24] Yet as sensitivity became more firmly associated with women, its real importance in the public world diminished significantly.

Although Sartre smugly asserted that his relationship with Simone de Beauvoir had cured him of male chauvinism, his life was marked by regular remissions into questionable thoughts and actions regarding women. Despite his praise of women's sensitivity and emotionality, Sartre admitted that it was always appearance and charm that first attracted him to a woman. He preferred to surround himself with attractive women, confessing with some embarrassment that he found feminine ugliness offensive. It is thus no surprise that Sartre's ideal woman was a fusion of natural sensitivity and desexualized physical beauty. The latter took some of the danger out of woman's connection to nature, while the former focused on woman as an aid to escaping from the inauthenticity of male civility.

Beauvoir herself has analyzed the male tendency to domesticate the power of nature that men see in women. The result is that "man, wishing to find nature in woman, but nature transfigured, dooms

23. Rosemary Radford Ruether, "Home and Work: Women's Roles and the Transformation of Values," *Theological Studies* 36 (Dec. 1975):647–59.
24. Jean Bethke Elshtain, *Public Man, Private Woman* (Princeton: Princeton University Press, 1981), p. 145.

woman to artifice. She is not only *physis* but quite as much *anti-physis*."[25] She must appear in a way that neutralizes her connection to nature. Although outward appearance was a major concern for everyone in bourgeois society, for women in particular, appearance became everything. The social duty of the bourgeois woman was "to make a good showing," and to gain satisfaction from being an object on display, not an agent doing things. The special emotional sensitivity of women went hand in hand with a special feminine style of deportment and dress which emphasized discretion, modesty, and respectability. Grace and gesture were crucial to her. In his own way, Sartre participated in the social situation that condemned women to lives of acting, to finding self-validation in their audience. Sartre's character Kean understood this: "Woman is a victim because she enjoys her beauty only through the eyes of others. Like an actor, she depends on the love of others" (K, 268).

By focusing on the issue of women's appearance, Sartre shifted the level of discourse from the biological to the social, from femaleness to femininity. Indeed, his references to femininity usually transcended the issue of biology completely. Ironically, his interest in analyzing the idea of femininity mostly arose in relation to men's personalities (e.g., Baudelaire's dandyism, Genet's homosexuality, Flaubert's passivity). Sartre shared Simone de Beauvoir's notion that in an important sense women are *made*, and *not born*. Bourgeois femininity was the result of social condition, not sexual anatomy.

> The essential characteristic of woman—of bourgeois woman—is that she depends very largely on *opinion*. She is idle and kept. She asserts herself by *pleasing*; she dresses in order to please; clothes and make-up serve partly to reveal and conceal her. Any man who happened to find himself in a similar condition would probably assume an appearance of "femininity." (B, 152–53)

Femininity is not a "natural" condition; it must be learned or created.

In his early study of the imagination, Sartre discussed women in the context of aesthetics rather than instinct or sexuality. He presented an implicit comparison between one's reactions to beautiful women, to actors, and to works of art. Sartre contended that in all these cases, we experience beauty or aesthetic pleasure only through an act of our own imagination. What is beautiful appears to us, moreover, only to the extent that we transcend the level of real physical existence. For exam-

25. Beauvoir, *The Second Sex*, p. 148.

ple, the beauty of a painting does not lie on the level of the physical object before us. What is *real* is "the brush strokes, the stickiness of the canvas, its grain, the polish spread over the colors" (*PI*, 247). Its *beauty* is not a matter of perceiving any of these things, but rather is "out of the world" (*PI*, 247). The real canvas permits the viewer to grasp the unreal beautiful object through it. Similarly, when an actor plays Hamlet, he uses his feelings, body, and gestures to create the feelings and conduct of Hamlet. If he is successful, the result is that Hamlet becomes real to the extent that the actor becomes unreal (*PI*, 250).

Such aesthetic experiences are examples of the transcendent power of consciousness to rise above the real world in its brute existence. Sartre said, "All apprehension of the real as world implies a hidden surpassing toward the imaginary" (*PI*, 245). Without this power of the imaginary, Sartre insisted, we would be "engulfed," "swallowed up," "crushed," and "pierced" by the real world (*PI*, 244). This is precisely the same kind of language Sartre used to describe the slimy, female aspect of existence.

Yet Sartre was able to appreciate women as beautiful, since their beauty was beyond the real, grasped only through the imagination. Woman's beauty was not threatening to him, since it only came into existence through the man's consciousness, which negates the real presence of the woman. "The real is never beautiful. Beauty is a value applicable only to the imaginary and which means the negation of the world in its essential structure" (*PI*, 252).[26] Furthermore, Sartre added paradoxically, "great beauty in a woman kills the desire for her" (*PI*, 253). He argued that to admire a woman's beauty meant that one must transform her into an "unreal," "imaginary" woman, whereas to desire her would bring one back to the plane of physical possession. "To desire her we must forget that she is beautiful, because desire is a plunge into the heart of existence, into what is more contingent and most absurd" (*PI*, 253). Given this analysis, it is obvious why Sartre preferred to admire women's beauty from a distance, without giving in to desire. The appreciation of beauty is a product of his own imagination skating lightly across the surface of reality, in complete control. Desire for a woman, however, "plunges" one into the reality of the woman's physical being and threatens to cloud the clarity of consciousness. This is not

26. Sartre pointed out that beauty is a matter of appearance rather than being. It requires a transcendent movement of consciousness beyond the imperfections of the real world. "To the extent that man *realizes* the beautiful in the world, he realizes it in the imaginary mode" (*BN*, 195).

to ignore the endless stream of love affairs throughout his life, but rather to suggest that his attraction to women and his relations with them reflected his imagining their ideal beauty rather than desiring their concrete reality. The sundering of beauty and desire is also a sundering of women into two categories, one real and the other imaginary. The result is not so different from the medieval elevation of the Virgin that arose out of fear of the carnality of real women.

Though sexual desire was incompatible with appreciation of beauty in Sartre's eyes, he did acknowledge in himself a primitive, magical kind of desire for beauty.

> I certainly had an appetite for beauty, which wasn't really sensual, but more magical. I should have liked to eat beauty and incorporate it. I suppose, in a certain way, I used to suffer from an identification complex with respect to all those good-looking people. And that explains why I've always chosen handsome men as friends. (WD, 282)

What a startling image: to eat a person's beauty. Perhaps what we have here is a way for Sartre to express the two sides of his feelings toward women. To eat the essence of the Other describes exactly what Sartre feared in women's sexual desire. It was woman's body that swallows up a man. In his "appetite for beauty," Sartre combined two images of women in himself: by an oral appropriation of the Other he would hope to internalize the transcendent quality of beauty.

## Women and Bad Faith

Unfortunately, the roles which women were forced to assume in order to create the image of beauty in the consciousness of men undermined the authenticity of their own behavior. It is perhaps no accident that Sartre used women's behavior as a frequent example of bad faith. One of the major illustrations of bad faith Sartre presented in *Being and Nothingness* involved the case of a woman going out with a man for the first time. In the course of the evening, the man takes her hand. The woman leaves her hand in his, "not noticing" what he has done and preoccupying herself with their lofty conversation. Sartre concluded that this woman was guilty of bad faith, since she was playing a role, acting as though she had a fixed or determinate nature, and evading her own freedom. More than that, there is a hint in Sartre to suggest he believed that bad faith was an especially prevalent predisposition of women.[27]

27. Lucien Fleurier is guilty of a similar form of bad faith regarding his homosexual seduction by Bergère: "Twenty times, these last few days, he had almost discovered what Bergère wanted of him

In Sartre's example, the woman in bad faith struggles with the tension between public appearances and private feelings. Such a woman knows very well the "intentions" and sexual desires of the man she is with, and that she is going to have to make a decision. It was bad faith for her to ignore the man's implicit desires and to concern herself "only with what is respectful and discreet in the attitude of her companion" (*BN*, 55). Sartre recognized that such public behavior was only a facade, an act which concealed private feelings. The woman's bad faith is her refusal to admit to herself the private meanings of her companion's public behavior or its sexual undertones. She does not look beyond the facade or read into his conversation "anything other than its explicit meaning" (*BN*, 55). For example, when he says, "I find you so attractive," she does not acknowledge to herself that this might have a sexual meaning. The explicit meaning was what was immediately apparent. The woman accepts this at its face value and endows it with an objective meaning which it does not really have. The man's polite public role thus obtains an objective quality or permanence. He appears to her "sincere and respectful as the table is round or square" (*BN*, 55). Such public playacting has little reality of its own, except to obscure deeper intentions.

The problem of the woman in bad faith is that she wishes for the authenticity and intensity found in private feelings, but she wants them to remain socially proper. Her dilemma is clear. "She is profoundly aware of the desire which she inspires, but the desire cruel and naked would humiliate and horrify her. Yet she would find no charm in a respect which would be only respect" (*BN*, 55). Respect which is only respect had no appeal to her, since it would be only public politeness for its own sake, an empty performance, a sham. On the other hand, the woman cannot tolerate undisguised, "naked" desire or affectivity. It would be a breach of the proper etiquette into which she has been socialized. It would be humiliating in the same way as being seen without her makeup on, or without her hair set. The woman recognizes that public behavior and private intention are in conflict. Her solution is to appreciate each as what it is not. She appreciates public respect only insofar as it conceals inner intentions; she can acknowledge inner intentions only insofar as they are not shown themselves but are embedded in public playacting.

In the same way that Freud spoke of the repression of socially unac-

---

and each time, as if on purpose, something happened to turn away his thought. And now he was there in this man's bed, waiting his good pleasure" (*CL*, 121). Sexual bad faith for Sartre is tied to the "feminine" or passive role in seduction.

ceptable behavior, Sartre spoke of the refusal of the person in bad faith to recognize desires for what they are. The woman recognizes the man's desire "only to the extent that it transcends itself toward admiration, esteem, respect and that it is wholly absorbed in the more refined forms which it produces" (BN, 55). The climax of the woman's bad faith occurred when her companion takes her hand. She wishes neither to acknowledge her reciprocal desire by consciously leaving her hand there, nor to reject the desire by removing her hand. She leaves her hand there, but she does not take note of doing so, because she has begun to discuss "the most lofty regions of sentimental speculation" (BN, 56). She disowns her identity with her body and sees herself solely as consciousness.

What Sartre ignores here, however, is that women are forced into bad faith by the attitudes of men in society. It is men who want female sexuality remolded by their own desire. As Sartre himself admitted, the seducer is as much an actor as the woman. He noted that for himself seduction was a play with rules. He would have been shocked and upset by a woman who broke the rules by prematurely showing too much sensual passion.

> I thought of women . . . as beings who first say No, then allow themselves gradually to be imposed on, still resisting but each time somewhat less. The woman would refuse and I would gently and patiently insist, each day winning a little more ground. . . . I was less keen on the woman than on the play-acting she gave me an opportunity for. (WD, 284)

But Sartre never accuses either himself or the man in his example of their own bad faith in the seduction. For both, the pleasure of the seduction comes from their thinking that they have manipulated and finally overcome the woman's resistance. Each convinces himself that the woman is responding spontaneously to his moves. Sartre saw the drama of his own seductions of women as "works of art" in which "the woman represented the raw material which I had to mold" (WD, 286). If he were to think that she was only following her own carefully planned set of responses, he would have been disappointed, for she would have undermined the central pleasure of seduction by essentially transforming him into what Sartre might have called a "transcendence transcended."

Sartre presented a complex analysis of actions of the woman in bad faith in terms of her distortion of the relation of facticity and transcendence within human reality and as a divorce of the body and the soul. The woman has disarmed the threatening aspect of her companion's actions by reducing it to its immediate being or facticity, severing the desire that transcends those actions. At the same time she "purifies the desire of anything humiliating" by considering the respect and esteem as transcendence, but "gluing it down with all the facticity of the present" (*BN*, 57). Sartre felt this woman was perceiving herself only as an inert, passive object to avoid seeing in herself possibilities she could project on the world. To the extent that women are objects for others, as Sartre thought, they would be especially vulnerable to bad faith.

Without disputing the philosophical depth of Sartre's analysis of female bad faith, it is possible to make a correlation between the axes of facticity and transcendence and the axes of public and private behavior which is characteristic of bourgeois society. The "facticity" of the situation relates to the immediate appearance of behavior, its discreet, respectful, refined form. In bad faith, this socially proper behavior is invested with a permanent reality of its own. The "transcendent" aspect of the behavior can be related to its private intention which cannot be directly expressed. The woman prefers to make sentimental speculations about romantic love, for this is socially proper, rather than to accept her bodily desire, for that is degrading to admit in public. In a sense, Sartre's cryptic description of human reality as "the being which is what it is not and is not what it is" (*BN*, 58) refers not only to an ontological structure of human beings but to a sociological one as well. Sartre implied that what people authentically are transcends their fixed social roles, their public behavior, and the images others have of them. In other words, they are (privately) what they are not (publicly), or they are not (privately) what they are (publicly).[28]

In his later work on Flaubert, Sartre acknowledged that bourgeois women's perspective has been so distorted by the oppressive world of patriarchy that it is hard for them even to envision a path of escape. They are "poisoned by the other world of the Other, the world of the 'first sex,' with an inevitable future which they cannot help foretelling" (*FI*, 1:431–32). Nonetheless, Sartre continued, women's bitterness and resentment at their own oppression may reach a point where they sever their passive identification with polite appearances. They may develop a corrosive power of observation in response to the pretensions of men's

---

28. There are a number of other cases where Sartre linked faked behavior with women, particularly frigid women. Thus when Sartre described his own struggle against childhood bad faith, he frequently compared himself to a woman. For example, he proclaimed, "I was a frigid woman whose convulsions crave and then try to replace the orgasm. Is she shamming or just a little too eager?" (*W*, 130). When he found it harder to charm the adults around him, he described his feelings as "the anguish of an aging actress" (*W*, 66).

public behavior. In contrast to the woman of bad faith he described in *Being and Nothingness*, who ignores her companion's sexual innuendos by focusing on the pleasant compliments he pays her, Sartre now described a more authentic "look" for a woman, one that unmasks the bad faith of men.

> Observing in a salon, that polite, assiduous husband whose wife knows his low tricks, observing the way he flirts discreetly thinking she doesn't see, hearing him repeat for the hundredth time the phrases she thinks he is inventing for the occasion, listening when his superiors approach him, and rejoicing in his slightly servile manner or his awkwardness; to others he may be reserved, but she is delighted that to her he is naked as a worm. . . . From his attitude, his clothing, every perceptible particular she expects the objective exposures of her oppressors, who are condemned in her eyes as ridiculous. (*FI*, 1:432)

In many ways, the otherness of women was simultaneously the most threatening and the most appealing to Sartre. When it came to describing the ontological structure of reality, he had first developed a dualistic model of transcendence and immanence that corresponded all too perfectly with the dualism of male and female. It was easy for him to identify the transcendent power of consciousness with his own male self and the threatening immanent qualities of the body and the natural world with the danger of an Other that, more often than not, was female. In his early works of literary imagination, he gave graphic expression to this philosophical misogyny.

But women were also the group with whom Sartre had had the most positive personal experience. He was an object of female attention, surrounded, adored, cared for, and pampered by women from his childhood to his death. Since childhood, he had also been uncomfortable with traditional models of masculinity, and his own sense of gender reflected an ambivalent identification with women. He appreciated in women a different way of being and seeing that contested the value of both the technological rationality he found dominating the male work world and the pretensions of bourgeois culture. He described a warmer, more sensitive attitude which, like the Jews', was less confined by the formality of civility. On this level, it was not surprising for Sartre to see himself as just as feminine as women and to acknowledge the special access to authenticity afforded by women's experience.

## SIX

# Passivity and Subversion:
# The Homosexual Other

The homosexual tries to be a deep reality, very deep. He tries to find a depth of being that heterosexuals don't have.[1]

—Jean-Paul Sartre

The homosexual is another outsider whose marginality to respectable society made him a source of fascination for Sartre.[2] Homosexual characters appeared in Sartre's early fiction and plays,[3] and the nature of homosexuality itself was an issue to which he paid more than casual attention in his philosophical and especially in his biographical works.

There are a number of likely reasons for Sartre's interest in homosexuality.[4] Some of them have less to do with homosexuals as concrete individuals and more to do with "the Homosexual" as another player in Sartre's mythology of otherness. In one way or another, all the embodiments of otherness that Sartre presented contain threats to the image of "civilized" sexuality upheld by Western civilization. At some level, fear of Jews, blacks, homosexuals, and women reflects an underlying fear of uncontrolled or perverted sexuality. Indeed, part of the mythology of

---

1. "Jean-Paul Sartre: The Final Interview," by Jean Le Bitoux and Gilles Barbedette, *Christopher Street*, July–August 1980, p. 36.

2. It was primarily the *male* homosexual in whom Sartre was interested. For a psychoanalytic approach to Sartre's treatment of homosexuality, see Leak, *The Perverted Consciousness*, Chapter 5.

3. For example, Bergère in "Childhood of a Leader"; Daniel Sereno in *The Roads to Freedom*; Inez Serrano in *No Exit*.

4. Sartre alluded to some slight homosexual inclinations in his own adolescence, but there is little indication that they played a significant role in his adult identity (A, 293).

each of these groups developed by Christian, white, heterosexual male society includes the libelous images of syphilitic and homosexual Jews, hypersexed blacks, seductive women, and a variety of other permutations. Although Sartre's mythology was rooted in an overall attraction to, rather than repulsion at, these groups of societal victims, he shared in a general sexualizing of the Other. Except for the problematic case of women, whose sexuality disturbed him, Sartre usually found the sexuality of the Other—the black or Jewish man or male homosexual—more authentic, more free, more virile.

Evolutionary models of culture in modern Western intellectual history have often supported the notion that the most advanced forms of human behavior and custom were those of European men. This was particularly true in the area of sexuality. European social thought has treated the sexuality of the Other as alternately primitive (the black, the native) or degenerate (the Jew, the prostitute, the homosexual).[5] Above all, homosexuality throws into question the accepted views of both sexuality and gender roles.

Sartre understood the persecution of these Others as only a thinly disguised projection of the "respectable" man's deepest anxieties. The Jew, the black, the homosexual frighten the respectable man because they represent the dark side of his own personality. He copes with his own wild impulses and instincts, "the vague swarming which is still himself, but a himself which is wild, free, outside the limits he has marked out for himself" (SG, 25), by labelling them "evil" and projecting them onto the Other (see CPM, 443). Whether the carrier of "evil" is the Jew, the black, the homosexual, or any other ethnic or religious group, he always experiences evil as other than himself. "Evil is the Other. . . . It is that which is always Other than that which is" (SG, 26). The negative side of one's own freedom is uprooted and transplanted to the Other. To the extent that evil represents choices that are negated and kept separate from oneself, those who symbolize evil for respectable society are also the rejected and negated members of society. Sartre observed:

> And whom does one strike in the person of the "dirty, greedy, sensual, negating" Jew? One's self, one's own greed, one's own lechery. Whom does one lynch in the American South for raping a white woman? A Negro? No. Again one's self. . . . If you want to know a decent man, look for the vices he hates most in others. . . . In the case of those who condemn Genet most

5. See Gilman's excellent discussion of this issue in *Difference and Pathology*, p. 213.

severely, I would say that homosexuality is their constant and constantly rejected temptation, the object of their innermost hatred and that they are glad to hate it in another person because they thus have an opportunity to look away from themselves. (SG, 29–30)

Conversely, the aspects of the Other that Sartre idealized and romanticized are precisely those that might rescue him from the weakness in his own sense of self and validate the parts of himself that were rejected by respectable society.

## Homosexuality and the Inversion of Sex Roles

Sartre's underlying conceptualization of homosexuality would probably not be regarded as terribly enlightened by today's standards and suffers, in any case, from the kind of excessively dualistic thinking that plagues many of his descriptions of human behavior. Sartre saw homosexual relations not as the kind of reciprocal love aimed at in romantic heterosexual love, but strictly divided into complementary active and passive partners, not unlike a sadomasochistic couple. In his view, it was therefore a truncated relation, the active partner demanding devotion without recognizing any reciprocal demands from the passive partner.

For Sartre, homosexuality most frequently represented a refusal of, and protest against, traditional models of masculinity. The common stereotypes of the effeminacy of male homosexuals and the unfemininity or masculinity of lesbians are based on the misleading assumption that a critical factor in homosexuality is the "inversion" of gender roles. Accordingly, the label "invert" has often been applied to the homosexual, as Sartre himself has done in a number of places. This inversion of sex roles, wherein a man sees himself as feminine in some essential way, is a common theme in Sartre's work. It applied not only to Flaubert and Genet, but also, as already mentioned, to Sartre himself. The man who sees himself as feminine is challenging some of the fundamental assumptions of the most powerful people in society.

It is true that some male homosexuals exaggerate ordinary gender roles in a different way by becoming, in effect, supermales. Such were the kind of men Jean Genet often took on as lovers. But Sartre was most interested in the opposite end of the spectrum, those men for whom passivity and femininity were dominant parts of their personalities. The result of this sort of personality constitution is that a major component of one's identity is determined by being a passive object of desire for others. It is this aspect of traditional femininity that the passive homosexual incorporates into himself.[6] To be a passive object for others, whether desirable or loathed, is the basis for victimization and oppression. Authenticity will always require finding some way to accept but also to transcend this experience of objectification.

Sartre's most elaborate examination of the issue of homosexuality came in his lengthy study of Jean Genet. In this case, he tried to understand the etiology of homosexuality in relation to Genet's childhood and his broader assault on bourgeois values. Sartre dismissed Genet's own account of innocent homosexual desires for a handsome boy arising spontaneously at the age of ten. Rather, Sartre insisted that the mode of sexuality chosen by a person was a response to certain dilemmas in his life. Homosexuality is never simply an accident of birth. Sartre extended to homosexuals Simone de Beauvoir's claim that women are made and not born. He argued:

> A person is not born homosexual or normal. He becomes one or the other, according to the accidents of his history and to his own reaction to these accidents. I maintain that inversion is the effect of neither a prenatal choice nor an endocrinian malformation nor even the passive and determined result of complexes. It is an outlet that a child discovers when he is suffocating. (SG, 78)

There are two major factors that contributed to Genet's childhood "suffocation." According to Sartre, Genet's mother gave him up for adoption, making him feel more like the discarded excrement of his mother's body than her beloved child. Genet's status as an orphan of sorts clearly appealed to Sartre, for he had his own similar feelings of illegitimacy. Out of this "unnatural" origin, Genet's sexuality took an unnatural turn. His own questionable origin made Genet question his legitimacy as a person, and later the legitimacy of the social identities of more respectable members of society.

Second, Genet was branded a thief when, in his childhood, he was once caught stealing. This event was so traumatic to him that it became sexualized in his mind and endlessly repeated in his later homosexual encounters. The result was a complete feminization of his sexuality. Through the Sartrean lens, Genet's homosexuality was not initially a matter of sexuality at all. Rather, Genet's response to being condemned

6. The inversion of sex roles is also evident in the character Inez in *No Exit*. From Sartre's point of view, she takes on the traditional male role as active looker, rather than the female role of object looked upon. Someone who seduces women is masculine in role. Inez does not require the mirror of another's look to assure her of her existence, as Estelle does. She is fully self-conscious: "I'm always conscious of myself—in my mind. Painfully conscious" (*NE*, 19).

was to effect "an ethical and generalized inversion" (SG, 81), of which his sexual inversion was only a later development. To submit to the sexual desires of strong males was Genet's sexual internalization of his submission to the societal judgment which the male represented.

Genet, like other passive homosexuals, responded to his original traumatic experience of being-for-the-other by continuing to identify himself totally as an object controlled and manipulated by the Other. According to Sartre, "Any man who places truth in his Being-for-the-Other finds himself in a situation which I have called prehomosexual. And this is the case, for example, of many actors, even if they enjoy sleeping only with women" (SG, 81). Thus homosexuality (or pre-homosexuality) is not determined by sexual behavior, but by a sense of oneself in relation to others. From the description of his attempt to ground his own self-definition in the opinions of others, we can see the same "prehomosexual" tendencies in Sartre's childhood, though they never became the dominant part of his identity.[7] Genet's homosexuality fascinated Sartre, since it was a model for how an invalidated identity could be turned against those who upheld societal standards and how it could be redeemed from shame.

Every person requires some confirmation of his or her identity through the judgments of others. Genet's problem was that the primary judgment he received from others was that of condemnation. "To Genet, the truth, separated from certainty, will be the intimidating, ceremonial, official thought of adults, judges, cops, decent people" (SG, 36). Those who criticized, judged, and rejected Genet as evil thereby denied him recognition of his existence as worthwhile and denied to themselves any recognition of the suppressed impulses of their own freedom. Genet's dilemma is that of all outsiders who have been rejected by "decent" people.

Whether the specific details of Sartre's interpretation of Genet are correct or not, his description reveals an analysis of the deeper existential significance of both homosexual and female sexuality. The traditional role of women, like that of passive homosexuals, links their identity with being sexual objects at the mercy of strong males. The experience of being an object for the Other is the origin of both forms of sexuality. Like Simone de Beauvoir, Sartre located the chief characteristic of female sexuality in the fact that "woman is an object to the

---

7. Sartre would likely respond that his subsequent life decisions retrospectively transformed these tendencies into something "inconsequential" rather than "premonitory" (SG, 78).

other and to herself before being a subject. One can expect that Genet, who is the object par excellence, *will make himself an object* in sexual relations and that his eroticism will bear a resemblance to feminine eroticism" (SG, 37).

To Sartre, the "look of the Other" that caught Genet in the act from behind and transformed him into a thief was no different than the piercing penis of a rapist. As a result, Genet reacted to his childhood crisis of being called a thief as though he had been raped. Indeed, he *was* raped by the look of the Other. As the victim of a "rape," moreover, he had been forcibly put into the position of a woman. Sartre believed that Genet's homosexuality was only the confirmation of the gradual transformation of his gender identity into that of a woman, that is, an object who exists for the sake of others, and whose identity is defined by the display of one's own flesh.

> This first rape was the gaze of the other, who took him by surprise, pene-trated him, transformed him into an object. . . . Genet has now been deflowered; an iron embrace has made him a woman. . . . He is the village whore. . . . Undressed by the eyes of decent folk as women are by those of males, he carries his fault as they do their breasts and behind. Many women loathe their backside, that blind and public mass which belongs to everyone before belonging to them. . . . Why be surprised if, after that, he feels more like an object by virtue of his back and behind and if he has a kind of sexual reverence for them? (SG, 79–80)

As a passive homosexual, Genet submitted to being penetrated from behind by both the look and penis of the Other. Through such be-havior, he was "metamorphosed into a contemptible female object. . . . The fairy is only a receptacle, a vase, a spittoon which one uses and thinks no more of and which one discards by the very use one makes of it. The pimp masturbates in her" (SG, 110). One might ask why women and passive homosexuals should care so much about their rears, since men have them, too. For Sartre, the male was always the looker, the female the one looked at. When a differential in power exists, the looker is also always the oppressor.

Genet's homosexuality represented a collapse of the ordinary mas-culine sense of the body. Sartre understood masculinity as an active force. A "manly" man is like a hunter, and his penis is his weapon. He experiences erection as "the aggressive stiffening of a muscle" and his sexuality as a mixture of "oppressive imperialism and generosity" (SG, 80). They represent his transcendent power, bursting forth explosively. In short, his masculinity manifests itself through doing. Whereas femininity manifests itself as a simple state of being and is focused on a woman's physical qualities, male sexuality has only a weak connection to a man's physical qualities. Sartre pointed out that a man "makes his woman love him for his power, his courage, his pride, his aggressiveness, in short he makes her desire him as a faceless force, a pure power to do and take, not as an object agreeable to the touch" (SG, 80–81). This idea was obviously a preferable position for someone like Sartre who was convinced of his appeal for women, despite his physical ugliness.

Genet's passivity was not only a flight from masculine sexuality in himself; he also used it to sabotage secretly the masculine power of his lovers. Hence, the great symbolic importance of Genet's receptive role in performing fellatio. Despite the homology to the sexual function of the female, the one who sucks is not entirely passive. In submitting to the penetrating hardness of the other's phallus, Genet discovered its secret weakness: "it melts on the tongue." Thus Genet could soften up even the toughest male.

> Emptied, drooping, a piece of wet rag, the virile member is no longer formidable. . . . In giving himself to the tough pimps, Genet becomes a trap; they are caught in his pestilential swamps and their virility abandons them. In the last analysis, fellatio is castration. . . . In the presence of the castrated male who rolls over on his back and releases him from his weight, Genet's consciousness remains alone and pure and, by a premeditated reversal, the penis of the passive homosexual, still erect because he has refused pleasure, bears witness to his vigilance. (SG, 129)

The images that Sartre used to describe Genet here are almost identical to the earlier ones he used in *Being and Nothingness* to express the discomfort caused by sliminess in general and women's bodies in particular. Genet's mouth dissolves the hard masculinity of his lovers just as the slimy overpowers what comes in contact with it. As in the case of genital sex with a woman, the draining of male desire represents a periodic castration of the male. The latter is trapped in Genet like the fly in the jam jar that Sartre referred to in discussing sliminess.

However, Sartre did not recoil from Genet's sexuality in dread or disgust. Indeed, he seemed to enjoy the idea of the powerful toughs being overcome by the seemingly powerless Genet. Sartre's identification with Genet rather than the toughs is quite different from his earlier discussion of women and sliminess. There he saw himself much more as a potential victim of slipping into the slimy and decomposing. Genet's "sliminess" may have been more acceptable to Sartre, since its target is those who symbolize the same inauthentic masculine power that Sartre likewise wished to dissolve. Like a female, Genet tames the tough male. "Tenderness is then born, a quiet, triumphant, maternal superiority" (SG, 129). Ironically, Sartre accepted female power most easily when it was embodied by a male in whom the danger of sliminess was only half real. Having refused sexual pleasure himself, Genet's consciousness is uncontaminated and his erection testifies to a masculine victory. At this moment, he feels the power that comes from being a masturbator rather than a copulator.

Sartre was also intrigued by the existential significance of the passive homosexual's practice of anal intercourse. His approach was to see how sexuality embodied the existential attitudes of an individual. For Genet, anal intercourse was an act of submission, as "the vanquished resistance of his sphincter" (SG, 108) represented the crushing of his will. This form of sex could only bring humiliation, pain, and suffering from being impaled, crushed, and perforated by another. It was a form of masochism rooted in his reaction to being abandoned by his mother in infancy. Yet in the end, it, too, produced a mixture of contradictory feelings. "The homosexual does not know, in the gripping ache of his pain, whether he is expelling excrement or opening himself to a foreign body. Rejection and acceptance are intimately mingled in the most immediate impression" (SG, 109). Genet was forced to identify with his anus, a nightmarish symbol of a hole that dissolves all that enters into it. At the moment of his own submission, Genet transformed the alien penis within him (and its owner) into excrement, expelling it from his own anus. Feeling like a piece of shit discarded by society, Genet succeeded in turning the phalluses of those who judged him into shit as well. By playing the passive role of a woman, he gives birth to his lovers as his mother did to him, excreting each one as a worthless object.

Sartre used Genet's homosexuality as an example of how an early experience of stigmatization reverberates into the very sexuality of a person. His intention was never to offer a complete theory of homosexuality, for Genet can scarcely be seen as a prototypical homosexual. Rather, Sartre understood Genet as a kind of sexual terrorist who used his body to undermine the values of those people in society who had condemned him. It was this aspect of Genet's vulgar sex life that enabled Sartre to overlook his own fear of holes that consume. Genet's anal sexuality struck at the central values of the respectable. As Guy Hocquenghem points out in *Homosexual Desire*, the homosexual's eroticizing of the anus not only violates what is most private, but threatens existing definitions of power. Anal privacy and cleanliness (*propreté privée*) is a precursor to private property (*propriété privée*). Thus there is a natural link between rejecting the privacy of the anus and rejecting private property, as Genet did. He is a thief only because of a particular social system of property which so defines him. Genet contested this system and the authority of those who support and enforce it. By shifting his sexual focus to the anus, he threatens traditional models of masculinity, since it is the phallus which confers identity on a man. As Hocquenghem puts it, "Seen from behind we are all women; the anus does not practice sexual discrimination."[8]

Genet's anal sexuality challenges the respectability of male power on two levels. First, it makes intercourse a preparation for defecation, reversing the initial humiliation of the submissive partner. Second, it reveals his partners' own other side. Through Genet's body, each realizes his own anal potential. The symbolic value of the penis as entitlement to and exercise of male power produces the fear that it will disappear or be taken away (impotence or castration). The symbolic threat to the anus, however, is never that it will be taken away. The real threat is that someone discloses that you have an anus, that it can be used by others. Such disclosure of the anus's sexuality challenges phallic existence. It evokes the fear of being seized from behind by the Other and submitted to his power. The anus as sexual object weakens the domination of the phallus and all it represents.[9] Sartre explained Genet's strategy as follows: "Since it is men who make the law and who arrogate to themselves the right to judge him, only the submission of men can redeem him, by humiliating in his presence his entire sex" (SG, 75). What Sartre saw in Genet's sex life was a corrosive assault on the presumptions of phallic power.

## Flaubert's Self-Transformation into a Woman

One of the striking aspects of Gustave Flaubert's personality was his self-identification with women, most dramatically portrayed in his famous exclamation: "La Bovary, c'est moi." Sartre thought it was important to examine just why Flaubert felt the need to "metamorphose himself into a woman" in his art (SM, 141) and why the character for which he is most famous might be described as "a masculine woman and feminized

8. Guy Hocquenghem, *Homosexual Desire* (London: Alison & Busby, 1978), p. 87.
9. Ibid., pp. 90, 89.

man" (*SM*, 142). In his monumental analysis of the evolution of
Flaubert's personality, Sartre took special notice of Flaubert's "femininity."

As in the case of Genet, Sartre traced the roots of Flaubert's sexual
identity to a childhood trauma. According to Sartre's description, Flaubert shared with Genet the feeling of being unwanted by his mother.
Flaubert's mother, Sartre conjectured, had wanted a daughter through
whom she could have relived her own childhood and made up for its
frustration and unhappiness. As a result, she greeted the birth of her son
Gustave as a disappointment, caring for him adequately, but without
tenderness or love. If Sartre is right, then Flaubert's later feminine
identification and passive sexuality were rooted in his unconscious
desire to be the beloved daughter of a mother figure (*FI*, 1:70).

Sartre characterized the earliest stage of human development as a
period of passivity, a time when all one's needs are taken care of.
Gustave remained arrested at this stage, and failed to develop a positive
sense of active agency or self-confidence. Subsequently, Sartre hypothesized, Flaubert's difficulties in learning to read brought condemnation
from his father, compounding the passive tendencies and nonvalorization of his self that had begun in infancy. His passivity and femininity
became protests against the fraternity of masculinity that ordinarily
binds father and son in the bourgeois family. Beneath Sartre's own
jealousy of the father-son relation he himself had missed was his conviction that fathers and their representatives impose certain roles and
expectations on their sons that must be rejected. To follow in one's
father's footsteps represents pursuing a path of social respectability and
acceptance, slipping into a role from which escape may be nearly
impossible.

Although Flaubert's personality was characterized by a clear inversion of those qualities commonly called masculine, in *Search for a
Method* Sartre rejected suggestions about Flaubert's possible homosexuality, emphasizing that "he was *not to any degree at all* an invert" (*SM*,
140). By the time he wrote *The Family Idiot*, however, Sartre was
slightly more circumspect in his appraisal. He still was reluctant to call
Flaubert a homosexual for several reasons. First, there seemed to be
little indication of actual homosexual behavior on Flaubert's part; and
second, Sartre did not want homosexuality to be used as an explanatory
essence from which Flaubert's passivity and femininity could be derived. Sexuality, Sartre countered, is a totalization of many factors.
Even though he acknowledged that Flaubert's friendships with his

closest male friends could rightfully be called "platonically homosex-ual" (*FI*, 2:35), he nevertheless saw passivity, not homosexuality, as the real issue.

> Gustave needs to be caressed more than to caress; he wants to be the hare rather than the hunter. . . . But this postulation of his passivity involves no decision on the sex of the aggressor. Rather we must recognize that it is the aggression that counts, and that circumstances alone will dictate the part-ner. (*FI*, 2:35)

Flaubert's femininity was related to his wanting to be a desirable object for the Other. It is here that Sartre saw the major dichotomy between male and female sexuality. To accuse Sartre of more sexist gender typing would be easy, but it should be remembered that "male" and "female" here indicate different modes of relation to others, both of which could be adopted by either men or women. At the same time, there is no denying that what intrigues Sartre about Genet and Flaubert is their need to violate the standard gender roles for men. "Masculine" desire, Sartre observed, comes from *taking* a woman. A woman, con-versely, has her sexual climax in *being taken* (*FI*, 2:33). "Feminine" desire is passive waiting, being embraced by the Other. Flaubert sought the latter; his desire was to be an "object of aggression, to become prey, to swoon under brutal caresses, to be dampened, made fecund, there-fore penetrated" (*FI*, 2:33). Like Genet, he sexualized his passivity, his need to be an object for others, and transformed his "masculine" body into "feminine" flesh. In so doing, he compensated for having missed the childhood experience of being a desirable object for the Other. He would not have seen himself as a homosexual, Sartre concluded, because it was not a man's embrace that he sought, but his mother's. Nor was he heterosexual in a traditional aggressive male way. It was not the role of the father who takes the mother that he sought, but rather to be the object of her caresses. He Oedipally rebelled against his father's wishes, but hardly wished to assume his father's place.

Many commentators have duly noted the connections between Flau-bert's struggles and certain issues in Sartre's own life. Indeed, the nature of gender and desire had a tremendous impact on both men's sense of their proper civilized behavior. In Sartre's case, the feminine world offered both hope and pitfalls. As a child, Sartre's experiences with his mother were moments of playing "hooky" from his grandfather's school of civility. But in another sense, it was his grandfather who made him feel like a little girl, always seeking the approval of others.

## Homosexuality as Artificial and Unnatural

The inversion of traditional gender roles in homosexuality often gives rise to the charge by "respectable people" that homosexuality is unnatural. Descriptions of the homosexual as either perverse or degenerate derive from the concern that the natural order of things has been violated.

Sartre believed that the concept of a "natural" order of things was only a creation of those people who hold power in a society. What deviates from their values and practices is repressed as subversive. He argued that Genet deliberately had emphasized and embraced the *unnatural* qualities of homosexuality as a means of contesting and scandalizing the social conventions by which he felt victimized.

Genet's difficulties began with a birth that made his relation both to society and to his own body strained and unnatural. Sartre imagined that, as a bastard and an orphan, Genet must have felt that his very existence "disturbs the natural order and the social order" and that he was "a fake child" (SG, 7). By renouncing her son, Genet's mother allowed societal bureaucracies to take over her role as mother. Because he did not know his mother, Genet lacked the comfortable relation with one's body that develops in the intimacy between mother and child.

> For want of having known the primordial relationship with naked flesh, with the swooning fertility of a woman, he will never have that tender familiarity with his own flesh. . . . He is said to be "contrary to nature." But the reason is that, as far back as he can remember, nature has been against him. (SG, 7)

Genet's hostility to nature subsequently manifested itself. For example, the idea of sainthood appealed to Genet since saints "go counter to their most legitimate desires in order to achieve within themselves an anti-nature" (SG, 11). Realizing that he could never be respectable, Genet tried to be as unrespectable as possible. He committed many of his crimes only because he rejected the concept of laws and rights. In this respect, Sartre compared him to "the young girl who was exasperated at having natural needs and forced herself to drink when she was not thirsty" (SG, 68).

Genet's outrageous behavior is a protest against the life-style of the well behaved. To the extent that social behavior is rooted in a prescription for the way things are intended to be, Genet's homosexuality is a rejection of the natural way to be. Sartre observed: "He cherished his inversion because it was against nature" (SG, 413–14). "The desire of Genet, who is condemned, outside of nature, impossible, becomes a desire for the impossible and what is against nature" (*SG*, 82). In other words, Genet sexualized his defiance of society and its rules. He had been treated as an exception to the rules; as a result his sexual desire and excitement came from what was most artificial and contrary to nature. "Genet's sexual desire contains within itself a fierce demand for its autonomy and singularity, in defiance of the rules, in defiance of nature, in defiance of life, in defiance of the species and in defiance of society" (*SG*, 82). Sartre was convinced that Genet's homosexuality, his "metamorphosis" into a woman, stemmed from this subversive desire to simultaneously attack notions of what is proper and expected (*SG*, 82).

Genet's self-identification as a woman fed his sense of artificiality and rejection of the natural. A passive homosexual is only a woman in his imagination. Genet needed to be a woman who was not really a woman, but rather an impostor, a fake woman. Thus, his homosexuality was not a desire to be a woman *per se*, but a man who *plays* at being a woman. So in escaping from one set of social roles, Genet assumes another one. He could refer to himself (herself) in the feminine in the character of Divine, but s/he actually felt discomfort with real women. "She does not wish to become a woman completely since she loathes women. She wants to be a man-woman: a woman when she is passive, a man when she acts" (*SG*, 291). If "she" were really a woman,

> she would become a *nature*, a species, she would wallow in being, her desire to be taken by a man would be licit, would take on flesh, would be a true, substantial desire. Divine wants to be a woman because "she" is not one and will never be one. She plays at femininity in order to taste the radical impossibility of feminizing herself. Everything about her is false: the names she gives herself are false, her simpering gestures are false, her desire for the male is false, her love is false, her pleasures are false. She has not the slightest desire to *be* a woman; what she wants is to be *fake*. (*SG*, 358)[10]

For the same reason, Genet wanted adolescent boys to play the roles of women in his play *The Maids*. Sartre believed the purpose was to create an "absolute state of artifice" by eliminating nature, to create a "defeminized and spiritualized female as an invention of man" (*SG*, 612). Genet was showing the impossibility for him of being a woman. Perhaps Sartre could tolerate feminine sexuality in Genet better than in

10. Cf. "A false woman harboring an imaginary passion for an appearance of a man and adorning herself in order to please him with appearances of jewels: is not that the definition of the homosexual?" (*SG*, 364).

actual women precisely because Genet was not really tied to nature, and indeed was committed to protesting it.

Genet's gender inversion occurred in the eyes of the Other. It was not for himself that he wished to be feminine. He did not want to change his body or sex. But through his gestures and language he wished to force the others to see him as a woman.

## To Subvert with Bad Taste

Sartre's intricate examination of Genet led him to question the deeper ontological significance of some homosexuals' love of "elegance," "bad taste," and "vulgarity." Genet's garish vulgarity, his taste for cheap costume jewelry and perfumes epitomized his attraction to the un-natural, to things that appear to be what they are not. A diamond that was *not really* a diamond reflected back the image of the woman who was *not really* a woman. It legitimized his being a "fake woman." "Violent perfumes justify the homosexual's artificialism: they are as far removed from vague natural scents as the homosexual wants to remove himself from the species" (SG, 363). In short, "falseness" is "a pro-foundly homosexual idea" (SG, 383). Paradoxically, respectable people support the "naturalness" of good taste as a way to cloak its groundless artificiality, while Genet used what was fake and artificial to actually criticize the fakeness of the standards of respectability.

Sartre sometimes used the idea of *antiphysis* to describe the human transcendence or conquest of nature and the creative transformation of the world. It was this power of *antiphysis* to break any primitive bond with nature that bad taste celebrated. Genet was delighted by loud, gaudy combinations of colors that could not be found naturally. Good taste honors nature and naturalness, but bad taste honors human pro-duction, the synthetic imitation of the natural product. "A synthetic pearl reminds us every moment, by its sheen, that man, who only yesterday was a natural creature, can produce in himself and outside of himself a false nature more sparkling and more rigorous than the true one" (SG, 362). Genet embraced *antiphysis* not to transcend nature, but simply to be against it. He was a fake child by his birth, a fake woman by his sexuality, and a fake person by his taste. In all ways, he was an unnatural thing and a violation of all social norms.

So it was that the fake and the imaginary were Genet's métier. Sartre called him "the lord of hoaxes, booby traps and optical illusions. Wherever objects are presented as what they are not or not presented as what they are, he is king" (SG, 360). It is here that Genet upheld the authenticity of his existence, for such objects demonstrate the true nature of human reality. The real hoax, trap, and illusion is to accept taste and civility as one's true reality. The true insight is to realize the "optical illusion" of human existence: it is what it is not and it is not what it is.

In one of his early stories, Sartre had already established a connection between homosexuality and the complex nature of tricks and illusions. When Lucien, the incipient antisemite described in "The Childhood of a Leader," visited the home of the homosexual Bergère, he was surprised by Bergère's enormous collection of practical jokes: "solid liquids, sneezing powder, floating sugar, an imitation turd, and a bride's garter." Bergère gracefully took the "perfectly imitated excrement" in his long, delicate fingers and told Lucien, "These jokes have a revolutionary value. They disturb. There is more destructive power in them than in all the works of Lenin" (*CL*, 114). What is revolutionary and disturbing about such jokes—fake shit to be delicately admired—is that they disrupt the relation of the natural and the artificial. Something artificial has been made to look natural, and something natural has been made artificial. They attack the pretensions of respectability and propriety, indicating ways in which things are not what they seem to be. Ultimately, Lucien flees from this world for the security of antisemitism and a worldview that offers real solids and things that *are* what they *seem to be*.

Sartre pointed out that aesthetic entertainment often makes use of such manipulation of appearance and reality for a special effect. In his early book on the psychology of imagination, he discussed the phenomenon of impersonation as an example of how the imagination can negate the natural world and entertain us with the experience of imitation. The woman who impersonates Maurice Chevalier gives the viewer two options, "to see Maurice Chevalier as an image, or a small woman who is making faces" (*PI*, 33–34). Unlike a portrait which is in some sense "natural," an imitation offers only a few simplified characteristics amidst a mass of opposing ones. "How is Maurice Chevalier to be found in these fat painted cheeks, that black hair, that feminine body, those female clothes?" (*PI*, 35). What is entertaining about an impersonation is that the impersonator expresses something of Maurice Chevalier without losing all of her own individuality. The imitated subject appears through the impersonator. "Thus primitively, an impersonator is one possessed. Here may lie the explanation of the role of impersonator in the ritual dances of the primitives" (*PI*, 37–38).

In his long discussions of Genet as aesthete, Sartre described the same process of transforming reality into appearance. "Beauty" is "the transformation of being into appearance" (SG, 377). Genet aimed to subvert the values of the "just" men by taking the details of his life which would disgust them and making them the basis for art. "He will constantly make use of his acts and needs and feelings to manufacture beautiful, disconcerting appearances, as the painter uses brush, paint and canvas to produce a beautiful image" (SG, 379). His project is to "disturb the good citizen . . . whisk away the ground from under his feet . . . make him have doubts about morality and Good." And so the dialectical process comes around. Genet takes the vulgar reality of his life and spins it into a palatable art. But it is the transformation of shit into art, shitty art, or one of Bergère's artistic turds. As the "good citizen" is enticed by Genet's artifice, moreover, the artifice of the citizen's own "goodness" may come into view, and he may realize that he is really not so different from Genet. In judging Genet, he judges himself.

Beneath Genet's restless transformations of himself, Sartre also admired his skillful maneuvering between the reefs of bad faith. Genet would never be a "sincere" homosexual who accepted his homosexuality as a destiny or essence from which all his acts flowed and which would negate his freedom. He does not try to *be* a homosexual in the way that Daniel attempts in the *The Reprieve*:

> Why can't I *be* what I am, *be* a pederast, villain, coward. . . . He . . . almost laughed aloud at the thought of how respectable he must look. . . . He was sick of thinking what he looked like, sick of looking at himself—especially as, when I look at myself, I am two people. Just *to be*. . . . To be homosexual just as the oak is oak. To extinguish myself. (R, 133)

But neither does he deny that he is a "queen" or a thief. Rather, Sartre's Genet accepts his homosexuality and thievery as the defiled identity he has received from society, but as artist he stands disidentified with that being, in the way Sartre hoped respectable society might become disenchanted with its presumptions of goodness and right.

### The Reader's Imagination as Compromised Masculinity

Genet's literature exploits the average male's fear that the homosexual threatens his own masculinity. As Sartre saw it, Genet's clever strategy was to make the reader experience his own homosexual feelings. To the extent that readers participate in the sexual activities of Genet's fictional characters and lend them the power of their own heterosexual imaginations, they begin by experiencing seemingly normal desires and passions. They soon find themselves duped, however, when these desires are progressively revealed to be deviant and perverse. The characters Bulkaen and Divine seem to be women, but in reality they are men. When Genet describes Divine in feminine terms, it is natural for the straight male reader to be aroused and to desire her. "The trouble is that this woman is a man" (SG, 501). Reading Genet is like meeting a charming woman, starting to caress her, and suddenly realizing that she is a man in disguise. In this case, the impersonation is neither amusing nor aesthetic. The reader of Genet feels

> the horror-stricken desire which nevertheless remains, unable to fade away, and which persists in seeking the woman in the unmasked male. . . . If I have the slightest inclination for men, even if it is repressed to my very depths, I am caught, constrained, in the shame of avowing my tastes to myself. If I really have no partiality for boys, then *I* become, in myself, the Other. Another uses me to desire what I cannot desire: my freedom lends itself, I am possessed by a homosexual zar and what is more, voluntarily possessed. . . . Homosexual because of the power of words, we taste for a moment, in the realm of the imaginary, the forbidden pleasure of taking a man and being taken, and we cannot taste it without horrifying ourself. (SG, 500–501)

In order to write, Genet removes himself from his sordid life on the margins of society, but to the reader, Genet is a way to experience oneself outside the protective shell of civility.

Genet's artistry was to take the vulgarity of his life and to trick the reader into swallowing it, by wrapping it in beautiful words and frosting it with an icing of poetry. As the reader's imagination is engaged, he realizes that Genet has tricked him.

> Since to read is to re-create, we re-create, for the sake of its beauty, the homosexual intercourse that is sumptuously bedecked with the rarest of words. But the words vanish, leaving us face to face with the residue, a mixture of sweat, dirt, cheap perfumes, blood and excrement. . . . Genet's art is a mirage, a confidence trick, a pitfall. In order to make us eat shit, he has to show it to us, from afar, as rose jam. (SG, 498)

By lending his imagination to Genet, the "good citizen" experiences homosexuality directly. He is tricked into considering the terrifying possibility of a feminization of his self and a devitalization of his masculine personality. Genet seeks to expose the paranoia and fear of the average male citizen when faced with deviant sexuality. His life demonstrates to Sartre that homosexuality is not an alien, grotesque aberration to be stigmatized, but a human possibility which calls into question the entire moral edifice of contemporary society.

The circle is complete. Decent folk used to think inside of Genet, that is, he internalized their values and became the outcast that they said he was. Now, when they read his work, he gets revenge by thinking inside of them. In reading Genet's books, we are changed into "homosexual subjects" and made to feel "an 'eccentric' experience that we cannot incorporate into the web of life and that will forever remain 'on the margin,' unassimilable, the memory of a night of debauchery when we gave ourselves to a man and came" (SG, 589). Clearly, the "eccentric" perspective one experiences from the margin is critical if one is ever to question the tempting, stable self offered by society. In providing this unassimilable experience, the unassimilable person—the Jew, black, homosexual—serves an indispensable role. Each preserves the possibility of a transcendent perspective on decent society's rules and values.

Genet's work takes one on a trip of homosexual imagination that decenters the moral grounding of heterosexual respectability. One element that contributes to this decentering is the outsider's deforming and reforming of language itself. Groups who have been defined as Other by respectable society must contend with the fact that the structure of ordinary language itself contains their condemnation. Society's language reflects the thoughts and values of its dominant groups (SG, 285). Consequently, homosexuals, like blacks, women, and others will often seek some kind of linguistic relief from the language of the oppressor, the language that names them as Other. In Genet's underworld of thieves and homosexuals, Sartre emphasized, slang enabled them to communicate without using the language of the "enemy." They thus neutralized the burden of society. For a passive homosexual like Genet, the language of slang was the linguistic equivalent of his sexuality. Slang recalled Genet's sexuality, since it "violates," "perverts," and "rapes" the language of ordinary respectable folk (SG, 288). It exchanged the improper for the proper.

> Argot is, in its words and syntax and by virtue of its whole semantic content, the permanent practice of rape. . . . Argot, by its refusal or inability to use the proper word, condemned itself to impropriety. . . . The victim of its acts of violence is the language of the just, the language which Genet is denied. (SG, 289)

Sartre provided an interesting example to show the underlying assumptions of these two languages. In its root, the word "infant" (*in-*

*fans*) embodies the essential characteristic of a newborn child, that is, it has no speech. Speech is an ability that signifies "civilized" human life. In learning to speak a child becomes civilized and enters a world of human meanings. Thus the word itself connotes the idea that a completed person is someone who speaks and reasons. In Genet's slang, a newborn was called a "crapper," calling attention to its "intestinal incontinence" (SG, 286). This description implies a very different understanding of an adult. The underlying assumption of this word is that the main characteristic of an adult is toilet training and anal control. As Hocquenghem has argued, the ability to regulate anal retention and release is "the necessary moment of the constitution of the self. 'To forget oneself' is the most ridiculous and distressing kind of social accident there is, the ultimate outrage to the human person."[11]

This last example summarizes much of Genet's symbolic power within Sartre's mythic universe. Genet's purpose for Sartre is to unveil the "crapper" in all of us. As a sodomist, his sexuality was a constant reminder of the crude organic quality of life and the power to decompose the protective shields of civility. Genet is a grown-up "crapper" who still refuses to control his anus. On the other hand, Genet launches an attack on artificial ways we design to separate ourselves from nature. As drag queen, he sabotages the world of civility by taking artificiality to an absurd extreme. He forces us to accept that there is nothing natural about the sense of order and stability we find in good taste. Everything is contrived and artificial. We are surrounded by fakes and optical illusions of our own design.

In *The Words*, Sartre described with some regret the ways in which his grandfather had taken a frightened and fatherless little boy and shown him how to speak and act like a well-behaved young man. Sartre's father had not had time to give his son a mission and purpose. In the short time that he remained alive after Jean-Paul's birth, however, he did manage to model one behavior for his son. Within a year of Jean-Paul's birth, his father's health rapidly declined due to enterocolitis and tuberculosis,[12] or what Sartre called "intestinal fever" (W, 8). At about the same time, the infant Jean-Paul's health was also failing due to "enteritis" (W, 8). Thus before the long civilizing process that would teach an "in-fans" to speak could begin, this father and son shared for a moment the inevitable results of their intestinal disturbances; probably they were both diarrheal. Beyond any desire for missions or purposes in

11. Hocquenghem, *Homosexual Desire*, p. 85.
12. Annie Cohen-Solal, *Sartre: A Life* (New York: Pantheon, 1987), p. 24.

their lives, the one factor that connected father and son—one dying and the other just born—was that both of them were "crappers." Of course, Sartre eventually recovered from his intestinal problems, but in other ways he remained a crapper on the bourgeoisie to the end.

Through his meditation on Genet's homosexuality, Sartre has probed once more the territory beyond the boundaries of civilized society's normative values. In homosexuality, we discover the suppressed Otherness of our own sexual desire. Thus the homosexual provides a vantage point from which to examine the social construction of "civilized" sexuality. Yet Genet's homosexuality is important to Sartre for reasons beyond the realm of sexuality. This passive homosexual has emerged from a set of circumstances in which his self was created and defined by the unwanted perceptions of the Other. His oppression, like that of Jews and women, is the result of finding himself outside the society of those whose identities are supported by the power of civilized men. Sartre saw Genet's attack on that power as coming from several directions. His revelation of his own anal potential showed that apparent weakness and passivity can still sabotage the monopoly of power held by the strong. His exploitation of the artificial and unnatural exploded the false identification of social norms with what is "natural."

# SEVEN

# The Dark Core of White Civilization:
# The Black Other

Negritude appears like the up-beat [unaccented beat] of a dialectical progression: the theoretical and practical affirmation of white supremacy is the thesis; the position of Negritude as an antithetical value is the moment of negativity. (*BO*, 49)

—Jean-Paul Sartre

For Sartre, the origin of racism is the fear of our own otherness. "In oppression, I am afraid of myself as Other" (*CPM*, 443). Those qualities and desires in ourselves that we resist and from which we are alienated are reflected back to us from the Other. It is the white racist's fear of his own uncontrolled sexuality and aggression, for example, that is behind the impulse to rape and kill that he sees in the black. The oppressor destroys any possible solidarity with the oppressed by perceiving them as "other." The oppressed thereby become both unfathomable and hateful. Yet this fearful otherness of the oppressed, Sartre reminds us, is an illusion of our own making. "What makes them others is that we have put them *a priori* in a situation where they can only appear to us as Others. And to the extent that we attribute feelings to them, they are feelings that we form first in ourselves" (*CPM*, 443; my translation).

At the same time that Sartre spoke eloquently for the rights of those groups of people who were disempowered by a society that defined them as "other," he never renounced the idea that such groups were indeed characterized by a fundamental otherness. This is not to say that he endorsed an essentialist view of such groups, for he was ever mindful that it is in response to their particular situations, that is, their *existence* in the world, that each of them developed the various qualities that set them off from the dominant values of European culture. In the cases of Jews, blacks, homosexuals, and women, Sartre rejected otherness and difference as a justification for dehumanization or oppression, but he clung to certain aspects of their otherness as the mirror in which he saw reflected his inverted image, and as a path of redemption from alienation.

In the years after the Second World War, Sartre turned his attention from the problem of antisemitism to that of racism in general. This was a natural transition, since Sartre believed that his analysis of recent antisemitism could be easily transposed in this new context. "Replace the Jew with the Black, the antisemite with the supporter of slavery, and there would be nothing essential to be cut from my book," he said.[1] In very general terms, this may be true, particularly to the extent that Sartre located authenticity for both Jews and blacks in their resistance to and negation of the white non-Jewish world to which Sartre himself belonged. But there were also significant differences which will be mentioned later.

Sartre's particular concern for the situation of blacks in the world came from several directions. After visiting the United States in 1945, he was disturbed by the plight of American blacks. His initial response, however, was to see the black problem in the United States as one rooted in class rather than race. He reported: "The black problem is neither a political problem nor a cultural problem: the blacks are a part of the American proletariat and their cause is the same as that of the white workers" (WS, 123). Sartre seemed oblivious to the cultural destruction and alienation suffered by American blacks at the hands of white society. He saw the solution to the racial problem in a coordinated revolt of the black and white working class against the ruling class. It would be several years before Sartre would fully appreciate the differences between class oppression and racism, and that "the selfish scorn that white men display for black men . . . has no equivalent in the attitude of the bourgeois toward the working class" (BO, 19). Ironically, a new generation of African intellectuals has criticized Sartre's position on blacks for distracting attention from the economic issues of class struggle in Africa by its focus on issues of black identity.[2]

---

1. Cited by M. Watteau, "Situations raciales et condition de l'homme dans l'oeuvre de Jean-Paul Sartre," *Présence africaine*, no. 2 (January 1948):228 (my translation).
2. Francis A. Joppa, "Sartre et les milieux intellectuels de l'Afrique noire," *Présence francophone*, no. 35 (1989):7–28.

Perhaps the source of Sartre's initial indifference to the specificity of racial oppression lay in the fact that American blacks had been away from their ancestral cultures, languages, and homelands long enough to have become Americanized in many ways. They had lost contact with many of the qualities Sartre would soon associate with "negritude" in its African or even Caribbean context. Certainly, Sartre had used a similar kind of argument to dismiss the importance of Jewish culture in explaining the identity of contemporary Jews. He could not believe that any national and/or religious ties held the Jews together any more (*AJ*, 64–67). His tendency, moreover, was to subsume other forms of oppression under the category of class conflict. Unfortunately, this meant that he sometimes overlooked or denied the very real racism and antisemitism of the *working* classes. In any case, Sartre gradually came to grips with the intersection of racism and African culture within black identity.

## Civility and Racism

*The Respectful Prostitute*, which premiered in 1946, was Sartre's effort to present the black problem in the United States. It was inspired by an actual 1931 case from Scottsboro, Alabama, in which nine blacks were condemned to the electric chair for raping two prostitutes, despite the fact that, under pressure, the prostitutes' testimony had changed several times (*WS*, 138). In the play, a white prostitute and a black man are thrown together, both victims of the racism and moral bankruptcy of those "decent people" in power.

The central tension of the play is focused on how Lizzie, the prostitute, will respond to a moral dilemma into which she has stumbled. Lizzie had just arrived in a Southern town by train. On the train, a group of drunken white men had provoked a fight with two black men and shot one of them. The second black man jumped off the train and later shows up at Lizzie's door asking for help. He pleads with her to exonerate him of false accusations that he had tried to rape her. A white man named Fred wants Lizzie to say that the black men had jumped her, that she had called the white men for help, and they were forced to shoot one of the black men after he flashed a razor. This false accusation will provide Fred's cousin Thomas with a defense for killing the first black man, and probably condemn the second black man to a lynching.

In the simplest sense, Lizzie must choose between black and white. In the course of the play, Sartre used the black and white characters to embody certain values and ideas of blacks and whites in general. The black in the play is not even given a name, but is simply referred to as "the negro." This is the only fact necessary to explain his role as victim. This black man's dignity and will to fight have been crushed by his realization of his hopeless situation. He has accepted the whites' claims to privilege and his own insignificance. Even when Lizzie gives him a chance to fight to save his own life, he refuses to shoot white people. Although he has not done anything wrong, he still feels guilty, since he has internalized the judgment of white society. This self-alienation is one of the tragic consequences of racism on its victims. The black inhabitants of French colonies were similarly alienated to the extent that they accepted their treatment and saw themselves as "natives" lacking any right to exist. "By considering himself as a mere natural product, as a 'native,' the slave sees himself through his master's eyes. He thinks of himself as an Other, and with the thoughts of the Other" (*LPE*, 243).

The attitudes of the white men in this play are very similar to those of the antisemite Lucien in "The Childhood of a Leader." What unites such white people and grounds their identities is their hatred of the black. One of the brutal ironies of the play is the level of cruelty and destruction that lies beneath the surface of white civility. Thus the black man observes with alarm that lynching creates a special friendliness among white people. "When white folk who have never met before, start to talk to each other, friendly like, it means some nigger's goin' to die" (*RP*, 252), he worries. White sociability rests on the persecution of innocent black men.

Although Lizzie does not want to get involved with someone else's troubles, she promises at first "to tell the truth" if she is forced to testify (*RP*, 252). It seems obvious to her that the black man is an innocent victim, and that Thomas is the one guilty of murder. As the play unfolds, Sartre shows that ideas of truth and guilt can be manipulated and redefined in the interests of those in power. Fred tells Lizzie, "There is no truth; there's only whites and blacks, that's all" (*RP*, 262). Certainly Thomas is not "guilty" of anything just because he shot a black man. "If you were guilty every time you killed a nigger—"(*RP*, 262) he jokes, suggesting that shooting a black is little worse than shooting a dog.

At the same time, the "decent men" like Fred see blacks and prostitutes as embodiments of evil. He tells Lizzie, "You are the Devil. The nigger is the Devil, too" (*RP*, 260–61). Just as white men are not guilty even when they have murdered innocent people, black men are guilty even when they have done nothing. They have no defense: "A nigger has always done something" (*RP*, 263). Like the antisemite's attitude toward the Jew, the racist attributes a fixed evil essence to the black as a foil to his own permanent sense of goodness and respectability. Throughout the play, respectability and civility are a veneer which disguises the real significance of people's actions, and which maintains both oppressor and oppressed in their respective positions.[3]

This hypocritical civility functions to negate Fred's and Thomas's sexual behavior. Fred, for example, tries to humiliate Lizzie for being a "ten-dollar whore," but overlooks the fact that it was his body and ten dollars which has just confirmed her in that identity. He becomes red and embarrassed at seeing Lizzie naked, and makes her turn out the light before they can have sex, a fact which Lizzie finds "nice and respectful" (*RP*, 256). As the light of morning illuminates the scene of their night together, Fred orders Lizzie to cover the bed because it "smells of sin" (*RP*, 253). He insists that she close the window, pull the shades, and not talk about what happened the night before. "What's done at night belongs to the night. In the daytime you don't talk about it" (*RP*, 257). Nocturnal indiscretions are not the subject of polite daytime chitchat. Though Lizzie reminds him that the sins that he wishes to cover up are really his own, she does not yet fully realize at this point the extent of his efforts to cover other people's sins.

This combination of brutal racism and demeaning sexual behavior is linked for both Fred and cousin Thomas. They deny their own sexuality and project it onto others like the prostitute and the black man who can be possessed for a small charge or destroyed at will. It is probably no coincidence that Fred feels an uncontrollable sexual urge toward Lizzie at the moment he watches a black man lynched.

> The nigger was swinging from a branch. I looked at him, and I thought: "I want her." It's not natural. . . . I looked at the nigger and I saw you. . . . I came running here, and I didn't even know whether I wanted to kill you or rape you. (*RP*, 279)

As for Thomas, it was after sexually harassing Lizzie on the train that he ended up killing a black man on the false charge of doing precisely what Thomas himself had *really* just done. Nevertheless, neither of

3. The play's title itself embodies the central tension between civility and vulgarity. Indeed, the first half of the French title (*La Putain*) was deemed so offensive to respectability that the play became known as "*La P . . . respectueuse*," after the censored posters in the Paris subways.

these things prevents him from being seen as a leader and a gentleman. Murder and rape are simply two different ways of maintaining one's sense of control in the world. They have little impact on the inauthentic person's cherished sense of respectability. As Fred explains, "He put his hand under your skirt, he shot down a dirty nigger, so what? You do things like that without thinking; they don't count. Thomas is a leading citizen, that's what counts" (*RP*, 263). What also counts is that Thomas is from "a good family," is "the finest fellow in town," and would be dishonored if Lizzie stubbornly refused to cooperate.

Fred's father, the Senator, acknowledges that the black man did not really try to rape Lizzie, but he tries to convince her that this fact was merely "a common truth," and that there are different kinds of truth (*RP*, 269). The most important truth for the Senator is that his nephew's life is more essential to the country than the black man's. The Senator does not see the black man as evil, like his son Fred, but rather as superfluous and insignificant. He tells Lizzie that a black man is born by accident, does not live like a real man, and would scarcely be missed if he died (*RP*, 270). He has no intrinsic right to live. The life of a white man like Thomas, however, is justified, valuable, and essential. He was born to lead.

> He is a hundred-per-cent American, comes from one of our oldest families, has studied at Harvard . . . employs two thousand workers in his factory. . . . He's a leader, a firm bulwark against the Communists, labor unions, and the Jews. His duty is to live, and yours is to preserve his life. (*RP*, 270)

Fred makes the same point in the final scene as Lizzie's brief moment of revolt is squashed. Lizzie is no better than the black man; she, too, has no right to live. Fred says, "Who are you? what do you do in this world? Do you even know who your grandfather was? I have a right to live; there are things to be done, and I am expected to do them" (*RP*, 281). Of course, this is the classic position of those who live in bad faith to protect themselves from the painful truth that they, too, lack any external justification for their being.

Gradually, Lizzie finds herself being seduced by the Senator's appeal to the ethic of respectability. A simple, perjured statement will buy her the whole town's love and admiration. But it takes only a second for her to realize that the respectability to which the Senator appeals is merely a trick, a mask for deceit. She says, "Until now I liked old men best, because they looked so respectable, but I'm beginning to wonder if they're not more crooked than the others" (*RP*, 274).

As the play ends, Fred promises to take care of Lizzie and give her a nice house across the river. First, however, Lizzie must swear that his sexual performance the night before was thrilling to her—for who other than a prostitute could realistically appraise his prowess (*RP*, 279). Having just learned the different uses of "truth" that forced her to lie moments before, Lizzie now wearily reassures Fred that their ten-dollar tryst was a real sexual thrill for her. Fred's ordered world is now back to normal.[4] In this play, the black man served only as the target of white racism. His being was defined by the judgments of others and his invalidated identity propped up their sense of entitlement.

Sartre intended to present a more theoretical examination of the oppression of American blacks during the period of slavery. An unfinished draft from about 1947 or 1948 is included in the Appendices of his *Cahiers pour une morale*.[5] Sartre had apparently read a number of books about the practice of slavery in the United States and tried to understand the slaveowners' ideological bad faith that transformed once proud African blacks into slaves that were less than human. He described a number of ways in which the reality of black slavery was masked by those who perpetuated the system.

With the memory of Nazi antisemitic racism still fresh, Sartre observed a number of techniques similar to those used by antisemites. One is the way in which people will participate in an oppressive institution with a clear conscience if they believe it is based on a fact of nature and is also legally endorsed by society. Just as the Nazis used the legal system to disenfranchise European Jews and strip away all rights from them, slavery also was institutionalized in a way that gave it legitimacy. It was regarded as merely a legal *right* to which Southern whites were entitled. Those who were born already owning slaves simply regarded them as a variation on the right to own property (*CPM*, 580).

The Nazis had justified the persecution of Jews by denying the full humanity of the victims. In the American South, slaves were likewise

---

4. According to Simone de Beauvoir, Sartre originally wanted to disturb the privileged white theatergoers who saw his play. Therefore, he deliberately chose to portray the situation as "both appalling and without remedy." Curiously, Sartre changed the ending when the play was made into a film. Lizzie continues her efforts to save the innocent black man to the end. Sartre sensed that the more democratic audience of a film needed hope more than discouragement. Beauvoir, *Force of Circumstance*, p. 115.

5. Perhaps this draft was to have been part of an article, "Concerning Slavery," which was announced by *Présence africaine* in 1949 but never appeared (*WS*, 216).

seen as less than human. The slaveowner had to create a large gap of otherness between himself and his slaves, for otherwise he might begin to identify with the possibility of his own enslavement. The owners explained that the black was suited *by nature* to be a slave. By reducing the black to a permanently fixed nature, the owner could obtain a permanently superior identity. But, insisted Sartre, the Southern white really knew nothing about the black. Rather, the traits that allegedly suit the black to slavery are precisely those that the white social system creates.

Sartre followed the same approach as he did in *Antisemite and Jew* in arguing that the qualities of the oppressed that the oppressor uses to justify oppression are in fact the product of oppression itself. Antisemites are not responding to preexisting qualities of Jews as much as Jews develop a certain character in response to antisemitism. Similarly, slavery produced certain traits in slaves that were then used to justify slavery in the first place. Sartre deconstructed several of the slaveowner arguments for slavery by showing their inner inconsistency. For example, slaveowners implied that since blacks were not Christians, they had no souls and were not fully human. They acted as though blacks were non-Christians *by nature*. But their refusal to teach their slaves Christianity indirectly acknowledged the slaves' potential to become Christians, thus negating the notion that the blacks' nature is fixed at a subspiritual level (*CPM*, 581). The slaveowners likewise said slavery was justified by the blacks' low intelligence. They treated illiteracy as a character trait fixed in nature. But in fact it was the laws that forbade teaching blacks to read that created their illiteracy (*CPM*, 581). Owners said blacks were suited to slavery because of their weak family ties; but the owners created this situation by separating families. If parents are not allowed to keep their children, Sartre noted, they will relax their attachment to them. In short, it was slavery itself that created an inequality between races. Slaves may have been ignorant, unbelieving, and unattached to family, said Sartre, but it was because slavery had made them that way. The whole social system elicited the traits that were then used to justify the system. In short, when white slaveowners described black character, it was not because the whites really understood the black. It was because they *made* the black (*CPM*, 583). White paternalism reduced black slaves to an infantile situation.[6] Like the Jew, the slave learned to survive by struggling to please and by accepting a

---

6. See Simone de Beauvoir, *The Ethics of Ambiguity* (Secaucus, N.J.: Citadel Press, 1975), pp. 37–38.

model of humility, devotion, and obedience to white law, customs, and power. Gradually, Sartre began to develop an appreciation of the insights that might be gained if the voice of the black were really heard.

## The Perspective of Black Writers

As Sartre reflected more seriously on the specific plight of the black, he became interested in how it was reflected in the work of black writers. In his 1947 treatise *What is Literature?* he presented black American writer Richard Wright as an example of literary "engagement." In black writers, Sartre could finally see testimony to the alienation of blacks in a white society. As in the case of Jews, blacks did not experience the world as abstract universal persons, but from the position of outsiders whom the ruling culture had defined as Other. This position of otherness in relation to the dominant powers in society provided the black writer with a particularly valuable vantage point. The black writer is one who "sees whites from the outside, who assimilates white culture from the outside, and each of whose books will show the alienation of the black race within American society" (WL, 71). Blacks thus represented the principle of negation which could both undermine and transcend the world of white privilege. For black writers, the world of whites likewise was "other," and they could only grasp from without "the proud security and that tranquil certainty, common to all white Aryans, that the world is white and that they own it" (WL, 74). If whites could learn to hear this black voice, they might be able to rise above their complacency and distorted narcissism.

Unlike the American experience with the descendants of black slaves who had been in America for a number of generations, the French colonial experience produced a different type of encounter with the black. In a brief essay written for the initial issue of *Présence africaine* (1947), Sartre pointed to the split in French attitudes toward their own blacks. The few blacks who lived in France were treated well enough and were well regarded. But the number of blacks from Martinique or Senegal who came to study in France was tiny. They had undergone a severe filtering and selection process. In "our" eyes, Sartre said, such students were only testimony to "our civilizing mission" (PN, 28), a way of honoring ourselves, and of forgetting the violences committed "down there." Sartre pointed to contradictory attitudes of the French.

> *Here*, blacks are handsome courteous foreigners who dance with our women; *down there*, they are "natives" who are not received in French

families and do not frequent the same public places. *Here* we go to their social gatherings and their balls; *down there* the presence of a black in a cafe of French people would create a scandal. *Here* they play the part of well-off students preparing for bourgeois careers; *down there* it is rare that a native worker is paid 150 Fr. a month. (WS, 2:187–88)

Thanks to black writers, whites could break out of their myopia and see themselves as others saw them. The white reader who identified imaginatively with the experiences described by black writers is made to feel indignant and ashamed and to "demand the liberation of colored people against the white race and against myself insofar as I am a part of it" (WL, 58). Just as Genet enabled his readers to experience their sexual submission and violation as a way to break through their bourgeois values, so the black writer gave the white reader a taste of the experience of oppression, and a realization that every white was complicitous with that oppression. Such black writing might legitimately be pervaded by hatred of whites, Sartre continued, since some hatred was merely a manifestation of the writer's demand for black freedom (WL, 57).

Sartre was especially impressed with Richard Wright's account of his childhood in *Black Boy*, which had been published in 1945. Ironically, this bitter account of the sufferings of a young American black boy presented a dark inversion of the privileged childhood of a young French boy which Sartre himself would later describe in his own autobiography, *The Words*. Just as Sartre saw his childhood as a kind of microcosm of bourgeois life, he saw Wright's childhood as an archetype of black experience. Thus black readers would recognize in Wright's account

the same childhood, the same difficulties, the same complexes. . . . In trying to become clear about his own personal situation, he clarifies theirs for them. He mediates, names, and shows them the life they lead from day to day in its immediacy, the life they suffer without finding the words to formulate their sufferings. He is their conscience and the movement by which he raises himself from the immediate to the reflective recapturing of his condition is that of his whole race. (WL, 73)

Though such statements led Frantz Fanon to criticize Sartre for disregarding the diversity of black experience and acting as though all blacks relived the same mythic pattern of suffering, Sartre was not daunted. The black's function as a reflection of white oppression and a symbol of hope was growing in importance to him.

Sartre's own revulsion at the attitudes of white racists and antisemites fueled his idealization of the otherness of their victims. He described a world populated by vile executioners like the racist Fred and the anti-semite Lucien, and virtuous victims like the nameless black and Jew who suffer at their hands. I have already shown how Sartre's treatment of the Jewish question involved accepting many classic antisemitic stereotypes of Jewish otherness, albeit with his own inverted explanation and endorsement. Sartre likewise maintained his own myth of the black, which consisted of two elements. First, the black represented the perpetual *negation* of Sartre's own white culture as well as freedom from the false stability and security claimed by the white European world. Second, Sartre developed a view of the autonomous core of black experience, which he borrowed and modified from the black writers' category of *négritude*. Colonialism had dehumanized the African by trying to wipe out native traditions, culture, and language. In response, Sartre emphasized a notion of indestructible and indelible blackness, implying that no amount of schooling in white (or any other) culture could ever (or should even try to) erase it.

The French black who claimed to be as much French as black was a victim of the same kind of self-denial and self-alienation that Sartre had seen in the assimilated Jew. Sartre insisted that the core of identity must be rooted in the same quality that is the basis for one's oppression and that is the focus of the dominant group's perception. Jews must first become aware of their difference from non-Jews, and blacks of their difference from whites. For either Jews or blacks, assimilation was ultimately impossible, thought Sartre, since it would require accepting an alien form of thought as one's own and trying to join a world of rampant bad faith. As a result of this rather Manichaean treatment of racial cultures, Sartre believed any attempt at a French-black cultural synthesis would either lapse into bad faith or represent only a temporary form of sabotage aimed at subverting French culture.[7]

Of course, in the case of blacks, assimilation was much less a possibility than for Jews, since their dark skin betrayed them at first glance. Unlike the Jew, who, after all, is "a white man among white men" and can act in bad faith to deny his Jewishness, the black cannot blend into colorless humanity. "He has his back up against the wall of authenticity" (*BO*, 18). This wall of authenticity was predicated on Sartre's insistence that French culture was always an alien and hostile strait-

7. This led to Frantz Fanon's question to Sartre: "What is all this talk of a black people, of a Negro nationality? I am a Frenchman. I am interested in French culture, French civilization, the French people. . . . What have I to do with a black empire?" *Black Skin, White Masks* (New York: Grove Press, 1967), p. 203.

jacket forced on black people, one which polluted the original purity of their existence. Given this assumption, it would be inevitable for Sartre to regard blacks as perpetual outsiders. Repeating the same strategy that had produced *Antisemite and Jew,* Sartre remained on the level of myth or symbol rather than history. Like the Jew, the black's primary mythic function was to embody simultaneously the victimization by, and the negation of, white European culture and the colonialism it supported.

Sartre's idealization of black culture, or negritude, had not been derived from any thorough understanding of the real nature of African culture, its philosophy, literature, or religion. In this regard, Sartre had followed the lead of Aimé Césaire, the black poet from Martinique who had coined the term *négritude.* Césaire had come to Paris to study at Sartre's alma mater, the Ecole Normale Supérieure. At the time Césaire was a student in the 1930s, assimilation into French culture was the only available path for blacks from the colonies who wanted to avoid being "natives" or "niggers" and to make the transition from "barbarian" to "civilized." "And so the best thing one could do for an African was to assimilate him; the ideal was to produce a Frenchman with black skin," Césaire explained.[8] Along with Léopold Senghor, Césaire responded to assimilationism with a demand for a separate black identity rooted in the African culture that colonialism sought to devalue and eradicate. Black identity needed to be grounded in a concrete consciousness of the situation of being a black. Negritude would constitute an ideology of resistance to the hegemonic claims of white cultural superiority. Césaire chose the term negritude as a way of redeeming the derogatory label *nègre,* which was mostly used to refer to African blacks, in contrast to the more assimilated Caribbean blacks who called themselves *noir.*[9]

Sartre followed Césaire's impulse to elaborate negritude as a kind of mythic structure. Césaire, after all, had not grown up in Africa, but rather pieced together a romanticized view of the black continent on the basis of his reading of white authors.[10] Sartre, in turn, absorbed negritude within his larger mythic world of outsiders who resisted the dominant cultural values of French society.

8. "Truer than Biography: Aimé Césaire Interviewed by René Dépestre," trans. Lloyd King, *Savacou,* no. 5 (June 1987):76.
9. A. James Arnold, *Modernism and Negritude* (Cambridge: Harvard University Press, 1981), p. 34. Among French Jews, a similar distinction exists between the derogatory *Juif* and the more assimilated *Israélite.* In *Anti-Semite and Jew,* Sartre discussed how antisemitism insidiously infects some assimilated Jews with antisemitic stereotypes that they see exhibited in *other* less assimilated groups of Jews.
10. Ibid., p. 44.

## The Recovery of Black Selfhood

Despite the fact that Jews, blacks, and women have all been the victims of social oppression, their respective places in Sartre's mythology of the Other were considerably different. Sartre's analysis of negritude in *Black Orpheus* (1948), for example, offered a striking contrast to his understanding of both femaleness (or femininity) and Jewishness. This important essay was prepared as a preface to Senghor's anthology of black poetry from the French colonies. What the black poets were doing, thought Sartre, was trying to undo some of the alienation that they had suffered under French colonial rule and to recover their indigenous sense of self.[11] It was in their quest for self, moreover, that Sartre saw reflected his desire for an authentic identity of his own. Although Sartre opened his essay by including himself among those who stand before the tribunal of black eyes, he clearly wanted to identify himself with black consciousness in some way. When he later writes, "In a word, I am talking now to white men, and I should like to explain to them what black men already know" (*BO*, 16), the narrating "I" has already displaced itself from the white readers. Toward the end of the essay, he confesses that it makes no sense for a white man to explain negritude, "since he has no inner experience of it and since European languages lack words to describe it" (*BO*, 35). Still, Sartre felt authorized to offer just such an explanation, for in some way he felt different enough from other white men to be an exception to his own advice.

In the African poets, Sartre understood the quest to recover the lost sense of authentic selfhood as an Orphic descent into black myths and customs of the past and into the depths of the black collective consciousness. Sartre referred to "primitive rhythms" of the black poets that linked them with their ancestors and that sought to awaken timeless instincts buried within them.[12] The black poet descended below words and meaning to "touch with his feet the black water of dreams and of desire and to let himself drown in it" (*BO*, 31). This black Orpheus[13] searched for the forgotten self from which he had been forc-

11. Sartre eventually criticized the poets of negritude for being too passive, suggesting that they were a form of consolation for the oppressed but failed to take direct revolutionary action. As Third World revolutions occurred, Sartre saw that the need and appeal of negritude had receded (*FI*, 2:176).

12. As Césaire recently explained, "Beyond the social self, one would find a deeper self on which all kinds of layers and ancestral alluvium had been deposited." "Truer than Biography," p. 73.

13. Fanon pointed out the bizarre irony of Hellenizing this search for black roots by transforming the black into the mythological Orpheus. He calls Sartre's essay "a date in the intellectualization of the *experience* of being black" *Black Skin, White Masks*, p. 134.

ibly separated, uncovering his negritude in "the mores, arts, chants, and dances of the African populaces" (*BO*, 29). Sartre supported the recovery and preservation of black culture in a way he had declined to emphasize or allow for Jews. But the central focus of negritude was more than just folkdances and the like. Negritude is not just the awareness of one kind of culture as opposed to another. It is not only the black's antidote to colonization, but also one of Sartre's antidotes to the poison of white culture in general.

As long as blacks were forced to participate in white culture, they became skilled playactors, alienated from themselves; they no longer experienced their negritude in its immediacy, but rather were in exile from their own cultural roots. Black poets were trying to break the stranglehold of white culture which separated blacks from "the swarming of instincts and the indivisible simplicity of Nature" (*BO*, 21). They had to get back in touch with their own blackness. Negritude could help each black restore his unity as a black, "to find death in white culture in order to be reborn with a black soul" (*BO*, 29). Sartre seemed to appreciate the attraction that African spirituality held for poets like Césaire, and he spoke approvingly of the feeling of mystical connection with nature in African culture.

At first, Sartre described negritude as a subjective experience which the white European could neither understand nor describe. It was the authentic inner reality of the black. Negritude, said Sartre, was not "a definite ensemble of vices and virtues, or of intellectual and moral qualities, rather but a certain affective attitude towards the world" (*BO*, 36). In existentialist terms, negritude was the blacks' *fundamental project*, their manner of living, their way of giving meaning to the brute facts of their experience. But negritude also came to represent the power to pierce the superficial crust of white culture and civility. Sartre's support of this concept helped to inspire many of the early struggles for liberation in Africa.

## Sartre's Black Mythology

Sartre's celebration of this resurgence of black selfhood obviously includes a number of stereotypical white notions about blacks, and Africa in general. To the extent that Sartre sought an alternative to European civilization, he looked to Africa and black experience.[14] He saw in

14. Pascal Bruckner, *The Tears of the White Man* (New York: Free Press, 1986), offers an interesting critique of the tendency in leftist European discourse to idealize the wisdom of the "Third World."

them simultaneously a negation of white civilization and a deeper sense of human reality that lay beneath white culture. Africa itself thus becomes a kind of underworld, beneath white civilization, geographically and culturally. Of course, unlike the racist who saw black culture as inferior to European civilization, and Africa in need of being "civilized," Sartre saw black experience as a symbol of the life-forces that European civilization had strangled. Just as he had reclaimed something of value in the stereotypes applied to Jews, Sartre also reversed the negative stereotype that saw natives as subhuman savages, and replaced it with his own positive mythology of a kind of tribal life that was truly in touch with the life-giving power of nature.[15]

It is hard to tell whether it was the black poets or Sartre himself who saw Africa as a primitive jungle that "plunges man back into the seething breast of Nature and at the same time, lifts him above Nature through the affirmation of his right to be unsatisfied" (*BO*, 31). In Sartre's account, the cold sterility of white culture, its customs, and science have built walls to keep blacks from feeling connected to this seething power of nature. The black was a kind of Rousseauian noble savage whom white civilization had violently separated from his land and innate black soul. Civilization has taken people away from the creative, vital source of life. European culture has substituted erudition for the true source of "folkloric inspiration" (*BO*, 30), while the black African remained in "the great period of mythical fecundity" (*BO*, 30) out of which negritude surged forth. One might ask where, besides the black poets, Sartre got his images of Africa. Much of his portrait of African life sounds like the kind of things Lévy-Bruhl described in his earlier *How Natives Think*, which had also influenced Sartre's interpretation of the culture of antisemitism. It is a mixture of sentimental romanticism and anticolonialist protest.

For Sartre, negritude represented more than the ground of black experience. In some way, it was also the inner core of human reality itself, once the veneer of (white) civilization was peeled away. Negritude was human reality before it has been deformed and choked by propriety and civility. The whites, too, had lost touch with their inner roots. Negritude was thus an escape from the prison of white culture. If Africa was the rejuvenating underworld of life instincts in Sartre's

15. There are other traits attributed to the natives to which Sartre reacted in a similar way. Yes, the natives were lazy; it was their form of sabotaging white exploitation. Yes, they stole; it was their resistance to those who stole their country and identity. Yes, they were religiously superstitious; but religious dance, ritual, and spirit possession were defenses against their humiliation and anger (*WE*, 19).

mythic scheme, Western culture was a kind of hellish underworld of suffering. Sartre reverses the traditional sense of white as clean and black as dirty, arguing instead that whiteness represents sterility and blackness the life-force of the earth. Whites need to be liberated from this sterility even more than blacks, he hinted.

Whiteness symbolized a suffocating finish over our natural humanity. In the black person, we could contemplate naked humanity, as it looks without our protective white suits. Sartre said, "Our whiteness appears to us a strange livid varnish that keeps our skin from breathing, white tights worn at the elbows and knees, under which we would find real human flesh the color of black wine if we could remove them" (*BO*, 14). Sartre looked to these black writers to enrich "our old ceremonious culture"; "embarrassed in its traditions and its etiquette, it needs something new; each black who looks for a way to depict himself with our words and our myths is a little fresh blood circulating in this old body" (*PN*, 29). Thus the black offers a life-giving transfusion without which a bloodless white culture will eventually die.

It is clear that Sartre used black and white as symbolic poles of the process of civilization. Whiteness represented what is bland, impotent, colorless, cold, lifeless, and inauthentic. Black represented virility, power, energy, and authenticity. It should, therefore, come as no surprise to find Sartre's description of the black peasant as "the great male of the earth, the world's sperm" (*BO*, 39). He was intimately in touch with nature. He experienced working the land, planting, and eating its fruits each as parts of making love to Nature (*BO*, 39). Sartre also referred to the androgynous balance in the black's link with nature. The "natural Eros" of the black man combined "the dynamic feeling of being an erect phallus, and that softer, more patient, more feminine one of being a growing plant" (*BO*, 40). This is a "spermatic religion" in which "creation is an enormous and perpetual birthing [*accouchment*]" (*BO*, 40). The black man "blends into all of Nature in as much as he represents sexual sympathy with Life" (*BO*, 42). Certainly, this sort of vegetative and sexual imagery is typical in poets like Césaire, though Sartre's sympathetic response to it is uncharacteristic.

White culture, by contrast, offered a desexualized, utilitarian attitude toward the world. The deity of white culture, said Sartre, was a technician or engineer who ordered chaos according to His rational will. Human beings are simply manufactured objects of a divine sculptor. The relation of creator to creature was not, on the whole, a sexual one, in contrast to the black poets for whom "Being comes out of

Nothingness like a penis becoming erect" (*BO*, 40). The white man could only scratch the surface of things, while the black man was linked to the roots of being. He had an instinctive relation to the land. The black was thus a mixture of "timeless instincts, a simple manifestation of universal and eternal fecundity" (*BO*, 46). In short, black culture expresses a deep-felt harmony with nature in contrast to the alienated consciousness of European culture which is constantly threatened by nature and any forms of otherness within it.

The profound link between negritude and the fecund and mystical power of nature was markedly different from Sartre's interpretation of the connection between nature and either Jewishness or femaleness. Although the Jew, like the black, was a victim of oppression and racism, and stood apart from white Christian civilization, Sartre did not see any relation between Jewishness and the power of nature. To be sure, Sartre strongly supported Jewish nationalist aspirations for a homeland and he described the founding of the Jewish state of Israel as "one of the most important events of our times, one of the few these days which let us keep on hoping" (*WS*, 225). But his support for Israel was as a refuge for the victims of antisemitism in Europe and throughout the world. It is hard to know what he thought of the potential impact of Zionism on the structure of Jewish identity insofar as it now offered Jews a mystical tie to the land that had been denied to them elsewhere. In *Antisemite and Jew*, it had been the antisemites who invoked the power of nature and connection to the land to affirm their identity. Sartre had admired the Jews for contesting the unfounded security of those who claim some special link to the soil of their birth. However, the Zionist mythology concerning the nourishing qualities of the land of milk and honey is every bit as powerful as the French antisemites' feelings for French soil and the black poets' connections to the life-giving power of Africa. In order for Sartre to grant what seems to be a legitimate parallel between negritude and Zionism in their attitudes toward the land and nature, he would have to rethink one of the central distinctions he had described between Jews and non-Jews.

There are clearly both parallels and divergences in Sartre's treatment of Jews and blacks. At the time Sartre wrote his treatise on antisemitism, he saw Jewish history as one of exile stretching indefinitely into the past. As a consequence of this exile, Jews have been homeless aliens, severed long ago from any real connection with a land or nature. True, blacks also knew the meaning of exile. Slavery separated blacks from their land, while colonialism separated the land from the blacks who had owned it. But the blacks were different from the Jews in that their link to the land was recent. They had lived freely in their own lands until the more recent developments of American slavery and European colonialism. Indeed, it was the colonialist who destroyed the idea of a sacred relation between natives and their land. Land could be taken by force and used for the alien colonist's own purposes. Against this background, the native's rootedness in the soil was not a manifestation of bad faith, but a form of resistance to white imperialism.

Sartre also handled the fundamental characteristics of Jewishness differently than those of negritude. Given the Jews' long history of exile, Sartre saw the Jewish identity completely as a product of the antisemite's perceptions. He might have comparably argued that negritude is the product of the racist's perception of the black's blackness. But he saw negritude as more than that. Conversely, he could have easily described Jewishness as a form of authenticity struggling against Christian civilization, just as the black struggled against the cultural dislocation produced by Christian colonialism. Like the black, the Jew represented an authenticity underneath white culture. Sartre sometimes implied such a conclusion, despite the fact that his stated position is ambiguous on this point.

When Sartre portrayed women as symbols of fertility and nature, he recoiled from this manifestation of nature. But when he explored the closeness to nature and instinct of the black, he found it more invigorating than fearful. The most likely explanation for this new tolerance, even respect, for nature and fertility has two parts. First, there is a strongly masculine dimension to Sartre's African imagery. When the power of nature is masculinized or at least androgynized, Sartre was better able to identify with it and was less fearful of being swallowed up by it. Second, Sartre's negative associations arise from an image of nature as a plenitude of being lacking the power of transcendence. As such, it is the embodiment of the in-itself, constantly threatening to ensnare the freedom of consciousness. But the fertility theme within negritude plays a different role. As the vulgar yet authentic core beneath white civility, this submersion in the explosive power of nature is indirectly a means of *transcendence* of an inert white culture. In a related image, Sartre described blackness as a phallus expanding in opposition to whiteness (BO, 33). Here, whiteness acquires the negative qualities of femaleness, that which is penetrated and overcome. Thus the different valences attached to nature in Sartre's thought are connected to the way in which nature has been gendered.

Nonetheless, it is still ironic that Sartre's ode to negritude focused on the phallic sexuality of the black, since it is not uncommon for racists to focus on this same issue, often to show that the black is more animal than human. Sartre himself had warned about the temptation to see in the Other one's own unexpressed desire. As in his treatment of the Jew, Sartre simultaneously endorsed a racist association and redefined it as a way to condemn the culture that produced this racism. The sexual potency of negritude is a reminder of the lost potency of a white culture that smothers its true energy beneath the shroud of civility. As Fanon pointed out, negrophobia is rooted in fear of the blacks' purported tremendous sexual powers, the fear that "our women are at the mercy of the Negroes," and feelings of sexual inferiority. Fanon traced this fear to the loss of sexual potency associated with civilization. "The civilized white man retains an irrational longing for unusual eras of sexual licence, or orgiastic scenes, of unpunished rapes, of unrepressed incest." He projects these onto the black, and fears the black accordingly.[16]

Fanon observed that while the antisemite often regards the Jew as an intellectual danger to society, the racist sees the black primarily as a biological danger. To a certain extent, Sartre employed a similar distinction, but transformed it to characterize the positive types of challenge posed by Jews and blacks to European society. On the one hand, the Jews' challenge is an intellectual one, since the Jewish emphasis on a rational approach to human thought and behavior threatens the antisemite's primitivelike mentality and mystical tie to nature. On the other hand, the blacks' challenge is rooted in just such a connection to nature. The creative power of nature that Sartre associated with the people of Africa revealed for him the emptiness of Europe's claims to civilization and the sterility of its technological rationality.

Much of Sartre's writing about blacks came in discussions about colonialism. It was common for the white supporters of colonialism to see Europeans' clothing as a sign of their advanced civilization in contrast to the nakedness of the native. Sartre likewise used the image of *naked* versus *clothed*, but for a rather different purpose. In his preface to Frantz Fanon's *Wretched of the Earth*, Sartre contrasted the reality of the colonies with the bourgeois citizens of the home countries. He

---

16. Frantz Fanon, *Black Skin, White Masks*, pp. 157, 165. Fanon overlooked the fact that antisemitism also created fear of Jews for reasons of sexual and biological threats. Thus Nazis in particular feared what they regarded as both cultural and biological pollution by the Jews.

called attention to the disguises whites used to clothe the truth of colonialism. "In the colonies the truth stood naked, but the citizens of the mother country preferred it with clothes on" (*WE*, 7). At first, certain promising "natives" were brought to the mother country to be "whitewashed." "They were branded with the principles of Western culture; they stuffed their mouths full with high-sounding phrases, grand glutinous words that stuck to the teeth" (*WE*, 7). In time, black writers and poets pointed out the hypocrisy of European humanism that still tolerated racism. The empire now had no clothes to hide the naked truth about it. It is true, perhaps, that Europeans are better attired in grand-sounding rhetoric, but beneath their wardrobe is naked oppression. Sartre admired Fanon for showing the white man naked. What Fanon disclosed was "the strip tease of our humanism. There you can see it, quite naked" (*WE*, 24). In the end, we are left facing two forms of symbolic nakedness: the naked hypocrisy, oppression, and bad faith of the white European *versus* the naked strength and groundedness of the black African.

The newly revealed nakedness of the whites represents a dramatic shift in the dialectic of otherness between black and white. White nakedness becomes visible to the extent that blacks experience the power of their own consciousness. For Sartre, black writers testify to the "look" of this black Other who reveals something crucial about the identity of whites. As blacks rediscover their own eyes and voices, whites realize "the shock of being seen" (*BO*, 13), thus reversing centuries of unidirectional objectification. Traditionally, it is a privilege of the oppressor to see without being seen and to speak without needing to listen, but now the blacks' "quiet and corrosive looks" see right through the whites, and make them "the objects of their speeches" (*BO*, 14). At one time tamed by whites, black eyes are now "wild and free" (*BO*, 14) in their gaze upon their former masters.

The experience of white shame that the "gazes" of black writers produce is not a response to a violation *of* civility, as in the case of Sartre's keyhole peeper, but rather to a violation *by* civility. It is the truth hidden by "humanistic" civility that now comes shamefully to light. As a white Frenchman, Sartre had to accept the part of his identity revealed by the black. To the extent that he could fully appreciate the black's insight, he indicted himself and attempted to experience himself as a European "native." Decolonization shifts the order of who controls the definitions of self and other. "In the past we made history and now it is being made of us" (*WE*, 27). "It's our turn to tread the path, step by step, which leads down to native level. But to become natives altogether, our soil must be occupied by a formerly colonized people and we must starve of hunger" (*WE*, 29). Most of all, to be "native" is to define oneself from the point of view of the Other. It is to be an object: occupied, ruled, enslaved, and studied as Other.

Sartre endorsed Fanon's analysis of the impending collapse of European civilization as it presently conceived itself. There had been a reversal in the relation between European and "native" that was destabilizing traditional assumptions of selfhood. The Third World was finding its own voice and was now speaking of the European as an object, the Other. The revolution of colonial countries would create a radical shift of identities. The natives were once "zombies" to whom the whites did not bother to speak. Soon it would be the natives who would ignore the colonists, not lowering their voices when the latter passed. "Now, at a respectful distance, it is you who will feel furtive, nightbound, and perished with cold. Turn and turn around; in these shadows from whence a new dawn will break, it is you who are the zombies" (*WE*, 13). Although the colonists and the natives have switched roles in this scenario, something is different. For the first time, the natives will show the colonists who they *truly* are to their Other, but it cannot be said that the natives learned who they *truly* were from the colonists, only who they were forced to be. For Sartre, it is always the oppressed and marginal Other who has the power to reveal the truth.

Never one to temper his own rhetorical images, Sartre gave his interpretation of negritude a messianic quality. He emphasized the historic oppression of the black and regarded negritude as a sacrificial "passion." "The black who is conscious of himself sees himself as the man who has taken the whole of human suffering upon himself, and who suffers for all, even for the white man" (*BO*, 42). Of course, this same image has been used to describe the historical experience of the Jews. Sartre saw the black, like the proletariat or the Jew, had a historical mission to fulfill. Out of black people's oppression was born "the sense of revolt and the love of liberty" (*BO*, 47) and their pursuit of liberation for all humanity. Thus negritude represented a lost innocence from the past and a prophetic hope for the future, quite analogous to Judaism's tribal past and messianic vision for the future.

Since white men have tended to see themselves as the standard for talking about Man, they have tended to associate their whiteness with truth, virtue, and "the secret white essence of beings." Sartre countered that, in reality, blackness is at the heart of being, unlike the "undercooked paleness" (BO, 15) of the whites, who lacked any justification for their racial privilege. Negritude is the dialectical negation of white supremacy, a creative destruction or revolution leading to the new synthesis of a raceless society. It symbolized a "colorless nudity" beyond both "white rags" and "black armor" (BO, 50). For the oppressed, becoming authentic first requires affirming themselves in their oppressed identity. But for the privileged it is necessary to remove their identity of white privilege and "to become a part of the totality from which those black eyes exile" them (BO, 15). As Sartre told two young American women, "If you are white and rich you will never think—hear me—think, reason, not just feel like a person who is poor and black."[17]

Although Sartre commended the black's return to negritude as well as the Jew's acceptance of being a Jew, he could not ultimately give much of a definition of either blackness or Jewishness. Instead, both terms can be used to signify the specific expression of existential authenticity for a particular group. Each expression includes a recovery of the past and a vision for the future. Each is both the discovery of what one is as well as a commitment to create one's own identity as a member of the group. It is *experienced* as one's essence but also as what one can never fully be; as what one cannot help being, but also as what one chooses to be. Surely, the tension in all these polarities is something with which all human beings must struggle. As a member of the dominant group, Sartre had no equivalent symbol for his own quest for authenticity. He needed the negation provided by these marginal groups to decenter temporarily the insincere humanism of the majority.

In the end, however, Sartre found relief in the dream of a synthesis beyond negation wherein self and Other would be reconciled. Like the Jew, the black "is walking on this ridge between the past particularism—which he has just climbed—and future universalism which will be the twilight of his negritude; he is the one who looks to the end of particularism in order to find the dawn of the universal" (BO, 51). Like Césaire, Sartre imagined that at some point in the future, in an ideal society, negritude (like Jewishness) would atrophy and disappear.

As African nations became independent in the postcolonial period, the idea of negritude came under attack for ignoring the real differences between black groups.[18] A new generation of French-speaking black

17. Gerassi, *Sartre*, p. 6.
18. After 1960, Césaire's popularity in newly independent African countries dropped quickly, and his own creative spark seemed to dim. Arnold, *Modernism and Negritude*, pp. 261, 269.

African intellectuals rejected Sartre's mythic world of negritude as outdated and dependent on the existence of colonialism. The source of unity of black people throughout the world, they said, was not necessarily a universal core of blackness, but the artificial unity imposed by shared suffering under colonialism. Had Sartre merely transposed his own argument in *Anti-Semite and Jew*—that the antisemite's hostility creates the Jew—to his analysis of blackness, he would probably have agreed that the ideology of blackness is primarily a response to racism. Although Sartre had never intended to endorse a racial or biological notion of negritude like Senghor's, his extravagant elaboration of the black soul led recent critics to accuse him of just this problem.[19] At the very least, observes Henry Louis Gates, Jr., Sartre's lyrical description of "the" African may be in danger of becoming a "racialist" generalization with its own distortions.[20] As Sandra Harding has further explained, the very concept of Africa as a single geographical and cultural unit is problematic, even in discourses of liberation, since "it emphasizes the 'otherness,' the alieness, of the ontologies, epistemologies, and ethics of people of African descent relative to those of people of European descent. It reinforces the contrast paradigm that has been so useful in projects of domination."[21] For this reason, Pascal Bruckner accused Sartre of being an "uncritical and naive Eurocentrist," in spite of Sartre's constant attack on European culture.[22]

Sartre was certainly aware of the kinds of criticism that would later be made of negritude. He warned that even people who proudly or defiantly bear the stigma of being black, Jewish, or homosexual, instead of accepting it in shame, still allow the oppressor to define them. "They continue to view themselves with the concepts and according to the pattern furnished by their persecutors" (SG, 54). The affirmation of one's black identity requires a category that first arose out of colonialist oppression (see *FI*, 2:175), thus "playing the game of the privileged class" (SG, 55).

Nonetheless, in the absence of a world where racial distinctions are drained of destructive power, authenticity requires acknowledgment of

19. Joppa, "Sartre et les milieux intellectuels," pp. 21f; Christopher L. Miller, "Theories of Africans: The Question of Literary Anthropology," in Henry Louis Gates, Jr., ed., *"Race," Writing, and Difference.* (Chicago: University of Chicago Press, 1986), pp. 281–300.
20. Henry Louis Gates, Jr., "Talking That Talk," in Gates, *"Race," Writing, and Difference*, p. 406.
21. Sandra Harding, "Other 'Others' and Fractured Identities: Issues for Epistemologists," in her *The Science Question in Feminism* (Ithaca: Cornell University Press, 1986), Chapter 7.
22. Bruckner, *The Tears of the White Man*, p. 185.

the oppressor's "game." As long as antisemitism and racism continue to flourish, the categories of Jew and black will remain oppressive constructions that cannot be avoided. Negritude, which for Sartre is tantamount to black authenticity, consists of a dual movement: first, an acceptance of one's being black for the Other, especially the Other whose racism has determined part of one's being; and second, a negative movement of resistance to the dominant cultural values that undergird that racism.

These two aspects of authenticity obviously parallel two of the dimensions of human reality described in *Being and Nothingness*. Beyond an acceptance of one's being-for-others, authenticity resembles the negative movement of being-for-itself, the power to detach itself from any given state of being. Negritude is an active principle of nothingness. Like consciousness itself, Sartre associates it with the power of negation, refusal, destruction, and ultimately freedom. On the other hand, the third aspect of Sartre's ontology, being-in-itself, is most often embodied for Sartre by the racist and antisemite who seek to establish essentialist definitions of both themselves and others. Complaints from blacks and Jews that Sartre's analysis pays inadequate attention to the unique cultural qualities of their groups may reflect Sartre's reluctance to admit anything with a stability resembling being-in-itself as a part of authenticity. Yet perhaps the only way for marginal groups to transcend the alternatives of definition by the Other and negation of the Other is to be able to assert some autonomous cultural identity. Albert Memmi points out that Sartre was preoccupied with the *oppression* of blacks and Jews. As a result, "he spoke as White and non-Jewish, and he didn't have to concern himself so much with the positive content of Jewishness or negritude,"[23] nor could he understand how and why one might retain a cultural or ethnic identity once oppression has been eradicated from society.

23. Quoted in Avner Perez, "Sartre, Memmi, et Fanon," *Présence francophone*, no. 35 (1989):106.

# EIGHT

## The Triumph of the Vulgar: Prophetic Religion and the New Community of Brotherhood

"Listen, you're haunted by this terrible regret. You'd like to be black, Jewish, a woman, a commie, and gay all at once. Don't you believe that's a little too much? . . . You have too much ambition." Sartre laughs.[1]
—Roger Stéphane

The bad faith and inauthenticity that permeate so much of modern life are symptoms of a fundamental alienation at the core of our concepts of self. Sartre's life and work raise two interrelated dimensions of this alienation. For those deluded by the extravagant claims of civilization into believing in their own rational autonomy and their distinguished superiority over the natural substratum of human life, the confrontation with vulgarity provides a painful flash of self-awareness. Sartre invites us to renounce the oppressive conditions of civility and to embrace the vulgar sides of ourselves that have been repressed, sanitized, or projected onto others. Not only does the denial of vulgarity result in an alienation from oneself; it has also contributed to a dangerous social alienation as well. The inability to accept our own otherness inevitably spawns social diseases such as antisemitism, sexism, racism, and homophobia.

Sartre realized at an early age that escape from the comfort and privileges of bad faith is very difficult to accomplish. In a sense, it required a reverse alienation from the bourgeois individualism and civility he had imbibed. As a result, Sartre constantly struggled with the

1. Quoted in Jean Cau, *Croquis de mémoire* (Paris: Julliard, 1985), p. 219 (my translation).

paradox of being (or identifying with) what he was not, and not being (or identifying with) what he was. He had exorcised his own negative self-image by projecting it onto the caricature he created of the civilized bourgeois Other. At the same time, he idealized a group of vulgar Others and tried to internalize their perspective as a way of filling the emptiness he found in his own sense of self, to find company among other outsiders. He progressively relied on them to help him define who he was. Simone de Beauvoir wrote: "The true perspective is that of the most disinherited. . . . It was through the eyes of the exploited that Sartre was to learn what he was."[2] And what he wanted to be.

In recent years, feminist theorists such as Carol Gilligan have shown the connection between gender identity and moral decision making.[3] Sartre, likewise, emphasized that ethical authenticity is determined by one's position in society. He saw that morality required a decentering of those in power and a redefinition of the meaning of otherness. Sartre tried to "alter" himself in order to speak critically about oppression. He wanted to appreciate the diversity of subjectivities of those who until now were only objects, looked at but not allowed to look back. As a writer, he had to identify himself with the marginalized perspective of women, Jews, homosexuals, blacks, workers, and all others who collectively symbolized the transcendent power of Otherness. In so doing he hoped to acquire the clearer vision of the marginal Other whose perspective provides an ethical indictment of those in power, that is, a view of a society's ethical "being-for-its-Others."

It is true that in *Being and Nothingness* Sartre presented the "look of the Other" as a perpetual decentering of the stability of the autonomous self. He described the sense of ontological shame that comes from realizing that one is an object for the other. However, the "look" takes on a very different quality when the social situation is factored in. Understood within its social context, the look of the Other performs a moral decentering as well as an ontological one. A "look" grounded in authenticity is one that identifies the oppression of racism, colonialism, antisemitism, and sexism. The "look" of the oppressed Other shows me how I may know myself *as oppressor*. This look reveals to the powerful that their own social position or power is accidental rather than justified or legitimate. From this point of view, Sartre suggested that the shame and fear white male bourgeois Christians may feel from the "look of the Other" is more than a phenomenological curiosity, especially if the

2. Beauvoir, *Force of Circumstance*, p. 7.
3. Carol Gilligan, *In a Different Voice* (Cambridge: Harvard University Press, 1982).

Other were a victim of one's own undeserved inherited power. For the group in power, authenticity requires both acknowledging and questioning the prior inauthenticity that grants privileges for some people but simultaneously oppresses others. Unfortunately, the "respectable" members of society often can see in the rejected and negated members of society only their own rejected and negated choices, the dark side of their own personalities. Gender, race, class are accidents of birth, but to deny the social impact and benefit of these accidents and their consequences for one's subjectivity is a sure sign of inauthenticity.

Sartre realized that his model of existential freedom and authenticity would degenerate into a humanism of bad faith if it did not take into account the power and privilege that diminishes members of some groups as Other. He rejected the notion of universal humanistic ethics based on some general democratic principle of seeing all people as just human beings. Advocates of this kind of humanism, as Roquentin observed in *Nausea*, are in love with abstract symbols and concepts rather than real people. "They all hate each other: as individuals, naturally not as men" (*N*, 158). It is no accident that Sartre places Roquentin's refutation of the Self-Taught Man's empty and presumptuous humanism immediately before Roquentin's encounter with the messy and concrete nakedness of the chestnut tree in the park. If humanism is to have any meaning, it must encounter the concrete nakedness of other people; it must become a "concrete liberalism" that considers all citizens concretely in their situations as Jews, blacks, women, or whatever (*AJ*, 146). This theme has been reiterated in recent "antihumanist" concerns that the discourse of Western egalitarianism might smother the voices of the Other.[4] Even when it was possible, Sartre opposed the assimilation of the minority into the majority's ideas and values, since such identification with the "I" of the majority would require a collapse of authenticity.[5]

The difference between bourgeois humanism and concrete liberalism was the difference between civility and genuine community. While Sartre had once considered the lonely creation of literature and culture to be the only road to "salvation" and "immortality," he was most content when he acted decisively as a member of a group. One of the

4. Gates, "Talking That Talk," p. 408.
5. Derrida's critique of Sartre's humanism in *Being and Nothingness* ("The Ends of Man," pp. 34–35) rests on a one-sided and incomplete picture of Sartre's thought and fails to acknowledge important links between Derrida and Sartre. See Christina Howells, "Sartre and Derrida: Qui perd gagne," *Journal of the British Society for Phenomenology* 13, no. 1 (1982):26–34.

happiest times of his life was his stay at the Ecole Normale when he and his friends "practiced violence" (*SH*, 21). Beneath the violence and practical jokes at the Ecole Normale, what made Sartre most happy was a sense of community, of sharing a common experience. Later, in his *Critique of Dialectical Reason*, Sartre developed this theme of the fusion of isolated individuals into a committed group who were united in brotherhood by their violent revolt against their oppressors.

Sartre had first noticed the difference between genuine social solidarity and the superficial world of bourgeois civility when he was a child. He was impressed with the crude democracy present in the movies. Sartre liked the fact that the movies were not removed from daily life. Movie houses were a place where one could talk, laugh, or eat. Sartre appreciated the unpretentiousness of the movies, the absence of the majesty that accompanied the theater. He found the "total disrespect" people felt toward the movies to be preferable to the elitism and hierarchical society represented by theater. Movies pierced the stultifying traditions of the theater and provided an experience accessible to all.

In time, Sartre came to see the shift in entertainment from theater to movies as a paradigm for the shift from nineteenth-century bourgeois values to postbourgeois modern society. The theater was all pomp and ceremony; the strata of society were replicated in the division of the balconies (*W*, 74). The movies lacked all this. They were the new symbol of "a century without traditions, a century that was to contrast with the others by its bad manners, and the new art, the art of the common man" (*W*, 75). Movies were clandestine, vulgar, egalitarian entertainment, shocking to "serious" people.

> The social hierarchy of the theatre had given my grandfather and late father, who were accustomed to second balconies, a taste for ceremonial. When many people are together, they must be separated by rites; otherwise, they slaughter each other. The movies proved the opposite. This mingled audience seemed united by a catastrophe rather than a festivity. Etiquette now dead, revealed the true bond among men: adhesion. I developed a dislike for ceremonies, I loved crowds. I have seen crowds of all kinds, but the only other time I have witnessed that nakedness, that sense of everyone's direct relationship to everyone else, that waking dream, that dim consciousness of the danger of being a man, was in 1940, in Stalag XII D. (*W*, 76)

On the ruins of civility and social stratification, a society of genuine relation to one another could emerge.

More than the movies, the communal experience of camp life as a prisoner of war marked Sartre deeply. According to Beauvoir, "It taught him the meaning of solidarity; far from feeling persecuted, he took great joy in this participation in communal life."[6] Indeed, Sartre remembered these experiences as models for communal behavior.

> It was a kind of impeccable relationship; day and night, we saw one another, we talked candidly and directly, as peers. There were, as you doubtless know, open toilets. Well, let me tell you, there's nothing quite like going to the toilet in the open, surrounded by your fellow prisoners, for breaking down elitism in whatever form it may exist. . . . This constant physical intimacy, with its constant communication around the clock, was a sign of the kind of communication that existed. (*SH*, 49–50)

Although it would be naive to think that Sartre lost his own sense of superiority in the prisoner of war camp, he did realize that he had something in common with the other inmates. The war caused him to reevaluate his relations with other people. Following the war, he said, "I abandoned my prewar individualism and the idea of the pure individual and adopted the social individual and socialism" (*LS*, 48).

In retrospect, Sartre divided his life into "an anarchistic individualistic part" and a later discovery of the importance of social existence through his experience in prisoner of war camp, the resistance, and liberation.[7] Ironically, it was in the camp that Sartre discovered a different use of theater from what he knew as a child. He wrote and directed the play *Bariona* as a Christmas event for his fellow prisoners. He remembered: "As I addressed my comrades across the footlights, speaking to them of their state as prisoners . . . I suddenly saw them so remarkably silent and attentive, I realized what theater ought to be—a great collective, religious phenomenon" (*ST*, 39). The playwright's challenge is that "he must create his public, he must fuse all the disparate elements in the auditorium into a single unity by awakening in the recesses of their spirits, the things which all men of a given epoch and community care about" (*ST*, 39). When Sartre used terms like "religious" or "spirit" in contexts like these, he rarely attached any theological or metaphysical content to them. Rather he was looking for a way to describe a transcendence of ordinary experience and the possibility of glimpsing a form of social connectedness that broke through everyday civility.

6. Beauvoir, *Force of Circumstance*, p. 5.
7. "An Interview with Jean-Paul Sartre," in Hugh J. Silverman and Frederick A. Elliston, eds., *Jean-Paul Sartre: Contemporary Approaches to His Philosophy* (Pittsburgh: Duquesne University Press, 1980), p. 239.

## Authenticity and the Prophetic Dimension of Religion

Throughout most of his life, Sartre portrayed religion as the epitome of bad faith and as an inauthentic response aimed at blunting human freedom and disguising the oppressive nature of social hierarchies. Yet despite his litany of complaints against religion and his rejection of belief in God, Sartre's attitude was not one of monolithic derision or contempt. Like the traditional theater, religion was morally objectionable to him when it became a system of encrusted rituals and ceremonies, or a doctrine implicated in legitimizing the suffering of society's victims. But Sartre also found himself somewhat attracted to elements in certain religious traditions and concepts that created and celebrated communal existence among equals.

In spite of the cynicism about religion that his Lutheran grandfather taught him, Sartre inadvertently discovered something positive about religion from Charles Schweitzer. Out of the split religious perspective of his family, Sartre emerged with a union of—in his words—"the critical spirit" and "the spirit of submission" (W, 63). While the spirit of submission to empty ritual and outdated doctrine was apparently the dubious legacy of Catholicism, the critical spirit was a valuable fruit of Protestantism. Luther's vulgar side was not lost on Sartre. He seemed to take pride in his grandfather's "coarse gaiety" and table talk, which tended to remind him of Luther (W, 62–63). Sartre appreciated this blunt, even crude, manner of expression. He credited Protestant frankness for this indifference to refinement.

In time, Sartre's criticism of religion developed in a "protestant" direction. Part of the hypocrisy he detected in bourgeois religion was its excessive concern with empty "works" and its lack of inner "faith." Given his attacks on religious ceremony and authority, it is not surprising that Sartre felt more warmly accepted among Protestants than among Catholics. He thought Protestants were more prepared to accept certain of his ideas, such as the inevitable existential solitude to which all human beings were condemned. But solitude and lack of genuine connection were also the inner truth of the bourgeois world he so despised.

As Sartre continued to grapple with the issues of moral and social responsibility, he admitted to being very impressed with the focus in the Protestant Reformation on a person's *total responsibility* before God. Such a religious idea, he thought, might lead to a sense of personal responsibility to and for society.

I believe that this total responsibility to God assumed by man is something truly admirable in Protestant religion—provided that it is really practiced. Consequently, Protestantism—if we are speaking of religion really practiced—seems to me wholly superior [to Catholicism] in this respect. (*CPM*, 295; my translation)

What appealed to Sartre about Protestantism above all else was its egalitarian, prophetic orientation. The power of a prophetic tradition is its focus on the redemption of the oppressed classes of society and its suspicion of wealth and power. It most often arises out of the lower social classes as a criticism of the official religious leaders and organization. In place of hierarchical relations, it emphasizes radical religious fellowship and equality. Sartre saw primitive Christianity as this kind of a communal expression among the oppressed people in the declining Roman empire.

Although the Catholic church represented the kind of hierarchical structure, dogmatic theology, and conservative values that Sartre opposed his whole life, the origin of this mammoth religious institution lay in a young messianic Jewish preacher who had dared to challenge the established hierarchy of his own day. He had broken with social custom in the interest of social change. Whatever the more grandiose claims made about Jesus, it is easy for all to agree that his ministry extended itself to the most marginal, disenfranchised members of his society, including those who might seem vulgar and repulsive to others. It was from this group of people that he sought to build a community based on acceptance and love of the Other. Even when Christianity later served as the ideology of an oppressive class, the subversive elements of Jesus' original message eventually helped to undermine it (*CPM*, 83).[8]

In short, Sartre clearly recognized that religion could serve as more than just a legitimation of an exploitative social and political structure. It could also be a powerful expression of revolutionary energy for which there was no other form of expression in certain periods of history. In the sixteenth century, for example, a religious framework was inescapable. Sartre recalled:

What struck me when I was studying the Reformation was that there is no heresy to which some form of social unrest is not, basically, the key, but it is

---

8. For an interesting application of Sartre's categories of analysis in the *Critique of Dialectical Reason* to the ministry and teachings of Jesus, see Roberta Imboden's *From the Cross to the Kingdom: Sartrean Dialectics and Liberation Theology* (New York: Harper and Row, 1987).

expressed in an ideology appropriate to the times. The Cathars, the Anabaptists, the Lutherans, and the rest are invariably some oppressed group seeking to express itself, but doing so in a religious form, because the age would have it so. (*ST*, 228)

Such religious expression by the oppressed led him to admire the Reformation idea that "every man is a prophet" more than the humanistic idea of the Enlightenment regarding the equality of all people. "This thesis of an absolute religious value that every man has for all men prompted me to prefer the Reformation, and especially the peasant prophets of those days, to all other historical situations and figures."[9] In the image of a "peasant prophet," Sartre once again found the vulgarity of the marginal and disempowered who alone had the unclouded vision to see the truth and communicate it with openness and honesty.

Historical moments of dramatic social and religious upheaval provided Sartre with material for at least two explicitly religious plays: *Bariona*, the Christmas play he wrote for his fellow inmates when he was a prisoner of war during World War II; and *The Devil and the Good Lord*, a play set around the time of the Reformation, which he wrote several years after the war. In both plays, the negative and positive possibilities of religion are presented. In the first play, the character Bariona is a Jewish leader, despondent over the sufferings of his people, yet cynical about their simple-minded superstition when they flock to worship the newborn Christ child. He chides them: "So all it takes is some boozed-up shepherds running across some half-cracked guy in the hills who drivels Lord knows what nonsense about Christ's coming for you to be drooling for joy and throwing your hats in the air?" (*WS*, 2:196). Yet Bariona, like Sartre, eventually can conceive a way of seeing Christ's mission that even he can accept. Christ the existentialist redeems mankind from suffering by showing that a person is not identical to his suffering. "Whatever you do and however you look at it, you surpass it infinitely; because it means exactly what you want it to. . . . Christ came to teach you that you are responsible for yourself and your suffering" (*WS*, 2:129–30). The play ends as Bariona leads his men in revolt against the overwhelming power of the Romans.

The original kernel of Christianity, therefore, is the same sort of corrosive power as that with which the forms of otherness eat away at the congealed structures of civilized society. For Sartre, the true nature of the spiritual as originally developed in the "Christian Revolution" was

9. Quoted in Liselotte Richter, *Jean-Paul Sartre*, pp. 86–87.

"a negativity, a contestation, and a transcendence, a perpetual construction, beyond the realm of nature, of the *anti-natural* city of
freedoms" (*WL*, 83). Unfortunately, this dynamic potential of the spiritual to reflect the perpetually renewed experience of all people was
quickly lost within a system of hierarchical elites.

In *The Devil and the Good Lord*, religious belief is presented, on the
one hand, as a feeble facade which cannot really respond to the problems of the people. The role of the church in the period preceding the
Reformation and the Peasant Wars was in opposition to the needs of the
poor. As in *Bariona*, it is still Rome that oppresses the people. Heinrich
the priest has been corrupted by the demands of the Church and
alienated from the people.

> Heinrich is a poor parish priest in the sixteenth century, raised by the
> Church, admitted to the priesthood, placing all his faith and his whole
> loyalty in the Church. But because of the situation of the Church in
> sixteenth century Worms, he falls into a dilemma: if he sides with the poor,
> he betrays the Church, but if he sides with the Church, he betrays the poor.
> (*ST*, 229)

The character Nasti, on the other hand, is both an advocate for the poor
and still religious. "Nasti would be the revolutionary, but because he is
living in the sixteenth century, he has a religious dimension. He therefore calls himself a prophet; in another age, he would have founded a
political party" (*ST*, 228). Nasti speaks of the church as "the community
of men" (*DGL*, 20), and proclaims: "All men are brothers and equals"
(*DGL*, 54). Such prophets, whom Sartre regarded as crucial to the
historical evolution of society, were the religious embodiment of dialectical negativity. They undermined society's acceptance of unjustifiable
social and religious distinctions.

Thus, Sartre opposed the priestly religion which takes refuge in the
conservative values of family, authority, hierarchy, but he was sympathetic to the kind of prophetic perspective that was committed to the
revolutionary ideals of liberty, equality, fraternity. Like other incarna-
tions of the vulgar Other, the prophet provided Sartre with an image of
revolutionary transcendence. The figure of the prophet is the kind of
outsider with whom Sartre could identify and whose role Sartre might
assume as a way of escaping from the priestly bourgeois identity he had
inherited.

In his theory of a literature of engagement, Sartre managed to redefine the job description of his own literary profession in terms that

would make him partner with the prophet and revolutionary. His ideal writer maintains the principle of negativity that is necessary for permanent revolution. The primary task of the writer is the "spiritualization" of the world (WL, 158). "Spiritualization," to Sartre, meant the constant renewal of society's structures, liberation from any rigidified order that has taken root, and a project for a future order. The spiritual dimension to which Sartre referred is not "otherworldly" in the traditional sense of reference to a supernatural realm. On the contrary, the writer confronts what is real—"the raw, sweaty, smelly, everyday world" (WL, 158)—and judges it in light of the possibilities of the future. Nonetheless, the utopian vision of the Sartrean writer is "Otherworldly" in a different sense. It represents the perspective one gains from the *world of the Other*, that is, one which envisions the transformation of the present structures of society.

## Sartre's Final Years and the Infamous Last Interviews

Sartre's uneasy relation with his body became acute in the final decade of his life. While his health was slowly declining, it was the loss of his eyesight in particular that had the most profound effect on his life. For a fiercely independent man like Sartre, the most practical consequence of blindness was a much greater dependence on others. It also meant that the major pillar of his identity was destroyed: he could no longer read or write. Sartre's illness was the final revenge of his body, now an opaque obstacle rather than a transparent vehicle for thought and action.

At first, Sartre attempted to understand aging in a similar way to how he had described Jewishness thirty-five years earlier. He denied that he had any internal sense of being old. Rather, being old meant being treated as an old person by other people. He told his young Jewish friend Benny Lévy, "I understand, from the others, what old age implies to those who watch it from the outside. . . . The fact that I am old for the other is to be old" (TH, 163). Sartre had discovered the form of otherness that all people may eventually experience. We see the aged as *other* to insulate ourselves from our own mortality. In Sartre's case, blindness made him, both literally and metaphorically, the passive object of others' objectifying looks, an Other to everyone.

Sartre also was aware of a gradual dissolving of his sense of self. He no longer had the same clear sense of "a synthesis of myself which should make one single man" (A, 432), or the continuity he had been able to see in his life earlier between what he had been as a young man and what he had become thirty or forty years later. When interviewed by Michel Contat at the age of seventy, Sartre expressed his distaste for old people. They repeat old ideas, and lose their freshness. Sartre preferred the company of younger people to keep him from becoming ossified.

During the seven years of Sartre's blindness, a young Maoist radical named Benny Lévy became deeply involved in Sartre's life.[10] Lévy was a combination of secretary, companion, collaborator, and disciple. Despite the fact that Sartre had never pursued or spoken very highly about friendships with men, Lévy seemed an attractive figure. He knew Sartre's philosophy well and could help Sartre retrieve parts of his own oeuvre that Sartre himself had forgotten; he was politically astute and engaged in political activism; and he had a little of the "feminine qualities" Sartre appreciated, such as being able to take a detour from "the main subject" to observe the little details in the world around him (A, 36). Lévy came dutifully to Sartre's apartment every day during this period to read to Sartre, to discuss ideas with him, and to work on a joint project that would spell out a political and moral vision for the future. Lévy's youthful energy and intellectual intensity seemed to stimulate and rejuvenate Sartre.

Sartre's relationship with Lévy is the subject of considerable controversy among those who knew Sartre during his final years.[11] Simone de Beauvoir led most of the old Sartreans in regarding Sartre's attachment to his project with Lévy as a pathetic effort to feel productive and useful after the loss of his sight. In Lévy, Sartre had found hope for the future. Lévy took Sartre seriously, albeit in his own contentious and abrasive way. If it is true that the Other teaches who one is, Sartre liked what he learned from Lévy more than what he learned from the looks of his older colleagues.[12] As an old man, Sartre had acquired the vulgarity of the aged that emerges as civility's mastery over the biological processes of the body begins to crumble. Some of his old friends found it difficult to have discussions with him and were embarrassed that this intellectual

---

10. Benny Lévy had gone under the name Pierre Victor while he was a Maoist, but had changed back to his original name during the time he was rediscovering his Jewish identity. Simone de Beauvoir's reluctance to recognize his new name in any of her accounts of this period probably reflects her own feelings about the religious change in him that produced the name change.

11. For a fuller account of this controversy, see Cohen-Solal, *Sartre: A Life*, pp. 488–519, and Ronald Hayman, *Sartre: A Biography* (New York: Simon and Schuster, 1987), pp. 438–75.

12. Sartre's earlier comments might easily apply to this situation: "If I am told that I am intelligent and witty or dull-witted and coarse this information refers to the effect I produce on others. To be witty, for example, is to entertain a well-defined social set in conformity with certain rules" (SG, 32).

giant could not eat without dropping food in his lap.[13] Beauvoir grew embarrassed when Sartre's loss of bladder and bowel control resulted in wet spots on his clothes or chair and soiled pants (A, 34, 66–67, 90–91). Though Sartre seemed indifferent or resigned to these accidents, Beauvoir was distraught. "It is horrible, your body betraying you while your mind is still sound" (A, 91). Whatever new thoughts Sartre may have had in his final years are overshadowed by Beauvoir's obsessively detailed reports of his humiliating physical decline.[14]

Lévy, however, ignored all this in the pursuit of their joint project. To Sartre's old companions, now staid and aging themselves, Lévy was an intellectual mugger. They dismissed any changes in Sartre's thought as merely the weakness of an old man unable to resist the pressure of a "merciless," "relentless" opportunist. Raymond Aron, who had had virtually no contact with Sartre for thirty years, took it upon himself to pronounce that the voice and thought of his *petit camarade* was not to be found in the conversations with Lévy. Ironically, Aron's complaint was not that the apparent shifts in Sartre's ideas were preposterous. On the contrary, he was sympathetic to Sartre's reconsideration of the role of violence, the nature of Jewish culture, and other issues. But Aron located Sartre's genius and imagination in his extremes and his mistakes. He insisted that *the old Sartre* would never have said what *old Sartre* said.[15]

In the recent so-called authorized biography of Sartre, John Gerassi, a member of the old "family" of Sartreans, guards the party line on the Lévy affair. Gerassi insists that the last two years of Sartre's life were dominated by "weird alliances" and opportunists who manipulated Sartre for their own purposes, even putting words in his mouth. In particular, he describes Lévy as a "fanatic, diminutive, warlord" and a "fake disciple" who claimed that Sartre "was really a Jewish philosopher all along." However, Gerassi's account of this matter is undermined by its own inner inconsistencies. In a conversation with Sartre during this period of allegedly weakened mental alertness, Gerassi asked Sartre if he had "renounced the dialectic and found God." While this is not at all what Lévy had ever claimed, Sartre replied that whatever he said to people like Lévy was all a game: "I tell them what they want to hear," laughed Sartre. At a time when people were not so interested in his work anymore, Sartre said he would do anything to "get people to read me,"

13. Cohen-Solal, *Sartre*, p. 501.
14. See Alain Buisine, "Les Mots et les morts," in Claude Burgelin, ed., *Lectures de Sartre* (Lyon: Presses Universitaires de Lyon, 1986), pp. 18–20.
15. Aron. *Memoirs*, pp. 452–55, 456–57.

even if it meant claiming that he had been influenced by the Talmud, Kabbala, or Koran.[16] On the one hand, Gerassi seems to be asking that the almost daily conversations with Lévy be dismissed as the manipulation of an enfeebled Sartre, while his own conversation in 1979 be privileged as one of Sartre's "rare moments of lucidity" and "amazing perspicacity." On the other hand, if we accept the lucidity and sincerity of this conversation, we would have to conclude that far from being manipulated, Sartre himself was an incredible opportunist and manipulator who was using people like Lévy to gain new audiences. Moreover, in assuming that he had special access to the "true Sartre," Gerassi never acknowledged that he, too, might be among those to whom Sartre told what they wanted to hear. Sartre was aware of the distress of his old circle over his relation with Lévy and may have responded to Gerassi in a way that he thought might defuse the situation a bit.

The center of the Sartre-Lévy controversy erupted with the publication of a three-part interview between Sartre and Lévy in early 1980, just months before Sartre's death in April of that year.[17] Sartre's old crowd from the journal he had founded, *Les Temps modernes*, lobbied Jean Daniel, the editor of *Le Nouvel observateur*, not to publish it. But Sartre himself called Daniel later to insist that it be published in full. The voice Daniel heard on the telephone was clear and forceful. Sartre was not only lucid; he knew the contents of the interview by heart.[18]

Simone de Beauvoir was especially enraged by this affair, and she reacted like both a spurned lover and the mother of a disobedient child. Up to this point she had paid little attention to Lévy's work with Sartre, never attending their discussions or asking Sartre much about them. In this case, once she and Sartre finally did discuss the manuscript, they quarrelled without reaching any agreement. She began to cry and threw the manuscript across the room. The explosion over this interview opened a rift in their relation that was little discussed between them thereafter. From her point of view, she explained much later, Sartre had painted himself into a corner out of foolish—almost senile—pride.

> Sartre persisted in his position because we were all against him. He persisted out of weakness. He had to shield himself behind some false strength and,

16. Gerassi, *Jean-Paul Sartre*, pp. 22–24, 20, 158, 22–23.

17. Benny Lévy, "Today's Hope: Conversations with Sartre," *Telos*, Summer 1980, pp. 155–96. Although the interviews with Lévy are commonly considered Sartre's last published words, there was one short additional interview with Sartre that was published in April 1980 in *Le gai pied* and translated as "Jean-Paul Sartre: The Final Interview," *Christopher Street*, July–August 1980, pp. 32–37.

18. Cohen-Solal, *Sartre*, p. 514.

since he was weak and broken, he had to flaunt it as much as possible. On the other hand, since he was no longer himself, he was doing all this on Victor's instigation. What Sartre never realized, and particularly not in those last discussions, is that Victor had pushed him to go against himself, to betray himself. He was completely blind to that. . . . So, since he was unable to judge things with an open mind, and could not trust himself, he stiffened: he had staked a lot on Victor, and he refused to see that he had been wrong. He thought I refused to follow his lead, he thought I failed to understand him. He thought I wanted to manipulate him, with the others at *Les Temps Modernes*, whereas, in fact, he was being manipulated by Victor and Arlette—to whom Victor had shrewdly gotten close after the crisis of 1978. He was terribly torn by this and did not want to face the truth.[19]

Nevertheless, the truth is not as easy to see as Beauvoir believes, nor are her own hands totally clean. Is it really fair to say that Sartre had simply become a dummy to Lévy's clever ventriloquist's act? Had Lévy cleverly taken on Arlette as a coconspirator to plant false ideas in Sartre's mind? Had Lévy edited the interview to make Sartre seem to believe things that he did not?[20]

Clearly, the publication of the Lévy interview was symbolic of something more, both to Sartre and to Beauvoir. It must be understood not only in terms of the ideas expressed in it, but also in terms of what it reflected about Sartre's relationships with Benny Lévy and to a lesser extent with Arlette Elkaim-Sartre.

First of all, the interview came out during a period when Sartre had not been heard from much. With his death shortly thereafter, this discussion became the last thoughts that the world would read of the great Jean-Paul Sartre, his final verdict on his own life work. Justifiably or not, it acquired a different stature, therefore, from the scores of other interviews Sartre had given throughout his life. But it is not as obvious that the nature and quality of the interview are so alien to Sartre as to lend credence to Beauvoir's "brainwashing" theory. Indeed, there are interesting new ideas that Sartre presents that cannot simply be dismissed as "flat rhetoric, sluggish thought, weak argument,"[21] or somehow un-

---

19. Ibid., p. 515.
20. It is interesting to note that Herbert Spiegelberg, writing *before* Beauvoir's attack in *Adieux* was published, found the Sartre-Lévy interviews to be not only an authentic extension of Sartre's thought, but also the basis for seeing Lévy as "Sartre's last 'hope' for his philosophical heritage." See "Sartre's Last Word on Ethics in Phenomenological Perspective," in Simon Glynn, ed., *Sartre: An Investigation of Some Major Themes* (Aldershot, England: Avebury, 1987), pp. 40–46. Though Lévy has certainly failed to fulfill such hope, Beauvoir's public denunciation did little to help his reputation.
21. Cohen-Solal, *Sartre*, p. 518.

becoming of Sartre, as old acquaintances of Sartre like Raymond Aron contended. Quality control in Sartre's interviews was always a bit spotty, and his moments of brilliant lucidity were sometimes interspersed with naive or banal pronouncements.

What most disturbed Beauvoir and other Sartreans about the interviews was Sartre's sympathetic view of certain religious themes. Beauvoir could only explain this kind of thinking as the influence of Lévy, who had in fact changed a great deal since Sartre first met him. She reminds us that "Like many other former Maoists [Lévy] had turned toward God—the God of Israel, since he was a Jew. His view of the world had become spiritualistic and even religious. Sartre jibbed at this change of direction" (A, 119). Once Lévy and Arlette Elkaim-Sartre began to study Hebrew together, Beauvoir feared the aging Sartre had come under the power of fanatical Jews. Although there is much that is questionable about Beauvoir's account of the alleged manipulation of Sartre by these Jewish conspirators, there is another factor that must be remembered. She had never shared Sartre's own fascination with the reality of being Jewish. What cannot be denied, however, is that this fascination had existed long before Sartre had met either Benny Lévy or Arlette Elkaim-Sartre, and it had little to do with Sartre's consistently atheistic position.

In fact, Sartre did nothing to repudiate his lifelong atheism in the interview. Nevertheless, he had long appreciated the power of religious *imagery* to express his ideas and had studied the work of historians, anthropologists, and sociologists of religion such as Eliade, Lévy-Bruhl, Mauss, and Durkheim.[22] He had already established a long history of appropriating such material for his own purposes.

Beauvoir's relation to religion was much less ambivalent than Sartre's, and her atheism apparently made such use of religious imagery seem hypocritical. When she published her own version of the last decade of Sartre's life in 1981, she included more than one form of response to this aspect of the Lévy interview. The narrative of Beauvoir's "farewell" to Sartre comprises only about a quarter of the volume in which it is published. The remaining four hundred pages are a series of interviews she had with Sartre in 1974. This was the only unpublished text of Sartre over which she retained control. The effect of this volume is to discredit the Lévy interview directly in the first part and to then

22. I have discussed a number of the religious images and themes throughout Sartre's work in my *Meaning and Myth in the Study of Lives: A Sartrean Approach* (Philadelphia: University of Pennsylvania Press, 1984).

bury it beneath a mountain of newly published interviews. As Terry Keefe accurately notes, Beauvoir displayed a "rigid determination to hang on to her own particular image of Sartre," as well as her privileged status in his life.[23]

Beauvoir's account of the Sartre-Lévy interview appears near the end of the narrative section that culminates with a description of Sartre's death, followed immediately by her preface to the Beauvoir-Sartre interviews. This preface provides an implicit comparison between Lévy's efforts and her own. On the one hand, she admitted that Sartre had sometimes been tired and had given poor answers to her questions, which she confessed had sometimes been silly. Consequently, she had chosen to omit the parts that she found uninteresting. Surely, this was the same problem that Lévy must have had. A published interview is rarely an exact transcript of the spoken conversation. On the other hand, Beauvoir wanted to establish that she respected Sartre's thought in a way that Lévy had not. Granting that she had edited the interviews, she also insisted that they preserved the spontaneity of Sartre's thought, including some of its ramblings and contradictions. "I was afraid of distorting Sartre's words or of taking away their finer shades of meaning. The conversations do not reveal any unexpected aspects of him, but they do allow one to follow the winding course of his thought and to hear his living voice" (A, 131). This, then, implied Beauvoir, is the authentic voice of Sartre, the one that does not offer religious surprises. She refused to consider that there might in fact be several authentic Sartrean voices, depending on when and with whom he was speaking.[24]

Although the last words of Sartre in Beauvoir's interviews are anything but religious, it is also true that this ending resulted either from Beauvoir's prompting during the original conversation, or—much less likely—her editing after the fact.[25] The natural ending for the interviews was Sartre's feelings about the approach of death. Sartre expressed a deep satisfaction with his life, an acceptance of his death, and his own

23. Terry Keefe, *Simone de Beauvoir: A Study of Her Writings* (Totowa, N.J.: Barnes and Noble, 1983), p. 65.
24. Cf. ibid., p. 70.
25. Although Beauvoir criticized Lévy's interviews for leading Sartre so much as to be manipulative, her own interviews are hardly free of interviewer "influence." As Deirdre Bair comments on them: "They are direct, personal, and honest, but they are also sentimental and redundant. . . . Beauvoir does prompt too much; she is peremptory in other places, instructing and correcting him as to what he really means with any number of answers to her questions; frequently, she cuts him off when she does not want to delve deeper into a subject that he appears happy to expound upon further." *Simone de Beauvoir: A Biography* (New York: Summit Books, 1990), p. 573.

narrative closure: "So when I die I shall be content. Displeased at dying that particular day rather than ten years later, but content. And up until the present, death has never weighed upon my life and probably it never will. It is on those words that I should like to end this chapter" (A, 433). Rather than ending the interview at this natural point, however, Beauvoir pushed Sartre further so as to leave no doubt about his final position on religion. The appearance of these earlier interviews a year after the Sartre-Lévy interviews could only reinforce the impression that any religious ideas later attributed to Sartre must have been planted by someone else. Significantly, the published ending of Beauvoir's interviews deals with the same issue of brotherhood that would come up in the Lévy interview, but totally and explicitly disengaged from any religious symbolism. Sartre told Beauvoir, "I don't need God in order to love my neighbor. It's a direct relation between men and man; I don't have to deal with the infinite at all" (A, 444). The two of them then agree that they have lived happily without paying any attention to the idea of God or talking much about it (A, 445).

Beauvoir had her own complex personal reasons for diminishing the importance of both Arlette and Lévy. After a lifetime of looking the other way in relation to Sartre's affairs with women, she had now to contend with his two Jewish "children." Sartre had adopted Arlette and thereby placed her in line as his legal heir and literary executor.[26] Lévy represented something worse than a rival lover. He gave Sartre intellectual stimulation in a way that Beauvoir had done earlier in Sartre's life. He had a relationship with Sartre that she neither shared in nor understood. Beauvoir's relationship with Lévy had already been poisoned several years earlier in a quarrel that erupted over a piece Lévy and Sartre had written about the Israeli-Palestinian situation. To Beauvoir, this piece of work was not only sloppy, but also another case of Lévy's alleged manipulation of Sartre. From then on, Beauvoir and Lévy stopped speaking and avoided each other. Beauvoir remarked, "Up until then, Sartre's real friends had always been mine, too. Victor [Lévy] was the only exception. . . . I was sorry that from then on, a part of Sartre's life was closed to me" (A, 111).

Arlette recalled Sartre had been very hurt and disappointed by Beauvoir's opposition, particularly since she had never attended or shown

26. According to Gerassi, Sartre said he had legally adopted Arlette because "he needed someone to keep distributing the royalties to the five women, all former lovers, whom he kept (including Elkaim herself), long after Castor too would be dead; and it was a perfect, courteous way of ending his sexual relationship with Elkaim without hurting her pride." *Jean-Paul Sartre*, p. 158.

any interest in his conversations with Lévy.[27] She simply rejected them outright without any way of judging what Sartre's state of mind might have been at the moment. Arlette had been at some of these interviews and pointed out that, if anything, Lévy had come to understand the evolution of Sartre's thought better than Sartre understood or remembered it himself.[28]

Within Beauvoir's charge that the Sartre in these interviews "was no longer himself" lay a bitter Sartrean paradox. Sartre had spent a lifetime saying that existential authenticity required some form of disconnection from who one had been and what one had thought. He regularly contradicted and repudiated positions he had previously taken. Nor were the Sartre-Lévy interviews the first time Beauvoir had complained that he was thinking un-Sartrean thoughts. Twenty years earlier she found herself bewildered by Sartre's work on *The Critique of Dialectical Reason*, which appeared to abandon some of the existentialist ideas they had shared in the era of *Being and Nothingness*. "He was moving into realms of philosophy that were—they were simply *not Sartre*."[29]

To say that Sartre *was not* being Sartre meant precisely that Sartre *was* being Sartre. As well-known Sartrean, Francis Jeanson, explained:

> In the last ten or so years before his death, Sartre's entourage, the Family, wanted to keep a certain image of him that was not the authentic Sartre, which was the Sartre who was constantly, all the time, in the process of becoming something new. . . . This bothered the Family, because their need was to hold him frozen, preserved as the Sartre he had been, the one they wanted him to be. But he eluded them; he was constantly slipping away.[30]

The person who can sincerely say "I now think what I thought before," or "I am what I used to be," has slipped into bad faith. For Sartre, to be authentic means perpetually to transcend oneself. I am never what I am, because my consciousness is something other than that of which I am conscious. Apparently, Sartre's fondness for "calling himself into question" and "thinking against himself" had its limits in the eyes of Beauvoir and others. The theoretical position of existentialism confronted the uncertainty of old age's toll on the mind. Beauvoir, the person whom Sartre had once called "authentic without trying" (WD, 336) had once more assumed the role of the Other who presumed to define Sartre for himself. She was now claiming that the "essence" of Sartre was nowhere to be found in his relation with Lévy. Of course,

27. Charmé, "Sartre's Jewish Daughter," pp. 28–29.
28. Cohen-Solal, *Sartre*, 501.
29. Quoted by Bair, *Simone de Beauvoir*, pp. 513, 516.
30. Quoted in ibid., p. 515.

there is no "essence" of Sartre, and all assumptions about the "real" Sartre's identity, be it existentialist, Marxist, post-Marxist or whatever, are founded on errors of thought.

The truth is that we can never resolve this controversy, nor can a few interviews radically alter the overall impact of Sartre's work. Whatever the deficiencies of the final interviews, however, they remain suggestive in relation to a number of the issues we examined in Sartre's earlier work.

The interviews reflected the consequences of his quarter-century relationship with Arlette and his shorter relationship with Lévy. Through them he began to move from a view of the Jews purely as victims, and to an appreciation of something else called Jewishness. When Sartre visited with Israeli Jews in the midsixties he discovered that while Jews might not agree upon exactly what comprised Jewish tradition, it did have a reality apart from antisemitism. He came away thinking: "I did not know what Jewish tradition was, but I did know that most of the Jews who were there were deeply attached to something—we would have needed much longer to bring out what that something was, but all the same it was a tradition." Sartre realized that it was attachment to this tradition that held together the Jewish people despite the contradictory ideas of different Jews, and he was deeply impressed by the "will to preserve the historical tradition in its deepest sense" that he observed in young Israeli Jews. [31] By the 1960s, Sartre had had ample opportunity to get to know Jews in a different way than he had before the war (*TH*, 126–27). His acknowledgment of certain inadequacies in his earlier theoretical position on the Jews was an honest reappraisal, not "a remorseful recantation" or apology forced out of him by Lévy, as some have claimed. [32]

Lévy's discussions, moreover, had introduced him to certain prophetic elements of Judaism, especially its moral critique of the existing structures of society. Sartre also learned about a religious tradition of deliberate distance from political power and the status quo: rabbinic Judaism. The exclusion of the Jews from genuine political power throughout European history enabled Judaism to maintain its moral independence with less danger of compromise. This was the perspective of the Other that Sartre believed was indispensable to move the morality of society forward.

Although Sartre acknowledged that Christianity was the tradition

31. "Jean-Paul Sartre in Israel: Impression and Opinions," *New Outlook* 10, no. 4 (May 1967):17–18.

32. For example, Bair, *Simone de Beauvoir*, p. 580; Hayman, *Sartre*, p. 471.

that his historical circumstance had provided him, he insisted that his feelings about the nature of morality and the future of mankind were closer to that of a this-worldly Judaism than an otherworldly Christianity. He liked the Jewish idea of "an end to this world and the appearance at the same time of another one, another world that will be made from this one but where things will be organized differently" (*TH*, 179). He was impressed by "the finality toward which every Jew moves more or less consciously, but which is ultimately supposed to reunite humanity" (*TH*, 179). For a number of years already, Sartre had been dissatisfied with Marxism. Indeed, he had told an interviewer in 1975, "I am no longer a Marxist."[33] Sartre appreciated the messianic rhetoric of Judaism as an alternative way to envision the forward progress of history.

There can be no mistaking Sartre's remarks for a theistic conversion of any kind. Nor was Sartre claiming in any sense to have discovered a hidden Jewish influence on his thought. Rather, what he found in his study of Judaism with Lévy was a parallel utopian vision of a new society based on the realization of what it means to be truly "human." In the Jewish idea of the messianic age, Sartre could see an approximation of his own vision for the advent of a new ethical existence for human beings, with each person existing for the other. At that moment, morality will have been incorporated into our thoughts and feelings. Sartre here echoed the ideas of Biblical prophets like Jeremiah as much as the early Marx.

As Lévy presented it to him, Jewish messianism also offered a religious counterpart to Sartre's own ideas of "revolution." Sartre agreed that the fundamental problem in social change was not simply economic, as the Marxists argue, but required a moral transformation of human relationships that could be "best conceived as a kind of Messianism" (*TH*, 179). In its own way, the exilic experience of the Jews had produced a culture that anticipated much of Sartre's own demand for a revolutionary break with the present state of society and a time when the suffering and oppressed groups of this society would be liberated. Only then would an authentic humanism be possible.

Sartre realized that the utopian changes he envisioned would require social relations to be based on a bond more basic than simply sharing the rights of citizenship and civil coexistence. He demanded a deeper bond, "the relationship of brotherhood [*fraternité*]" (*TH*, 170). As a

33. Quoted in Hayman, *Sartre*, p. 467.

model for this relationship, Sartre reached back even further into religious history. Here Sartre introduced a discussion of primitive totemism. It would be hard to see Lévy's influence here, since he reacted
rather uncomfortably to Sartre's move in this direction, repeatedly
badgering Sartre and contesting the value of such mythological imagery
to express this point. Sartre suggested that what linked the members of
primitive tribes in a relationship of brotherhood was their experience of
common descent from the tribe's totem animal. "This is what must be
recovered today, because it was a true brotherhood; it was a myth,
perhaps, in one sense, but it was also a truth" (*TH*, 171).

Unlike Freud, who had also studied primitive totemism, Sartre did
not see the totem as a symbol of the power and authority of a dictatorial
father. Indeed, he rejected Lévy's suggestion to see brotherhood as the
idea that we are all *sons* of a single *father*, the mythic basis of the
patriarchal religions of the West. On the contrary, he insisted that the
primordial sense of brotherhood or kinship in primitive tribes is rooted
in the pre-Oedipal idea of birth from a common womb. To be members
of the same species is to share the same parent, to be born of the same
mother (or totem animal) who engenders them all. Religious myths
arose, said Sartre, to give expression to this sense of common origin. To
bring about a future recovery of the sense of brotherhood will mean to
reexperience this attachment through a common mother, that is, to
achieve a sense of solidarity rooted in a sense of global family.

This experience may be the next dialectical stage beyond the brotherhood based on the oath of violence described in the *Critique of Dialectical Reason*. That earlier form of brotherhood arose out of a unified
revolt against the oppressors who refused to recognize one's humanity
and who defined one as Other. Since revolutionary brothers came
together in a kind of Oedipal revolt against the paternalistic power of
society, it was not surprising that Sartre saw the bonds between them as
totally self-generated. He wrote: "We are brothers insofar as, following
the creative act of the pledge, we *are our own sons*, our common
creation" (*CDR*, 437). Whatever bonds of love existed among these
revolutionary brothers, their sense of fraternity was expressed mainly in
an indirect way, through their shared violence against the group's
enemies and traitors.

However, Sartre clearly had an inkling of another kind of brotherhood. Jeannette Colombel notes that the posthumously published
*Cahiers pour une morale* sees brotherhood as an ancient link between
people, thousands of years old. It is based on acceptance of otherness as

the highest moral value. In his conversations with her, Sartre often grappled with finding a foundation for morality not based merely on a rational principle of obligation. It was brotherhood that offered this foundation. Although the sharp differences and heterogeneity that characterize people clash with the idea of equality, Colombel continues, the idea of brotherhood supposes it. Difference is acknowledged and embraced. This kind of brotherhood does not arise out of the violent revolt of the oppressed, but rather from the bond of tenderness linking mother and child. From the mother's first look at her child, we can learn the attitude of unconditional acceptance that makes brotherhood possible.[34] Sartre demonstrated great sensitivity to the power of the mother-child relation in his analysis of Gustave Flaubert, where he wrote: "In order to love life, to wait each minute for the next with confidence, with hope, one has to have been able to internalize the Other's love as a fundamental affirmation of the self" (FI, 1:392). This appreciation of one's unique value in the earliest period of life will lay the foundation for all subsequent relations with the Other.

What Sartre seemed to be groping for as the symbolic foundation for renewed human relationships is what many feminists have rediscovered in the image of the goddess, and others in what is being called "postmodern spirituality."[35] With the powerful image of a female totem like this, humanity might begin to transcend the divisions of self and other, or create a relational model of self with more fluid boundaries. Sartre explained:

> All of us are brothers in the clan inasmuch as we are born of the same woman, who is represented by the totem. They are all brothers in the sense that all are born from the womb of woman; and at that point the individuality of the woman is not a question. She is simply a woman, with the womb that will engender, the breasts that will nourish, the back that perhaps will carry. This mother can just as easily be a totemic bird. . . . When I see a man, I think: he has the same origin as myself, like me he comes from Mother Humanity, let's say, Mother Earth as Socrates says, or Mother. (TH, 171)[36]

34. Jeannette Colombel, *Sartre* (Paris: Librairie Générale Française, 1985–86), pp. 739–43.
35. Catherine Keller, "Toward a Postpatriarchal Postmodernity," in David Griffin, ed., *Spirituality and Society: Postmodern Visions* (Albany: SUNY Press, 1988), pp. 63–80. Please note that I am not ascribing any *theological conversion* whatsoever to Sartre; I am merely calling attention to the addition of a powerful new *religious metaphor* to the long list of other religious images that he had used throughout his life.
36. In *War Diaries*, Sartre had already considered, albeit somewhat critically, the idea of universal womb as the "final dialectical avatar of the idea of human species" (WD, 27).

We can only speculate about the direction Sartre might have taken this idea, and it is certainly not without its problems. The figure of an anonymous mother defined by womb and breasts alone is still far from correcting stereotypical associations to woman. Still, if Jewish messianism offers a way to imagine social and ethical progress in this world, then perhaps this goddesslike figure might offer a symbolic model with which to reclaim the goodness of nature, women's bodies, and our connections to each other. The physicality of the image can keep us focused on the "raw, sweaty, smelly everyday world" (WL, 158) where change must be born. Sartre's image of the womb as our shared connection is a welcome change from his earlier view of women's bodies as slimy, devouring holes.

Most exciting about Sartre's allusion to the image of an engendering mother goddess is its potential for helping to build a model of cooperation between self and other. For a long time, Sartre's search for connection with the Other was crippled by a model of the self based on the male experience of separation from the original attachment to the mother, and transcendence of one's origins.[37] This same model of selfhood produced Sartre's radical individualism. The totally free individual was also totally alone, living in constant dread of the objectifying power of the Other. It is no wonder that Sartre reported never feeling fondness for a man his own age (with one exception in his youth) or desiring an affective connection with one (A, 280). Sartre's reconsideration of the concept of family as a model for human relations was now leading him to a new understanding of self and other. Perhaps the sense of peoplehood among the Jews, their residual "tribal" self-image, impressed him in a similar way.

In *Being and Nothingness*, Sartre described God as "the concept of the Other pushed to the limit" (BN, 326). As such, the concept of God represents the inevitable alienation that comes from being unable either to know or control the part of oneself that appears to the Other. The only solution to this dilemma is to dismantle the wall that separates self and other. At the time of *Being and Nothingness*, Sartre saw this effort as futile and the universal "desire to be God" as doomed to failure, since it was tantamount to a desire to be simultaneously self and other. The concept of the goddess as developed by many contemporary feminists refers not to any metaphysical or supernatural entity, but to a metaphor

37. See Linda Singer, "Interpretation and Retrieval: Rereading Beauvoir," *Women's Studies International Forum* 8, no. 3 (1985): 231–38.

for a nondualistic attitude toward other people and toward reality itself. It was in this spirit that Sartre saw this image as an alternative to the polarized world of *Being and Nothingness*.

The qualities that Sartre idealized among the inhabitants of the margin were the ones he thought necessary for a new form of social existence. The spontaneity, sensitivity, vitality, and other traits that drew him to Jews, women, and other outsiders needed to be developed in all people. He proposed that eventually Others would cease to be threatening once they were encountered in a spirit of "transparency."

> I think that what spoils relations among people is that each keeps something hidden from the other, something secret. . . . I think transparency should always be substituted for what is secrecy. I can imagine the day when two men will no longer have secrets from each other, because no one will have any more secrets from anyone, because subjective life, as well as objective life, will be completely offered up, given. (*LS*, 11)

The rise of the bourgeoisie in Europe had been marked by a greater focus on the inner workings of the self. As the idea of a private realm of the self became established, the protection of that realm through a carefully defined system of public behavior also appeared. Sartre complained that our concern with the private has destroyed our feelings of solidarity in anything but a superficial sense of civility. He lamented, "The bourgeoisie imprisons us within the cocoon of private life and defines us, with snips of the scissors, as *individuals*, which means, as molecules without history who drag themselves from one instant to the next" (*S*, 223).

Civility's preoccupation with honor and fear of shame has only kept people from revealing themselves. The true revolutionary must strip away the rules and conventions that preserve the differences between those in power and those not. The way to disarm the look of the Other is to bask in it nakedly. "A man's existence must be entirely visible to his neighbor, whose own existence must be entirely visible in turn, before true social harmony can be established" (*LS*, 13). Perhaps the absence of totally frank discussion between people is the result of distrust and fear, but Sartre may also have underestimated the difficulty of penetrating the opaque face of otherness and achieving this ideal of transparency.

The circumstances of the last interview present a useful metaphor for the struggle for identity that persisted throughout Sartre's life. He found himself accused of not being who he had always been to his old friends, of speaking as a "we" with one young North African Jew, and seeming to be someone he could never really have been, a father of another North

African Jew. Thus Benny Lévy and Arlette Elkaim-Sartre offered Sartre something that Simone de Beauvoir could never give him.[38] Beauvoir came from the same bourgeois background that he himself had fled. In addition, their youth offered Sartre a link to a new generation.

It is true that Sartre had resisted any fathers and the authority they represented. A psychoanalyst had told him that the original title of *The Words*—*Jean-sans-terre*—really meant *Jean-sans-père*. At the end of that book, Sartre said he still felt like a man without a ticket on the train. But it is the train episode he had written for Freud[39] that seems more appropriate for the last decade of Sartre's life. Maybe he did not have a ticket and no one was waiting for him at his destination, but he thought a young companion who had read his works could make the ride more enjoyable. Maybe, like Freud, he realized it was time for him to be a father after all, not simply out of a narcissistic desire for immortality,[40] but out of a sense of caring for the next generation.[41]

Early on, one of Sartre's loyal followers, Francis Jeanson, identified the importance of the theme of bastardy in Sartre's work. The bastard represents the person who has been *othered* rather than *fathered* by society. Of course, Sartre was not literally a bastard, nor even—strictly speaking—an orphan. Rather he was a totally legitimate and accepted child who made himself into a bastard by rejecting his inherited identity as false. In this sense, Sartre hoped to reveal the "fundamental bastardy" of every person.[42] He once described himself as a "false bastard" and certainly saw himself as someone who did not, or perhaps refused to, belong. It was a way for him not to be who he was and to identify with other outsiders. Born a respectable bourgeois, white, male, Christian, European, he felt alienated from all that that meant. The idea of bastard is a negative identity: I am *not* someone's son. Sartre thus developed an identity based on affirming who he was not. He was the non-Jew who adopted Jews, the male who felt a woman inside him, the white who understood what it meant to be black, the old man who hung out with thirty-year-olds. This was the only way for him to escape accepting who he was: a bourgeois, white, male, European intellectual.

Out of the devalued identities of the vulgar Other, Sartre was able to

---

38. Arlette said that he had been both pleased and amused to have a Jewish daughter though he could not quite explain why. Charmé, "Sartre's Jewish Daughter: An Interview," p. 26.

39. See Chapter Four, above.

40. Just as his own aging grandfather had seen his survival in his grandson Jean-Paul, so, too, the now-aging grandson may have seen the same thing in Lévy.

41. Sartre himself was unwilling to admit that his relation with Lévy had any "father-son sentiments" (*LS*, 78).

42. Frances Jeanson, *Sartre* (Paris: Seuil, 1975), pp. 6–7.

piece together a model of personal authenticity and a vision of authentic human community. In the end, religious *metaphors* provided the best expression for some of his thoughts about authenticity. To begin to catalogue the elements in Sartre's mythology of authenticity would require mention of the prophetic messianism of the Jews; the sense of brotherhood grounded in the primitive image of the mother-goddess that might be a way out of dualisms of subject/object and public/private; the vibrant beat of African tribal religion that drowned out the sound of white culture and reconnected one to nature and sexuality; the "saintliness" of Genet's attack on the bourgeoisie. Such metaphors do not constitute a roadmap to authenticity, but merely glimpses and hints. To the extent that Jews, women, blacks, homosexuals and others approached the heroic resistance necessary for authenticity, they acquired mythic significance and came to express a path to genuine community, one where the Other is brother.

Of course, one should not get carried away with Sartre's invocations of religious imagery. Certainly, he never altered the conclusions he reached while waiting for a bus when he was eleven. The concept of God as a palpable supernatural force still seemed old-fashioned at best and alienating at worst. In either case, it was hardly worth arguing about. A feisty Sartre once told a Catholic priest, "You are mistaken when you accuse me of being *against* God: how could one be against what does not exist? I am *without* God and I'm proud of it" (WS, 1:149). To the end, Sartre maintained that the social dangers of religion still threatened to undermine the very utopian visions of brotherhood for which he dimly realized religion could also provide the most potent symbols.

Ultimately, Sartre left the record of his own life as a symbol of the quest for authenticity. Earlier in his life, using another religious image, he admitted that he had not achieved authenticity himself. He wrote in his journal: "I'm not authentic, I have halted on the threshold of the promised lands. But at least I point the way to them and others can go there. I'm a guide, that's my role" (WD, 61). More importantly, perhaps, Sartre tried to point the way *out* of our enslavement to bad faith and our futile work on the pyramids of civility. The security of "Egypt" constantly tempts us to return while the reality of the promised land is endlessly deferred. For now, at least, authenticity is found in the restless movement between these two worlds.

The itinerary of Sartre's life was a search for new ways to relate to himself and to others. He challenged the assumptions that underlie the oppression of various groups as Other, and celebrated the vitality to be found in the vulgar and marginalized parts of our own lives as well as those groups whose identities have been vulgarized and marginalized. While it is apparent that Sartre's own mind was conditioned by the influence of his culture, class, and race, his valiant attempt to free himself from such roots remains noteworthy. The mental habits of bad faith do not disappear easily. After their exodus, a whole generation of Jews needed to wander the desert between Egypt and the promised land, so that those whose minds had been formed in slavery would pass. Sartre, too, wandered in that territory in between, and like the Jews, he looked out upon a "promised land" in which groups with other cultures and languages must ultimately have a share.

Throughout his life, Sartre left a trail of unfinished projects, and it is possible, even likely, that his new suggestions about the possibility for authentic relations with others would never have received any definitive exposition, even if he had lived longer. Nonetheless, Sartre continues to point in challenging directions and it may be worthwhile to explore where they lead. As Gilles Deleuze has said in the epigraph with which this book began, Sartre was neither the beginning nor the end of something, but was always engaged in the middle. His sense of commitment never wavered, even when he was wrong, yet he was also not afraid to change his course, even up until the very end. As time goes on, people may return to Sartre and find that his search for authenticity still remains—at the very least—a breath of fresh air.

# BIBLIOGRAPHY

## Works by Jean-Paul Sartre

*The Age of Reason.* Translated by Eric Sutton. New York: Vintage Books, 1973.

*Anti-Semite and Jew.* Translated by George J. Becker. New York: Schocken Books, 1965.

*Baudelaire.* Translated by Martin Turnell. New York: New Directions, 1950.

*Being and Nothingness: An Essay in Phenomenological Ontology.* Translated by Hazel E. Barnes. New York: Philosophical Library, 1956.

"Black Orpheus." *Massachusetts Review* 6 (1964–65): 13–52.

*Cahiers pour une morale.* Paris: Gallimard, 1983.

"The Childhood of a Leader." In *Intimacy.* Translated by Lloyd Alexander. New York: Berkley Medallion Books, 1960.

*The Condemned of Altona.* Translated by Sylvia and George Leeson. New York: Vintage Books, 1960.

"A Conversation about Sex and Women with Jean-Paul Sartre." *Playboy,* January 1978.

*Critique of Dialectical Reason.* Translated by Alan Sheridan-Smith. London: NLB, 1976.

*The Devil and the Good Lord: Nekrassov; Kean.* New York: Vintage Books, 1960.

*The Emotions: Outline of a Theory.* Translated by Bernard Frechtman. New York: Philosophical Library, 1948.

"Existentialism Is a Humanism." In *Existentialism from Dostoevsky to Sartre.* Edited by Walter Kaufmann. Cleveland: Meridian Books, 1969.

*The Family Idiot.* 3 vols. Translated by Carol Cosman. Chicago: University of Chicago Press, 1981–89.

*The Freud Scenario.* Edited by J.-B. Pontalis, translated by Quintin Hoare. London: Verso, 1985.

"La Gauche, le désespoir, et l'espoir: Entretien avec Jean-Paul Sartre." *Le Matin* (supplement), no. 843, 10–11 Nov. 1979, 3–5.

*L'Idiot de la famille.* 3 vols. Paris: Gallimard, 1971–73.

*Imagination: A Psychological Critique.* Translated by Forrest Williams. Ann Arbor: Ann Arbor Paperbacks, 1972.

"Interférences: Entretien avec Simone de Beauvoir et Jean-Paul Sartre. *Obliques*, nos. 18–19 (1978).

"An Interview with Jean-Paul Sartre." In *Jean-Paul Sartre: Contemporary Approaches to His Philosophy*. Edited by Hugh J. Silverman and Frederick A. Elliston, 221–39. Pittsburgh: Duquesne University Press, 1980.

"Jean-Paul Sartre: A Candid Conversation with the Charismatic Fountainhead of Existentialism and Rejector of the Nobel Prize." *Playboy*, May 1965.

"Jean-Paul Sartre: The Final Interview." *Christopher Street*, July–August 1980, 32–37.

"Jean-Paul Sartre et Michel Sicard: Entretien." *Obliques*, nos. 18–19 (1979): 9–29.

"Jean-Paul Sartre in Israel: Impression and Opinions." *New Outlook* 10, no. 4 (1967): 14–23.

"Jean-Paul Sartre on His Autobiography." Interviewed by Oliver Todd. *The Listener*, 6 June 1967, 915–16.

*Lettres au castor, 1926–1939.* Paris: Gallimard, 1983.

*Life/Situations: Essays Written and Spoken.* Translated by Paul Auster and Lydia Davis. New York: Random House, Pantheon Books, 1977.

*Literary and Philosophical Essays.* Translated by Annette Michelson. New York: Collier Books, 1977.

*Mallarmé, or The Poet of Nothingness.* Translated by Ernest Sturm. University Park: Pennsylvania State University Press, 1988.

*Nausea.* Translated by Lloyd Alexander. Norfolk, Conn.: New Directions, 1964.

*No Exit; The Flies; Dirty Hands; The Respectful Prostitute.* New York: Vintage Books, 1949.

Preface to *The Wretched of the Earth*, by Frantz Fanon. New York: Grove Press, 1968.

"Présence noire." *Présence africaine*, no. 1 (Nov.–Dec. 1947): 28–29.

*Psychology of the Imagination.* Translated by Bernard Frechtman. New York: Washington Square Press, 1966.

*The Reprieve.* Translated by Eric Sutton. New York: Alfred A. Knopf, 1959.

*Saint Genet: Actor and Martyr.* Translated by Bernard Frechtman. New York: New American Library, 1963.

*Sartre by Himself.* Translated by Richard Seaver. New York: Urizen Books, 1978.

*Sartre in the Seventies: Interviews and Essays.* London: Andre Deutsch, 1978.

*Sartre on Theater.* Edited by Michel Coutat and Michel Rybalka, translated by Frank Jellinek. New York: Pantheon Books, 1976.

*Search for a Method.* Translated by Hazel E. Barnes. New York: Vintage Books, 1968.

*Situations.* Translated by Benita Eisler. Greenwich, Conn.: Fawcett Publications, Inc., 1965.

"Today's Hope: Conversations with Sartre." *Telos*, Summer 1980, 155–96.

"To Show, To Demonstrate." Interviewed by Madeleine Chapsal. *Yale French Studies*, no. 30 (Winter 1962–63): 30–44.

*The Transcendence of the Ego: An Existentialist Theory of Consciousness*. Translated by Forrest Williams and Robert Kirkpatrick. New York: Noonday Press, 1957.

*The War Diaries of Jean-Paul Sartre*. Translated by Quintin Hoare. New York: Pantheon Books, 1984.

*What Is Literature?* Translated by Bernard Frechtman. New York: Harper and Row, 1965.

*The Words*. Translated by Bernard Frechtman. New York: George Braziller, 1964; reprint, Greenwich, Conn.: Fawcett Publications, 1969.

*The Writings of Jean-Paul Sartre*. Vol. 2, *Selected Prose*. Edited by Michel Contat and Michel Rybalka. Evanston, Ill.: Northwestern University Press, 1974.

## Works about Sartre

Barnes, Hazel E. "Beauvoir and Sartre: The Forms of Farewell." *Philosophy and Literature* 9 (April 1985): 21–40.

———. *Sartre and Flaubert*. Chicago: University of Chicago Press, 1981.

Beauvoir, Simone de. *Adieux: A Farewell to Sartre*. New York: Pantheon Books, 1984.

Bell, Linda A. *Sartre's Ethics of Authenticity*. Tuscaloosa: University of Alabama Press, 1989.

Buisine, Alain. *Laideurs de Sartre*. Lille: Presses Universitaires de Lille, 1986.

Burgelin, Claude, ed. *Lectures de Sartre*. Lyon: Presses Universitaires de Lyon, 1986.

Cau, Jean. *Croquis de mémoire*. Paris: Julliard, 1985.

Caws, Peter. "Flaubert's Laughter." *Philosophy and Literature* 8 (October 1984): 167–79.

Charmé, Stuart. "From Maoism to the Talmud (with Sartre along the Way): An Interview with Benny Lévy." *Commentary* 78, no. 6 (1984): 48–53.

———. *Meaning and Myth in the Study of Lives: A Sartrean Approach*. Philadelphia: University of Pennsylvania Press, 1984.

———. "Sartre's Jewish Daughter: An Interview." *Midstream* 32, no. 8 (1986): 24–28.

Cohen-Solal, Annie. *Sartre: A Life*. New York: Pantheon, 1987.

Collins, Margery L., and Christine Pierce. "Holes and Slime: Sexism in Sartre's Psychoanalysis." *Philosophical Forum* 5 (Fall/Winter 1973): 112–27.

Colombel, Jeannette. *Sartre*. 2 vols. Paris: Librairie Générale Française, 1985–86.

Cranston, Maurice. *Jean-Paul Sartre*. New York: Grove Press, 1962.

Danto, Arthur. *Jean-Paul Sartre*. New York: Viking Press, 1975.

Davies, Howard. *Sartre and "Les Temps Modernes."* Cambridge: Cambridge University Press, 1987.

Derrida, Jacques, "The Ends of Man." *Philosophy and Phenomenological Research* 30, no. 1 (1969): 31–57.

―――. "An Interview with Derrida." In *Derrida and Differance*. Edited by David Wood and Robert Bernasconi, 71–82. Evanston, Ill.: Northwestern University Press, 1988.

Erickson, John. "Sartre's African Writings: Literature and Revolution." *L'Esprit Créateur* 10, no. 3 (1970): 182–96.

Flynn, Thomas R. *Sartre and Marxist Existentialism*. Chicago: University of Chicago Press, 1984.

Gerassi, John. *Jean-Paul Sartre: Hated Conscience of His Century*. Chicago: University of Chicago Press, 1989.

Glynn, Simon, ed. *Sartre: An Investigation of Some Major Themes*. Aldershot, England: Avenbury, 1987.

Hayman, Ronald. *Sartre: A Biography*. New York: Simon and Schuster, 1987.

Howells, Christina. "Sartre and Derrida: Qui perd gagne." *Journal of the British Society for Phenomenology* 13, no. 1 (1982): 26–34.

Imboden, Roberta. *From the Cross to the Kingdom: Sartrean Dialectics and Liberation Theology*. New York: Harper and Row, 1987.

Irele, Abiola. "A Defense of Negritude." *Transition* 3, no. 13 (1964): 9–11.

Jeanson, Francis. "Hell and Bastardy." *Yale French Review*, no. 30 (Winter 1962–63): 5–20.

―――. *Sartre*. Paris: Seuil, 1975.

―――. "Sartre et le monde noir." *Présence africaine*, no. 7 (1949): 1–27.

Joppa, Francis A. "Sartre et les millieux intellectuels de l'Afrique noire." *Présence francophone*, no. 35 (1989): 7–28.

La Capra, Dominick. *A Preface to Sartre*. Ithaca: Cornell University Press, 1978.

Leak, Andrew N. *The Perverted Consciousness: Sexuality and Sartre*. New York: St. Martin's Press, 1989.

Le Doeuff, Michele. "Simone de Beauvoir and Existentialism." *Feminist Studies* 6, no. 2 (1980): 277–89.

Lévy, Benny. "Sartre et la Judéité." *Études Sartriennes II–III, Cahiers de sémiotique textuelle* 5–6 (1986): 139–49.

Marks, Elaine. "The Limits of Ideology and Sensibility: J. P. Sartre's *Réflexions sur la question juive* and E. M. Cioran's *Un Peuple de solitaires*." *French Review* 45, no. 4 (1972): 779–88.

McMahon, Joseph H. *Humans Being: The World of Jean-Paul Sartre*. Chicago: University of Chicago Press, 1971.

Molnar, Thomas. *Sartre: Ideologue of Our Time*. New York: Funk and Wagnalls, 1968.

Pacaly, Josette. *Sartre au miroir*. Paris: Librairie Klincksieck, 1980.

Perez, Avner. "Sartre, Memmi, et Fanon." *Présence francophone*, no. 35 (1989): 83–115.

Poster, Mark. *Existential Marxism in Postwar France: From Sartre to Althusser*. Princeton: Princeton University Press, 1975.

Prince, Gerald. "L'Odeur de la nausée." *Esprit créateur* 17, no. 1 (1977): 29–35.

Pucciani, Oreste F. "Sartre, Ontology, and the Other." In *Hypatia*. Edited by William M. Calder III, Ulrich K. Goldsmith, and Phyllis B. Kenevan. Boulder: Colorado Associated Press, 1985.

Richter, Liselotte. *Jean-Paul Sartre*. New York: Frederick Ungar Publishing Co., 1970.

Rosenberg, Harold. "Does the Jew Exist?: Sartre's Morality Play about Anti-Semitism." *Commentary* 7 (January 1949): 8–18.

Schroeder, William Ralph. *Sartre and His Predecessors: The Self and the Other*. London: Routledge and Kegan Paul, 1984.

Silverman, Hugh J., and Frederick A. Elliston, eds. *Jean-Paul Sartre: Contemporary Approaches to His Philosophy*. Pittsburgh: Duquesne University Press, 1980.

Smoot, William. "The Concept of Authenticity in Sartre." *Man and World* 7 (May 1974): 135–48.

Stern, Alfred. *Sartre: His Philosophy and Existential Psychoanalysis*. New York: Delta Books, 1969.

Sungolowsky, Joseph. "Criticism of *Anti-Semite and Jew*." *Yale French Studies* 30 (1963): 68–72.

Theunissen, Michael. *The Other*. Translated by Christopher Macann. Cambridge: MIT Press, 1984.

Walker, Margaret. "The Nausea of Sartre." *Yale Review* 42 (Winter 1953): 251–61.

Watteau, M. "Situations raciales et condition de l'homme dans l'oeuvre de Jean-Paul Sartre." *Présence africaine*, no. 2 (January 1948).

## Other Works

Adam, Barry D. *The Survival of Domination: Inferiorization and Everyday Life*. New York: Elsevier, 1978.

Arendt, Hannah. *The Human Condition*. Chicago: University of Chicago Press, 1958.

Arnold, A. James. *Modernism and Negritude*. Cambridge: Harvard University Press, 1981.

Aron, Raymond. *Memoirs*. New York: Holmes and Meier, 1990.

Bair, Deirdre. *Simone de Beauvoir: A Biography*. New York: Summit Books, 1990.

Bakan, David. *The Duality of Human Existence*. Boston: Beacon Press, 1966.

Baudelaire, Charles. *Flowers of Evil and Other Works*. New York: Bantam Books, 1964.

Beauvoir, Simone de. *Ethics of Ambiguity*. Secaucus, N.J.: Citadel Press, 1975.

———. *Force of Circumstance*. 2 vols. New York: Harper and Row, 1977.

———. *Memoirs of a Dutiful Daughter*. New York: Harper and Row, 1959.

———. *The Prime of Life*. New York: Harper and Row, 1976.

———. *The Second Sex*. New York: Bantam, 1970.

Becker, Ernest. *The Denial of Death*. New York: Free Press, 1973.

Berger, Peter. *The Noise of Solemn Assemblies*. Garden City, N.Y.: Doubleday, 1961.

———. *The Precarious Vision*. Garden City, N.Y.: Doubleday, 1961.

Bloch, Maurice, and Jean H. Bloch. "Women and the Dialectics of Nature in Eighteenth-Century Thought." In *Nature, Culture, Gender*. Edited by Carol P. MacCormack and Marilyn Strathern. Cambridge: Cambridge University Press, 1980.

Brown, Norman O. *Life Against Death: The Psychoanalytic Meaning of History*. Middletown, Conn.: Wesleyan University Press, 1971.

Bruckner, Pascal. *The Tears of the White Man: Compassion as Contempt*. New York: Free Press, 1986.

Césaire, Aimé. "Truer than Biography: Aimé Césaire Interviewed by René Dépestre." Translated by Lloyd King. *Savacou*, no. 5 (June 1987).

Clor, Harry. *Obscenity and Public Morality*. Chicago: University of Chicago Press, 1969.

Corbin, Alain. *The Foul and Fragrant: Odor and the French Social Imagination*. Cambridge: Harvard University Press, 1986.

Cuddihy, John Murray. *No Offense: Civil Religion and Protestant Taste*. New York: Seabury Press, 1978.

———. *The Ordeal of Civility: Freud, Marx, Lévi-Strauss, and the Jewish Struggle with Modernity*. New York: Basic Books, 1974.

Eliade, Mircea. *Cosmos and History*. New York: Harper, 1959.

Elias, Norbert. *The History of Manners*. New York: Pantheon Books, 1978.

Elshtain, Jean Bethke. *Public Man, Private Woman*. Princeton: Princeton University Press, 1981.

Emerson, Ralph Waldo. *The Complete Works of Ralph Waldo Emerson*. New York: Houghton, Mifflin, 1904.

Fanon, Frantz. *Black Skin, White Masks*. New York: Grove Press, 1967.

———. *The Wretched of the Earth*. New York: Grove Press, 1968.

Freud, Ernst L., ed., *Letters of Sigmund Freud*. New York: Basic Books, 1975.

Freud, Sigmund. *Autobiographical Study*. New York: Norton, 1963.

———. *Civilization and Its Discontents*. New York: Norton, 1962.

———. *The Interpretation of Dreams*. New York: Avon Books, 1970.

————. *Jokes and Their Relation to the Unconscious*. New York: Norton, 1963.

Gates, Henry Louis, Jr., ed. *"Race," Writing, and Difference*. Chicago: University of Chicago Press, 1986.

Gilligan, Carol. *In a Different Voice*. Cambridge: Harvard University Press, 1982.

Gilman, Sander L. *Difference and Pathology: Stereotypes of Sexuality, Race and Madness*. Ithaca, N.Y.: Cornell University Press, 1985.

Goffman, Erving. *Stigma: Notes on the Management of Spoiled Identity*. Englewood Cliffs, N.J.: Prentice-Hall, Inc. 1963.

Gramont, Sanche de. *The French: Portrait of a People*. New York: Bantam Books, 1969.

Groethuysen, Bernard. *The Bourgeois: Catholicism vs. Capitalism in Eighteenth-Century France*. New York: Holt, Rinehart and Winston, 1968.

Harding, Sandra. *The Science Question in Feminism*. Ithaca: Cornell University Press, 1986.

Hocquenghem, Guy. *Homosexual Desire*. London: Alison and Busby, 1978.

Hyman, Paula. *From Dreyfus to Vichy: The Remaking of French Jewry, 1906–1939*. New York: Columbia University Press, 1979.

Keller, Catherine. "Toward a Postpatriarchal Postmodernity." In *Spirituality and Society: Postmodern Visions*. Edited by David Griffin. Albany: SUNY Press, 1988.

Laing, R. D. *Self and Others*. Baltimore: Penguin, 1969.

Lévy-Bruhl, Lucien. *The "Soul" of the Primitive*. New York: Frederick A. Praeger, 1966.

Lynd, Helen Merrell. *On Shame and the Search for Identity*. New York: Harcourt, Brace and World, Inc., 1958.

Memmi, Albert. *Portrait of a Jew*. New York: Orion Press, 1962.

Millett, Kate. *Sexual Politics*. New York: Avon Books, 1971.

*The Complete Essays of Montaigne*. Translated by Donald M. Frame. Stanford: Stanford University Press, 1958.

Moore, Barrington, Jr. *Privacy: Studies in Social and Cultural History*. Armonk, N.Y.: M. E. Sharpe, Inc., 1984.

Nietzsche, Fredrich. *The Gay Science*. Translated by Walter Kaufmann. New York: Random House, 1974.

————. *On the Genealogy of Morals*. New York: Vintage Books, 1969.

Oring, Elliot. *The Jokes of Sigmund Freud: A Study in Humor and Jewish Identity*. Philadelphia: University of Pennsylvania Press, 1984.

Ortega y Gasset, Eduardo. *The Revolt of the Masses*. New York: Norton, 1932.

Ortner, Sherry. "Is Female to Male as Nature Is to Culture?" In *Woman, Culture, and Society*. Edited by M. Rosaldo and L. Lamphere. Stanford: Stanford University Press, 1974.

Renaud, L.-P. *Notions Pratiques de politesse, de tenue, et de savoir-vivre*. Paris: Charles-Lavauzelle and Co., 1952.

Robert, Marthe. *From Oedipus to Moses: Freud's Jewish Identity*. Garden City, N.Y.: Anchor Books, 1976.

Ross, Andrew, ed. *Universal Abandon? The Politics of Postmodernism*. Minneapolis: University of Minnesota Press, 1988.

Ruether, Rosemary Radford. "Home and Work: Women's Roles and the Transformation of Values." *Theological Studies* 36 (Dec. 1975): 647–59.

Samuel, Maurice. *The Gentleman and the Jew*. New York: Alfred A. Knopf, 1952.

————. *Jews on Approval*. New York: Liveright, 1932.

Schneider, Carl D. *Shame, Exposure, and Privacy*. Boston: Beacon Press, 1977.

Sennett, Richard. "Destructive Gemeinschaft." *Partisan Review* 43, no. 3 (1976): 341–61.

————. *The Fall of Public Man*. New York: Vintage Books, 1978.

————. *The Psychology of Society*. New York: Vintage Books, 1977.

Singer, Linda. "Interpretation and Retrieval: Rereading Beauvoir." *Women's Studies International Forum* 8, no. 3 (1985): 231–38.

Slater, Philip. *The Pursuit of Loneliness*. Boston: Beacon Press, 1970.

Spivak, Gayatri Chakravorty. *In Other Worlds: Essays in Cultural Politics*. New York: Routledge, 1988.

Trilling, Lionel. *Sincerity and Authenticity*. Cambridge: Harvard University Press, 1972.

# INDEX